Land and Revolution in Iran, 1960–1980

Modern Middle East Series, No. 7
Sponsored by the Center for Middle Eastern Studies
The University of Texas at Austin

Land and Revolution in Iran, 1960–1980

By Eric J. Hooglund

University of Texas Press, Austin

First Edition, 1982

Requests for permission to reproduce material from this work should be sent to: Permissions, University of Texas Press, Box 7819, Austin, Texas 78712.

Library of Congress Cataloging in Publication Data
Hooglund, Eric J. (Eric James), 1944–
    Land and revolution in Iran, 1960–1980.
    (Modern Middle East series)
    Bibliography: p.
    Includes index.
    1. Land reform—Iran. 2. Iran—Politics and government—1941–1979.
I. Title. II. Series: Modern Middle East series (Austin, Tex.)
HD1333.I7H66   333.3'1'55   81-21959
ISBN 0-292-74633-4   AACR2

To Safijān,
Turaj,
and my kāko, J. B.

Contents

Tables

Preface

In 1962 the government of the former shah of Iran initiated a land reform program which was to have important social, economic, and political consequences for the rural population. Implemented in three distinct stages over the course of a decade, the redistribution altered an agricultural system characterized by feudal relationships between absentee landlords and sharecropping peasants and enabled nearly one-half of village families to acquire at least limited land ownership. Simultaneously it permitted the central government to penetrate the villages and control them politically to an extent not achieved by any previous regime since Iran's re-emergence as an independent state early in the sixteenth century. The primary motivations for this land reform program were political, rather than economic or developmental. Thus, from the beginning there were contradictions between the rhetoric of its stated goals and the actual results which ensued. The most serious of these contradictions related to the peasants who were supposed to be the principal beneficiaries of the program; due to the methods by which the reform was undertaken, the overwhelming majority of peasants did not benefit in any measurable material sense from the redistribution, and within a few years their economic position began to worsen. This situation led to widespread peasant disillusionment, not just with land reform but also with all other government policies affecting villages. Consequently, when the *ancien régime* was confronted with a serious and mass opposition movement in the urban areas in 1978, not only did it fail to generate any support from the peasantry, but, significantly, tens of thousands of participants in the protest demonstrations which speeded the downfall of the monarchy were rural young men who had recently migrated to the cities from the very lands "given" to their fathers by the excoriated shah.

The objective of this book is to examine these developments in detail. I believe such a study to be not only useful, but even necessary because so many misperceptions about Iran's land reform are prevalent both in the scholarly community and among the general public. These misperceptions have tended to be reinforced by the virtual lack to date of any serious analysis of the program's actual results. This dearth, however, has not discouraged widespread speculation about the presumed attitudes of the peasants toward land reform, the shah, and, more recently, the revolution. Consequently, a lot of the "common knowledge" about rural Iran has more of a mythic than real quality. Thus, a secondary aim of my study is to try to dispel some of this misinformation.

The field research methodology for this book consisted of what anthropologists like to call "participant observation" and the more standard political science technique of interviewing based upon preformulated questions. The first approach, carried out in one village in central Iran during the winter and spring of 1972 and another village in the south during the academic year 1978–1979, provided much insight into rural society and the relative complexity of non-mechanical agricultural techniques.

Living in a foreign culture, naturally, entails certain frustrations as one learns to adjust to unfamiliar norms and expectations, as well as endure the inevitable suspicions that attach to being an obvious outsider in an otherwise homogeneous social system. However clumsy my adaptation may have been at times, the process certainly was facilitated by the patience, tolerance, and understanding that seem to be characteristic traits of so many Iranian peasants. Living in an Iranian village also has its rewards. The warm and close friendships that I developed with several villagers will always remain a cherished part of my life.

The book, however, is not intended as a case study of any particular village, but rather as an evaluation of the land reform's social, economic, and political impact upon rural Iran in general. In order to obtain the comparative data necessary for such an assessment, I visited scores of villages in various parts of the country. During these field trips I sought to determine what common and/or differential patterns existed from locality to locality with respect to three broad areas of inquiry: the actual manner of distributing land; changes resulting from the implementation of land reform; and peasant attitudes both to the reform and the increasingly widening scope of governmental activities in the villages. Initially my research technique was to utilize formal questionnaires. However, since respondents often were quite articulate and provided lengthy explanations full of fascinating detail which no questionnaire could record, I gradually found it more effective to adopt a less rigid approach. Depending upon the particular circumstances, I would take notes as a peasant spoke or wait until an appropriate time to write up as much as I could recollect.

The field research for this book was undertaken during the academic year 1971–1972, the summer of 1977, and from June 1978 to July 1979. The initial part of the field work formed the major portion of my doctoral dissertation at the Johns Hopkins University School of Advanced International Studies in Washington, D.C., under the direction of Majid Khadduri and William G. Miller. Bill Miller was the most important influence in encouraging me to pursue my interest in Iran which had developed during 1966–1968 while a Peace Corps volunteer teaching English in a small town junior high school in East Azarbayjan province. During my first research trip, I was fortunate to meet the late Dr. Nader Afshar-Naderi, who then headed the Rural Studies Group at the Institute of Social Studies and Research in Tehran. Dr. Afshar provided me with access to the resources and facilities of the institute and arranged for introductions to several of Iran's most prominent scholars of rural sociology. The ideas and publications of these individuals have been a continuing influence upon my own thought about Iran ever since. In particular, I owe an intellectual debt to Mostafa Azkia, Hushang Keshavarz, Khosrou Khosrovi, and Javad Safi-nezhad. Azkia and Safi-nezhad, especially, have been both warm friends and valuable critics of my work.

My second research trip to Iran, during the summer of 1977, was in connection with a project I was undertaking on the effects of land reform upon the peasant work teams which had managed production under the now defunct sharecropping system. At this time I was able to renew the friendships of my earlier experience, as well as to observe the many changes which had taken place in rural areas during the previous five years. I was quite unprepared for the evidence of large-scale youth migration from villages to towns and cities. The implications of this movement for both agriculture and rural society were the bases of many stimulating discussions with Iranian specialists. It was at this time that I began to contemplate a long-term study of the consequences of land reform.

My third field trip to Iran coincided with a visiting assistant professorship at Pahlavi University in Shiraz (Shiraz University since January 1979) and provided the opportunity to gather the data necessary to revise my original doctoral dissertation into the present book. During this fourteen-month period I was also able to witness an unanticipated upheaval: the Iranian revolution. Since I was living in a village at this time, I was able to gain insight into peasant attitudes toward the revolution and initial expectations of the new Islamic government. Due to the unstable political situation and the often heavy component of anti-American feeling in Iranian nationalism, this stay had more frustrations than any previous one. At the same time, however, it was intellectually more challenging than any earlier experience. And there were inestimable personal satisfactions in the development of many warm and close friendships.

All of my field research experiences have been much richer because of the presence of my wife, Mary Hooglund, who is not only a friend and companion, but also a fine scholar. As a social anthropologist who shares with me an interest in Iran, she has always been prepared to offer valuable perspectives from her own discipline. As a woman she has been able to interact freely with village women in a society where social segregation of the sexes is fairly rigid. Her insights gained from personal experiences have been useful in helping me form my own judgments.

Funding for my first field research in 1971–1972 was provided by a Fulbright-Hays Doctoral Dissertation Research Fellowship. In 1977 I was awarded one of the Iran Bicentennial Fellowships administered by American Friends of the Middle East (since renamed Amideast) out of funds given by the government of Iran to the U.S. government on the occasion of the two hundredth anniversary celebrations of American Independence. During 1978–1979 I was fortunate to hold a Fulbright-Hays Lecture Fellowship during part of my stay. Special thanks are due to Dr. Pari Rad, executive director of the Commission for Cultural Exchange between Iran and the USA, and to Mr. Jack Schellenberger, head of the Tehran Office of the International Communications Agency, for their support in this period. I also received a small grant for travel expenses and manuscript preparation from Bowdoin College.

Several friends and colleagues have read various drafts of this book and made helpful suggestions for changes. In this respect I am particularly indebted to Ervand Abrahamian, George Alkalay, Mostafa Azkia, James Bill, Richard Cottam, Constance Cronin, Mohammad Fard-Saidi, Michael Fischer, Daniel Goodwin, Amir Hassanpur, Leonard Helfgott, Mary Hooglund, Nikki Keddie, and John Langlois.

Finally, I would like to say that Iran for me is far more than a field research site. All the time I have spent there has been a rich personal experience. It would not be possible to acknowledge all the friends and acquaintances who have helped to make Iran such a pleasant place to live. However, the warm hospitality of certain people does need to be cited. These include Esfandiyar and Elspeth Hyains Ahmadi, Donald and Vicki Arbuckle, Jabbar Bagheri, Jalal and Piri Bagheri, Hushang and Gertrude Conway Banan, Shirin Fallahi, Ali Ghaleh-Golabi, Bijan and Mahin Keshmiri, Fatimeh Moqqadam, Khalil Musavi, Gertrude Nye-Dorry, Ephraim Polussa, Chantal Rezai, André Singer, Mehdi and Joanne Soraya, Brian Street, Thomas Thompson, Jalal and Anne Betteridge Sadeghi, and Ali Shaykholeslami. Also, special recognition is due to the families of Esfandiyar Ahmadi, Mostafa Azkia, Jalal Bagheri, Esfandiyar Gholami, Amir Hassanpur, Sayyid Ayyub Jafari, Hushang Keshavarz, Jalal Sadeghi, Javad Safi-nezhad, Gohartaj Sepanta, "Baba" and "Mama" Shaykholeslami, and Asghar Tala-minai.

Needless to say, none of the persons or institutions named above are responsible for the substance, interpretation, or conclusions contained in this study. I accept full responsibility for any errors of facts or judgment.

E. J. H.
Brunswick, Maine

Introduction

The Iranian land reform program affected a greater proportion of the rural population than have any similar undertakings in the Middle East since the redistribution of agricultural land as official government policy began in Egypt in 1952. In comparison to such self-avowed revolutionary countries as Egypt, Iraq, and Syria, where less than 10 percent of villagers acquired land, in pre-revolutionary Iran approximately one-half of all village families—90 percent of peasants who actually held traditional rights of cultivation—were able to become proprietors of the land they farmed. On a superficial level such results are impressive. Consequently, it should not be surprising that by the mid-1970's the Iranian effort had acquired an international reputation as an innovative and successful attempt at reforming the structure of land ownership. However, it must be admitted that the standards for measuring land reform success have not been very rigorous. Too often the basic fact that some land actually was redistributed has been accepted as sufficient evidence for assessing achievement. While redistribution per se undoubtedly can be a positive action, its occurrence as a statistical phenomenon reveals little about the impact of land reform upon the economic, political, and social structure of affected rural societies.

In order to evaluate the effects of any particular land reform, it is necessary to examine the details of the program with the objective of determining which groups benefited; how much land was acquired per family and at what cost; which groups were excluded and upon what rationale; and what new class alignments, if any, resulted. Such information is a virtual prerequisite for understanding the economic developments—both positive and negative—which are the consequence of land redistribution and for distinguishing them from economic developments which occur due to other and unrelated factors. Equally important are the insights provided by appropriate data into any changes in social structure which derive directly from land ownership alterations. Only when one has a thorough grasp of any new social and economic relationships being created is it possible to assess the overall significance of land reform upon villages.

With respect to the Iranian experience, it has now been one decade since the land reform program was officially declared completed in 1971. Yet, its apparent "success" up to now has been measured only in terms of the actual number of peasants receiving land; that is, there has been no significant evaluative study of its results. In fact, only two books dealing directly with the subject have been published. One is little more than a sychophantic panegyric for the former shah of Iran and can be dismissed without further comment.[1] The other work is a genuine scholarly endeavor by Professor Ann K. S. Lambton of the University of London.[2] Although Lambton is a preeminent authority on rural Iran and the value of her study cannot be overemphasized, the book is essentially a description of the implementation of the land reform laws in some three hundred villages between 1962 and 1966. As such, it does not address any of the important issues suggested above, nor does it attempt to assess the overall significance of the program.

The purpose of this book is to fill in some of the gaps in the knowledge about Iran's land reform. I have attempted to provide answers for such crucial questions as the following: how much land was actually redistributed; what was the average size of plots obtained by peasants; what percentage of all villagers received land; how was rural social structure affected by land reform; and what have been the political consequences. The answers to these questions build a necessary foundation for proceeding to an interpretation and assessment of land reform's impact upon the villagers. The analysis will demonstrate that while the statistical success of the program as measured in terms of the percentage of sharecroppers becoming landowners was undeniable, the practical success as measured in terms of actual positive benefits occurring to the peasants as a result of redistribution was virtually nonexistent.

The scope of this book is narrow. The primary focus is upon the villages, which were the natural objects of land reform. The reader should not assume that the inadequate attention paid to the relationship between the land reform program and Iran's domestic and foreign politics is any indication that I attach minor significance to this subject. To the contrary, I believe that one cannot understand the reasons for land reform's inception in the 1960's without an appreciation for the overall national and international political climate. But this is a separate, albeit important, study in its own right. I hope that my analysis of the impact of redistribution upon the economic, social, and political patterns of rural Iran will serve as an initial step toward an understanding of land reform's wider import and stimulate further research on the part of persons interested in Iran.

The book is divided into two parts. Part I presents the background of the land reform program initiated in 1962. The physical environment's conditioning of agricultural methods (Chapter 1) and the nature of village society (Chapter 2) are discussed first. Then there is an examination of the idea of redistribution within a historical perspective (Chapter 3). Finally, there is an analysis of the legislation which comprised the three stages of land reform (Chapter 4).

Part II is a discussion of the results of land reform. Chapter 5 addresses itself to the important questions of how much land was redistributed; which villagers received land; and the size of holdings acquired. Next, the changes in economic structures (Chapter 6) and village political patterns (Chapter 7) which evolved after land reform are examined. Finally, the conclusion (Chapter 8) analyzes how peasant attitudes toward the consequences of the land reform program influenced village views and behavior during the revolutionary upheavals which toppled the monarchy.

Before proceeding into the book, I should comment upon the transliteration scheme used in the text for Persian words. My preference is for the system devised for the American Library Association by Nasser Sharify (*Cataloging of Persian Words*, Chicago, 1959). This system employs a full range of diacritical marks to distinguish vowels and to differentiate multiple representations of the same consonant sound. However, colleagues unfamiliar with Persian have insisted that all the dots and dashes are distracting to most readers. Thus, I have chosen to omit all diacritical marks except for the macron over long *a* (*ā*) and apostrophes to indicate the glottal stop (the letter *ayn*) and the *hamzeh* in medial or final position. Three deviations from this system should be noted. For those Persian words which are found in *Webster's Third International Dictionary* or in *Webster's Geographical Dictionary*, I have tended to use the common English spelling; in the transliteration of personal names, I have followed the preferences of individual Iranians; and in all cases I have omitted the macron over long *a* in geographical names.

PART I. THE BACKGROUND OF LAND REFORM

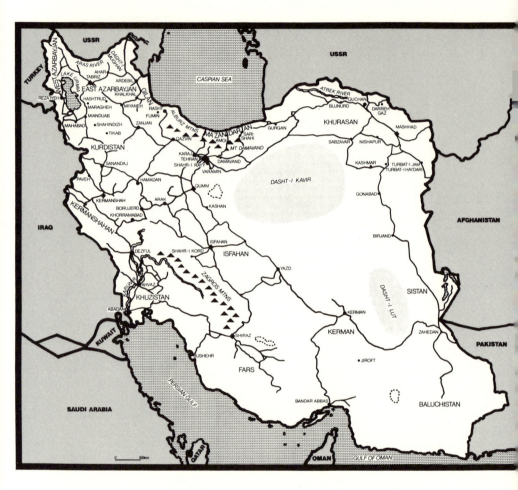

1. The Rural Setting

PHYSICAL ENVIRONMENT

In order to understand better the political, social, and economic relationships which this study explores, initially it would be useful to describe some of Iran's outstanding natural morphological features, since geographical conditions have an important influence on rural society. The country is large, extending over 636,000 square miles. High plains, surrounded by higher mountains and an arid climate, typify most of Iran. The Zagros Mountains cut some 1,400 miles across the land from Azarbayjan in the northwest to Baluchistan in the southeast. They are higher in the north, where many peaks exceed 10,000 feet, and generally decrease in height toward the south. Numerous plains averaging 3,000–5,000 feet above sea level are interspersed between the series of parallel ranges which comprise the Zagros. The mountains terminate in a coastal lowland bordering upon the Persian Gulf and the Gulf of Oman.

Rimming all of northern Iran are the Alburz Mountains. This range is less extensive than the Zagros, but contains some of the country's most spectacular mountains, including the highest peak, volcanic Mount Demavand, which crests just under 19,000 feet. The Alburz follow the southern shore of the Caspian Sea. A narrow, fertile plain is squeezed in between the mountains and the sea. This coastal strip is the only region of Iran which receives abundant rainfall.

The center of the country consists of several closed basins collectively referred to as the Central Plateau. Average elevations on this plateau are between 2,000 and 3,000 feet. More than half of the plateau is covered by the uninhabited salt deserts, the Dasht-i Kavir and the Dasht-i Lut. Beyond the deserts extending north to south along the Afghanistan frontier are the eastern highlands, a range of low, barren mountains.

The climate of Iran is one of extremes. Summers are hot and, excepting the coastal plains, dry. Temperatures reach 100° F on the plateau and sometimes may exceed 120° F in the southern lowlands. Winters are cold, although heavy snows and subfreezing temperatures are generally confined to elevations above 5,000 feet. The coastal strips along the Persian Gulf and the Gulf of Oman generally experience milder winters than the rest of the country. Strong winds occur in all seasons, but are most pronounced in summer.

Precipitation is scant. Only in Gilan and Mazandaran provinces along the Caspian Sea and on selected mountains above 10,000-feet elevation does annual precipitation exceed 20 inches. The plains and valleys of the Zagros Mountains generally receive 10 or more inches of precipitation annually, while on the Central Plateau there are yearly variations of 4–8 inches. Excepting the Caspian littoral, rainfall is seasonal. Most precipitation occurs between October and May; in many areas there is no rainfall at all during the hot summer months.

The arid climate and mountainous terrain make agriculture difficult. Only 10 percent of the total land area, or some 42 million acres, is arable. However, more than half this amount (29.4 million acres) lies fallow each agricultural year. Of the land seasonally in production, 41 percent is irrigated. In addition to the cultivated land, there are about 24.7 million acres which are used as natural pastures for grazing domesticated animals. Woodlands, consisting principally of the forests of the Alburz Mountains, cover 11 percent of the land. Fully half of the country is made up of deserts, mountains, and other unusable land.[1]

Geography, then, has shaped the agricultural system. Farming methods and types of crops grown largely are determined by climate and terrain. Control of scarce resources such as water or rights in water often has been as important as land ownership, since in many areas land which is not adequately watered is worthless. The level of production, regulated by natural conditions, affects the distribution of population; the more arid regions obviously can support fewer people than can districts receiving sufficient rainfall.

SETTLEMENT AND AGRICULTURE

Approximately 55 percent of Iran's 35 million inhabitants are rural. The rural population of 18 million includes nearly 2 million people — 10 percent of the total rural population—who migrate with their large flocks of sheep and goats between regular summer and

Table 1. *Number and Size of Villages, 1966*

Size by Population	Number of Villages	% of All Villages	Total Population
1–50	21,624	32.4	484,140
51–250	27,367	41.0	3,595,785
251–500	10,140	15.2	3,588,185
501–1,000	5,170	7.7	3,561,320
1,001–2,000	1,862	2.8	2,511,150
2,001–5,000	593	0.9	1,708,290
Totals	66,756	100.0	15,488,870

Source: Khosrou Khosrovi, *Jām'ehshināsi-yi rustā'i-yi Iran*, p. 9, Table 1.

winter pastures.[2] The remaining 16 million of the rural population live in an estimated 67,000 villages. The exact number of these villages has yet to be determined. During the 1966 national census a total of 66,756 villages were enumerated. For this census a village was defined as a permanent settlement inhabited by at least one family and having up to 5,000 residents.[3] Both this definition and the 1966 statistic will be utilized in this study. It should be noted that scholars accept the official figures as generally accurate, although one that undercounted the total number by a minimum of several hundred to a maximum of 5,000 villages.[4] The number and size of villages are summarized in Table 1. These figures reveal that over 70 percent of all villages are very small, containing fewer than 250 inhabitants.

The villages are found in all regions: in valleys, against mountains, on open plains, along seacoasts, beside rivers, even in deserts. The major determinant of village location is the availability of water. Thus, the heaviest concentration of settlements occurs where rainfall in most years amounts to at least 10 inches. These regions include Azarbayjan, Kurdistan, Kermanshahan, Gilan, Mazandaran, northern Khurasan, and parts of Fars. In some areas of Gilan and Mazandaran, where precipitation exceeds 40 inches annually, population is dense and villages are close together. In Azarbayjan, which normally receives 20 inches of rainfall per year, there are numerous villages, many with populations of several thousand. In contrast, settlements in the more arid central, southern, and eastern parts of the country tend to be small and separated by extensive stretches of uninhabited land.

Regardless of location, villages generally are similar in layout and construction. Compact settlements in which individual dwellings adjoin are characteristic of rural Iran.[5] A wall of dried mud reinforced with straw often surrounds villages. In the central and eastern parts of the country, walls may be up to 10 feet high and have built-in watchtowers, thus securely enclosing villages within a fortress (*qal'eh*). There has been, however, a general tendency to let village walls fall into disrepair since the 1950's.

The homes of the peasants are also surrounded by walls, albeit lower ones. A courtyard arrangement with the house facing southwest is typical. The average peasant family lives in one room constructed of sun-dried mud brick along one edge of the courtyard. The roof may be a flat one supported by wooden beams (western Iran), sloping and built entirely of wood (Caspian), or dome-shaped and made of mud-brick (central, east, and south Iran). The exterior is almost never painted. Usually there are neither windows nor electricity. Furnishings are sparse, consisting almost entirely of bedding and cooking utensils. If a family owns animals, a smaller stable room in which to shelter them will be found near the house. Peasants of better circumstances may have two rooms to live in, more furnishings, a well or pool in their courtyard, and a private latrine in one corner. Most peasants, however, must depend upon a distant water source and communal latrine.[6]

Depending upon actual size, villages contain a variety of buildings in addition to the peasants' homes. Grocery and butcher shops, tea houses, public baths, mosques, flour mills, and schools are common in the largest villages (population 2,500–5,000). Even a small village of 250–300 people has shops, and sometimes a primary school, mosque, and/or community bath house. Orchards of fruit and/or nut trees are also commonly found in villages. Sometimes noncultivating owners may maintain residences for either permanent or, more typically, seasonal use. These homes consist of large walled courtyards in which are located a several-room, two-story mud-brick house, various out-buildings, and gardens.

Surrounding the village are the cultivated fields. Traditionally, the village with its fields was divided into six equal parts, or *dāng*s. Each *dāng* consisted of a number of agricultural units which were measured in terms of the area which could be tilled, sown, or watered in a given period. One widespread measurement was the *juft*, the amount of land which could be ploughed by a team (*juft*) of oxen during one day. A *juft* of dry-farmed land varied from 4 to 6 hectares (about 10–15 acres), while a *juft* of irrigated land averaged about 2 hectares (5 acres). The actual size, however, was of only minor significance. The primary objective was that all *jufts* be qualitatively, rather than quantitatively, equal.[7] Thus, the *jufts* of a *dāng* often displayed great variety in size and shape in order that all might be equal with respect to soil fertility and proximity to irrigation water. It was even unnecessary that a *juft* be a contiguous unit; it could be scattered in several strips among the good, average, and poor land of a *dāng*.

A ploughland could be in one of three productive states: *daymi*, *ābi*, or *āyish*. These terms refer to whether the land is dry-farmed, irrigated, or left fallow in a given agricultural season. The major areas of *daymi*, or dry-farmed, land are Azarbayjan and northern Khurasan. Since there is scant precipitation in these provinces during the summer, *daymi* techniques have evolved to take advantage of rainfall during the other seasons. For example, wheat, about two-thirds of which is dry-farmed, is planted in early fall after the fields have been prepared. The snow which covers the ground in the winter serves as a protective layer for the seed against the cold. When warm weather causes the snow to melt, most of the water soaks into the ground, causing the seeds to germinate and sprout. The rainfall during the spring is ordinarily sufficient to enable the wheat to grow and ripen. The wheat is ready for harvest in June when the dry season begins.

Ābi, or irrigated, agriculture is also widespread. Indeed, for most of the villages of central and east Iran, agriculture without the aid of irrigation would be impossible. Rivers, streams, springs, and wells are all sources of irrigation. The most common form of irrigation, however, is the *qanāt*. *Qanāts* are artificial underground water channels. They are limited to land with some slope.[8] Their function is to tap water which has seeped into the ground, usually at the foot of a mountain, and conduct it through a relatively straight tunnel which eventually intercepts the surface of the land. By careful design, the *qanāt* surfaces in the area of the village crops. This ancient and ingenious system is very costly; not only is a *qanāt* difficult to construct, but it also requires constant maintenance in order to function properly. Despite this, *qanāts* still retain an advantage over the increasingly popular power-operated deep wells, since they can tap underground water at relatively long distances from the villages.[9]

Very elaborate irrigation schedules are followed for all *ābi* land. Depending upon the crop, each field must get a fixed quantity of water at periodic intervals. If wheat is irrigated, for example, it may receive one twenty-four-hour period of watering every twelve days or twelve hours of water every six days. Other crops may need more or less water over the same time interval. Rice plant roots, for example, need to be continuously submerged in water throughout that grain's growing cycle. Rice cultivation is thus largely limited to the rain forest climate conditions of Gilan and Mazandaran.

The third state in which cultivable land may lie is *āyish*. *Āyish* is fallow land. In many villages, as much as one-half of all cultivable land may be *āyish* in one season. Lack of sufficient water for irrigation is the main reason for the prevalence of *āyish*. The usual pattern in irrigated areas is to rotate a given field between *āyish* and *ābi* in such a way that it lies fallow every third year. In dry-farmed areas, it is common to plant the land with winter wheat in the fall, then leave it fallow during the summer after the wheat has been harvested.

Daymi land does not always lie fallow during the summer, however. Whenever a village has sufficient water for irrigation, some or all of the *daymi* land is ploughed up after the wheat and barley harvest, then sown in such summer crops (*sayfi*) as lentils, chick peas, yellow split peas, tomatoes, eggplants, onions, garlic, cucumbers, melons, and even spring wheat. In this way *daymi* land is converted to *ābi* land for part of the year. Villages with good water supplies practice this form of double cropping annually. There are, however, severe limitations upon *sayfi* crops. For example, summer is generally a rainless season. Water sources such as streams dry up, while *qanāt* flow is low. Additionally, most *sayfi* crops require more water per acreage than do wheat and barley. Nevertheless, most villages within the vicinity of towns are often able to produce good vegetable harvests which the peasants market in order to supplement their income.

Irrigation is also vital for the fruit orchards which are found adjacent to many villages. Orchards (*bāghs*), however, are not computed as part of the village ploughlands. With rare exceptions, the orchards are walled. Sometimes they are the property of one or more village families. More frequently, orchards belong to absentee landlords. Orchards are usually quite small in relation to the cultivable lands of a village. Grapes, apples, apricots, pomegranates, quinces, pears, and peaches are common fruits in western and northeast Iran. Citrus fruits grow along the Caspian and in parts of Fars. Dates are important throughout southern Iran. Nut trees such as pistachio, almond, and walnut are also popular in various areas.

The fields and orchards usually comprise only a part of the land belonging to a village. Beyond the cultivated area, sometimes adjoining the fields and sometimes a considerable distance away, lie the natural pastures. These may be registered under a private owner or be considered communal property. In the latter case, all the villagers can graze their animals on the village pastures. If the pastures are private, the owner usually levies a pasture due in return for the right of usage. This may take the form of a small cash payment for each animal or some percentage of the produce of each animal.[10]

Animals are often important in the rural economy. This is especially so in western Iran, where a peasant's livelihood may depend as much upon flocks as agriculture. Cattle, goats, and especially sheep are the grazing animals kept by peasants. The cattle—both water buffaloes and oxen—are still used for agricultural work in many areas. Goats provide hair from which ropes, tents, and coarse rugs are made. The wool of sheep is especially valuable for Persian carpets; villagers also use wool to make winter clothing. All three animals provide milk from which is obtained yogurt, cheese, and clarified butter, important staples in the peasants' diet. The manure is used for fertilizer, or sometimes collected and dried in cakes to use as fuel. A few chickens and donkeys also frequently are found in villages, and, more rarely, there may be horses as well.

The preceding overview should give a basis for understanding the rural background in which some of the political, social, and economic factors of land reform operated. The next chapter will describe the structure of rural Iran preceding the implementation of land reform in 1962, while the succeeding chapters will attempt to analyze how land reform policies affected this structure.

2. Agrarian Society, Circa 1960

The outstanding characteristic of village society in the 1950's and early 1960's was its domination by large landowners. Usually absentees, these landowners managed their agricultural properties through appointed agents who contracted with the villagers to undertake cultivation in return for a specified share of the crop. Invariably these arrangements provided the landowners with the largest share of the harvest and left for the peasants amounts barely adequate for subsistence. The unequal nature of the crop division was replicated in all other relationships involving landowners and villagers. That is, those who owned productive land could—and did—demand various dues and services from the peasants who worked on the land. Scholars have referred to this agricultural regime as feudal. While all feudal systems tend to have certain similar features, it should be noted that there are differences between historical European feudalism and Iranian feudalism of the twentieth century, as well as between Iranian feudal conditions as they prevailed in past eras and at later periods.[1] A discussion of these differences, however, is beyond the scope of this study, although the interested reader is encouraged to refer to the sources mentioned in note 1. Of more relevant concern are the nineteenth-century rural socioeconomic developments out of which evolved Iranian feudalism as it existed in the mid-twentieth century.

The most significant development for agriculture from the middle of the nineteenth century onward was the gradual but progressive involvement of the Iranian economy with the international economy.[2] This process affected the rural areas in four closely interrelated ways. First, there was a shift in production from food to essentially non-edible cash crops. Whereas early in the nineteenth century grains for domestic consumption had constituted the major agricultural crop, by the end of the century cotton, opium, and tobacco, all of which were grown primarily for European-controlled

markets, had become the dominant crops.[3] Naturally, this production shift did not affect all areas uniformly, and some regions were
essentially bypassed due to their remoteness from the local markets
which functioned as initial collection points in the overall trade
structure. Also, it is reasonable to assume that the unsettled international conditions occasioned by two world wars interspersed by a
world economic depression retarded the change to cash crops, although to date the lack of scholarly research on Iran's economic history in this period precludes drawing any definitive conclusions.

The second effect of Iran's developing relationship with the international economy was an increase in the profitability of agricultural production, especially of cash crops.[4] Prior to the 1950's,
landowners made virtually no substantive capital investments in
land as a means of increasing production and thus profits. Rather,
they succeeded in maximizing their profits by expanding the cultivated acreage of cash crops and by extracting a greater surplus from
the peasants. Initially, expansion of the area sown in cash crops was
accomplished simply by substituting a crop such as cotton or opium
for grains or legumes. Later, fertile but previously uncultivated land
was brought into production. However, increasingly during the last
half of the nineteenth century larger landowners acquired more agricultural land at the expense of smaller owners.[5] This expansion in
the size of large landholdings was a third consequence of Iran's as-
similation into the international economy.

The fourth effect was the worsening of peasant living standards
compared to those in the early part of the nineteenth century.[6] This
development can be attributed to the efforts of large landowners to
maximize their profits by retaining a greater portion of the crop.
Various subterfuges were devised which effectively permitted landlords to keep up to three-quarters of the entire harvest by the twentieth century. While peasants tried to resist the imposition of unfavorable sharecropping agreements, the rapid increase in rural population
—it doubled between 1900 and 1960—without any concomitant increase in the amount of land under cultivation resulted in more
competition for restricted opportunities and inevitable peasant submission to exploitative work arrangements. The peasants' economic
dependence facilitated their political acquiescence to a highly disadvantageous agricultural regime.

As a consequence of all these developments, a hierarchy of distinct social groups had emerged in the villages by the middle of the
twentieth century. This hierarchy consisted of the landlords and
their agents at the top and an intermediate strata of various middlemen. At the bottom were the majority of all villagers, comprised of

both peasants who possessed traditional rights to sharecrop the land-lords' fields and those who did not. The purpose of this chapter is to describe the hierarchy and examine the relationships of the different groups to one another.

PATTERNS AND PRIVILEGES OF LANDOWNERSHIP

In twentieth-century Iran, landownership was measured in villages, rather than areal extent, and fell into two broad categories. Large owners consisted of all individuals and institutions holding the equivalent of at least one six-*dāng* village, while small owners included all those whose productive properties equaled less than a complete village. As a group, the large owners controlled about 55 percent of all cultivated land.[7] However, they accounted for less than 2 percent of all owners.[8] Since large owners controlled a disproportionate amount of land relative to their numbers, they tended to wield considerable political power in the areas where their properties were located.

One can identify three different groups among the large land-holders: individual owners, institutions, and renters. Individual landlords usually owned several villages. The most extreme example was that of the shah, who held some two thousand whole and partial villages as personal possessions prior to inaugurating a voluntary redistribution program in the 1950's. More typically, large land-lords owned between twenty and forty villages. Such owners included members of the royal family, important government officials at both the national and the local level, high-ranking military officers, leaders of the larger pastoral tribes, prominent members of the clergy, wealthy merchants, and individuals whose primary occupation was the personal supervision of their properties. All of these owners were absentees. Landlords who lived in Tehran rarely, if ever, visited their villages and entrusted all matters to salaried agents. Those who resided in provincial cities and towns generally took a more active interest in village affairs. In the case of the latter absentee owners, it was not uncommon to maintain in one of the villages a house in which part of the year was spent. There was even an occasional landlord who preferred living permanently in one of several owned villages.

There were two classes of institutional landownership, government (*khāliseh*) and *vaqf* (endowed) properties. The number of government-owned villages varied throughout the first half of the twentieth century, but the general trend was for their sale.[9] Still, as late as

1960, the government owned at least 1,500 villages in whole or part. The majority were located in Khuzistan province, but there were also notable concentrations in the southeast near Iran's border with Afghanistan and Pakistan and in the northwest near the Turkey-Iraq border. *Vaqf* agricultural lands, in contrast, were both more numerous and more widely dispersed.[10] Indeed, *vaqf* holdings constituted the largest single category of rural landownership, amounting to nearly forty thousand properties distributed mostly as fractional parts of villages, although several hundred complete villages were also included. *Vaqf* properties had been endowed in perpetuity according to provisions of Shi'i Islamic law for charitable or religious (i.e., maintenance of mosques, shrines, and theological schools) purposes. They were managed by an administrator who was entitled to keep 10 percent of all annual revenues as a personal remuneration. While *vaqf*s have been associated rather closely with the clergy, control over them actually has been an issue between the government and the religious establishment at least since the beginning of the twentieth century. Especially after the establishment in 1934 of the Endowments Office within the Ministry of Education, the government was able to assert progressively stricter supervision over the appointment of *vaqf* administrators and the allocation of *vaqf* income.[11]

The third category of large landholders were the renters. These were individuals who leased several villages on a seasonal basis in return for a specified rent, retaining all revenues in excess of the rental fee as profit. Virtually all government-owned villages were rented in this fashion. *Vaqf* administrators also frequently contracted out their properties to renters, as too did certain private owners who for various reasons preferred to handle their villages through third parties. While renters did not have legal rights to the land, in practice they were the landlords of the villages during the period of their leaseholds and as such enjoyed all the prerogatives normally associated with landownership.

Large landowners exercised considerable political power in the regions where their properties were located. In their own villages, especially, landlords were the sole and unchallenged authority. If a landlord was displeased with a peasant for any reason, said peasant could be denied the right to cultivate. Peasants even could be evicted, since in practice their residence in the village was at the pleasure of the landlord. The landlord permitted peasants to cultivate a portion of the land on a crop-sharing basis. The landlord received most of the crop, sometimes as much as 80 percent. In many areas the landlord also levied certain dues upon the peasants. The most burdensome of these was *bigāri*, any kind of compulsory labor which peasants were required to perform on demand without remuneration.[12]

In general, landlord-peasant relations were characterized by tension. Owners tended to regard peasants as inferior beings whose function was to make profits. Suspicious of the peasants and convinced that they would rob and cheat whenever an opportunity arose, the typical landlord dealt severely with them at all times.[13] Peasants also were mistrustful of the landlord. Since poverty was a constant part of life, the dues levied by the landlords often represented a burden they could ill afford. The insecurity of cultivation rights and the frequent abuse suffered from the landlord's agents aggravated their situation. In such circumstances, many peasants feared their landlord and dreaded the possibility of being summoned before him.[14] If peasants found their situation unbearable, sometimes the only perceived option was to flee the village to resettle in another rural area or a city.

There were some checks to landlord arbitrariness. Especially after having owned a village for several years, the landlord tended to have a paternalistic attitude. For example, in drought years, landlords sometimes allowed peasants a larger share of the harvest than normal to prevent starvation. Invariably, this kindness was remembered during a bumper crop; accordingly, a larger share was deducted for the owner. In very bad years, loans and advances sometimes were provided to the peasants. Landlords who lived on or near their properties tended to have a stronger interest in aiding the peasants. Most large landlords, however, preferred to reside in cities and to visit their estates only at harvest time to collect their dues.

All large landowners were absentees. Even the few who lived in villages resided in only one of several which were owned. Thus, absentee landlords depended upon agents to oversee their interests in the villages. This bailiff, called a *mubāshir*, was entrusted with the affairs of the landlord, and especially those relating directly to agricultural production. He was the "guardian of the landlord's profits,"[15] and his own rewards depended upon the success of the crops. A good harvest would usually bring a handsome bonus. His salary, in cash and / or kind, was generous by village standards. The *mubāshir's* relations with the peasants were rarely easy. If he was honest and conscientious in his duties, his strict supervision would arouse resentment. If he was dishonest, the peasants often became the victims of extortion against which they had no redress, since the *mubāshir* was also the intermediary through whom complaints to the landlord were relayed. *Mubāshir*s often acquired land as a result of their position and became local petty landlords.[16]

In addition to serving as bailiff, the *mubāshir* sometimes functioned as village headman, or *kadkhudā*. Each village had a *kadkhudā*, whose primary responsibilities included maintaining internal security and representing the village in dealings with outsiders, especially government officials and nomadic tribes. Since *kadkhudās* were chosen by the landowners, it was common for one individual to combine the positions of *mubāshir* and *kadkhudā*. However, in many villages there were separate *mubāshirs* and *kadkhudās*. In some cases the landlord permitted the *mubāshir* to select the *kadkhudā*; in such villages the latter invariably was subordinate to the *mubāshir*.[17] In other villages, especially those with several owners, the *mubāshir* and *kadkhudā* were political rivals, competing to curry favor with the landlord(s); the lines of authority between the two were unclear, each tending to check the power of the other. Experience in agricultural matters was the most important qualification for a *kadkhudā*. In the majority of villages, landlords chose a farming peasant to be *kadkhudā*. His compensation often included the right to keep the entire harvest from a part or whole ploughland which he cultivated. The landlord sometimes gave him a monthly or yearly salary. More frequently, the *kadkhudā's* payment came out of the harvest. This usually was included among the dues levied upon the harvest before division between landlord and peasant; in many Azarbayjan villages, the peasants paid a fraction of their own share directly to the *kadkhudā*. Often, he was entitled to a certain number of days of free labor service (*bigāri*) from each peasant.[18]

The *kadkhudā's* customary functions included the maintenance of order within the village. Thus he served as the local judge, settling disputes between villagers and inflicting punishments for minor civil offences such as thefts.[19] These powers were given legal validity in 1935. The next year another law provided that all *kadkhudās* be officially appointed by county governors, albeit upon the recommendation of the village owners.[20] These laws were part of overall efforts to reassert central government control over provincial and rural areas. In the twenty-seven years from the passage of this legislation to 1962 when land redistribution began, government officials gradually but steadily penetrated the countryside. In this process, the *kadkhudā* acquired a role as intermediary between the villagers and the government.[21]

Among the officials with whom the *kadkhudā* dealt on behalf of the peasants were the military representatives. Compulsory male military service had been established during the reign of Reza Shah (1925–1941). Since all eligible men were not necessary for service in any one year, military recruiters consulted with the *kadkhudā* about which men would be drafted from each village.[22] Peasant families who had cultivation rights often suffered economically from a two-year absence of a healthy, working male. Thus, they were reluctant to have their sons drafted, in contrast to the poorest families, who viewed military service as a more positive opportunity. *Kadkhudā*s could exploit these class differences to punish and reward families upon the basis of the nature of their own personal relations with the peasants. Particularly dishonest *kadkhudā*s even allowed bribes to influence their decisions.[23]

Those *kadkhudā*s who used the military draft system to gain personal advantages also practiced other forms of extortion against the peasants. Since a *kadkhudā* was recognized by both the landlord and the government as the resident authority of the village upon the basis of his services to them rather than to the villagers, he was relatively free to behave arbitrarily with the peasants. Usually those peasants who dared to complain to authorities could expect reprisals from the *kadkhudā*. Nevertheless, there were some limits operating upon *kadkhudā*s. If extortion were too overbearing, the peasants might flee in desperation to remoter regions or to the cities, thereby adversely affecting the village's pool of labor, at least temporarily. More significantly, however, the small size of most villages and the fact that *kadkhudā*s were usually cultivators meant that they would have some sympathy with peasants' problems. In addition, most *kadkhudā*s were natives of the villages they headed and had kin ties with several families. Thus, *kadkhudā*s were usually inclined to cooperate with, rather than to harass, the peasants. Many *kadkhudā*s therefore were compelled to mediate the conflicting interests of landlords and peasants.[24]

While large absentee landlords and the village authorities who derived power from them dominated the rural areas politically, their control was not necessarily absolute or uniform. There were tens of thousands of small owners (those whose holdings equaled less than one complete six-*dāng* village) throughout the countryside, many of whom had variable local influence.[25] There were two distinct classes of small owners: nonfarmers and peasant proprietors. The small owners who did not personally cultivate their land included merchants, financiers, bureaucrats, teachers, professionals, members of the clergy, and certain skilled craftsmen. A majority of these owners lived and worked in towns; in general, they tried to manage their land after the fashion of the larger owners.[26] Similarly to large landlords, small owners relied upon agents who resided in the villages. Since small owners typically shared ownership of a village with at least one other person—ownership of large villages could be divided among up to ten different landlords—it was not always possible to reach agreement upon a single *mubāshir* or *kadkhudā*. Thus, some villages had two or more *kadkhudās*, and sometimes several bailiffs as well, at various periods. Some of the small owners were relatively wealthy and / or held important positions in provincial government; both of these factors were political assets for anyone aspiring to exercise regional influence. Indeed, in certain areas, an owner of five *dāngs* of a large and prosperous village could be politically and socially more influential than an owner of one or more complete villages which were small and unproductive.

In contrast to the absentee small owners were the peasant proprietors who cultivated their own land. While peasant owners may have accounted for up to one-half of all small owners (there are no reliable statistics), they represented only an estimated 5 percent of all peasants.[27] Peasant-owned villages were located in all parts of the country, but typically they were found in areas that were relatively isolated and not easily accessible. In general, peasant proprietors were quite poor; their holdings were small and rarely provided more than a bare subsistence livelihood. Although peasant proprietors were considered to have a higher social status than landless peasants, they enjoyed neither the prestige nor the influence of absentee owners, large or small.

Throughout the first half of the twentieth century there was a close relationship between landownership and rural political power: those who owned the most land, measured in villages, generally exercised the most power. Nonowners aspiring to acquire influence necessarily had to ally themselves with the landed elite and their representatives who ruled the villages. Naturally, only landless individuals who had independent sources of wealth were in a position to exchange favors with owners. People whose money, and consequently, influence, was not directly connected to personal landownership were found in virtually all the larger villages (population 1,000–5,000) as well as many smaller ones. They sold, rented, or loaned various goods and services to the villagers and constituted an intermediate class between landlords and peasants.

BETWEEN LORD AND PEASANT

In virtually all Iranian villages there were some residents who neither owned nor sharecropped cultivable land. As a group, these people were called *khwushnishin*s, literally "those who sit comfortably." The term derives from the fact that those who did not cultivate or own land were considered to have an easier life, since they did not need to worry about all the problems associated with farming. Although the use of *khwushnishin* was relatively widespread, there were other terms which conveyed a similar meaning, e.g., *oftābnishin* ("he who sits in the sun") in Khurasan. The term *khwushnishin*, however, has become accepted in Persian academic literature to refer to all rural people who neither owned, rented, nor sharecropped land.[28]

The *khwushnishins* were not a homogenous class; rather, they consisted of three quite distinct groups. First, there was an elite minority of middlemen (tradesmen and creditors) who probably comprised only 6 percent of all *khwushnishins*. A second group, which included 10 percent of the *khwushnishin* population, were the nonagricultural workers, who provided various services and manufactured necessary products for the villagers. The third group—and the overwhelming majority—may be termed the agricultural laborers; they had no regular occupations but were dependent upon seasonal farm work for their livelihoods. Except that they too neither owned nor cultivated land, those in the first group were totally dissimilar to the other *khwushnishins*. In order to emphasize their importance in the rural economy, the traders will be discussed separately in this section; the other *khwushnishin* groups will be discussed later in the chapter.

Khwushnishin tradesmen played a prominent role in the rural economy primarily because landowners were disinterested in the buying, selling, and lending of goods, services, and capital in the villages. Their minimal participation in those activities probably can be attributed to the fact that most were absentee landlords who preferred to live in the cities and towns. Whatever the reasons, their limited involvement provided nonowners the opportunity to gain an important degree of control over village economic transactions. These *khwushnishins* included itinerant peddlers, village shopkeepers, local moneylenders, bazaar merchants, wholesale dealers, and rentiers of wheat grinding mills and the cattle used for ploughing.[29] Representatives of all these types of *khwushnishins* might be found in the largest villages (above 2,500 population), whereas small villages (less than 500 population) contained only one or two shopkeepers. Most of the hamlets (less than 200 population) were too small to support any *khwushnishin* residents engaged in specialized services. However, wandering peddlers (*pilehvars*) made their way to the smallest and most remote mountain villages, where they sold and bartered their wares.

The village shopkeeper (*baggāl*) was the most common tradesman with whom peasants typically came in contact. Frequently, the shop was only one tiny room, but it was stocked with an extraordinary variety of goods.[30] The most important commodities consisted of those necessities—tea, sugar, rice, and cotton cloth—which were not produced locally. Transactions were usually on a barter, rather than a cash basis, the shopkeeper receiving grain from the peasants as payment for the goods.[31] He might sell some of this grain in the nearest market town, but he usually retained a significant portion to be used as commodity loans.

The peasants generally exhausted their supplies by midwinter. Lacking food, they were forced to seek credit in order to survive until the first harvest (at the beginning of summer in the case of winter wheat). The shopkeeper provided this credit in the form of grain sufficient to meet the basic requirements of each family. Such loans in kind were converted into monetary terms. For example, if a peasant received on credit 10 *manns*[32] (65.4 pounds) of wheat valued at 22 *riāls* per *mann*, his debt was reckoned at 220 *riāls*. At harvest time, however, the abundant supply of grain would cause wheat prices to slump back to around 18 *riāls* per *mann*; thus, the peasant would need to repay 12.25 *manns* for the original 10 which he borrowed.[33] It was also standard practice for shopkeepers to charge interest on these loans. Minimum interest rates averaged 3–5 percent per month. Thus a loan contracted in February could accrue up to 20 percent interest by June when harvesting began. More frequently, however, monthly charges were 7 percent or higher.

Many shopkeepers engaged in a variety of other profitable economic endeavors. Some provided short-term cash loans to the peasants for which they generally charged a single flat interest fee. Terms for such loans were usurious, sometimes as high as 100 percent.[34] Other shopkeepers exploited the peasants' poverty by purchasing crops in advance of the harvest (a practice known as *salaf-khari*). For example, a shrewd bargainer who was aware of a peasant's economic circumstances might offer 2,000 *riāls* ($26) for each *kharvār* (654.6 pounds) of wheat to be delivered after it was harvested several weeks in the future. This amount of wheat, however, could fetch up to 2,900 *riāls* ($39) per *kharvār* on the market at harvest time. Peasants who were in desperate need of cash but were unwilling or unable to obtain credit had no alternative to accepting such unfavorable terms.

The various buying, selling, and lending activities discussed above were practiced to varying degrees by all tradesmen who had regular commercial dealing with villagers. From the peasants' point of view, the credit policies were the most exploitative. There was no redress from the imposition of extortionate interest rates. Significantly, the landlords, as long as they continued to receive their customary dues, did not interfere with peasant-creditor relations. Indeed, the landowning class often cooperated with the wealthier merchants, and their agents were usually on cordial, and even kinship, terms with village shopkeepers. Some landlords, especially the smaller ones, were even in the habit of extending short-term credit at exorbitant interest rates to their own peasants.[35] Such conditions created a cycle whereby the peasants remained impoverished and indebted, while their creditors maintained control of rural economic transactions.

Certain *khwushnishin*s who provided specialized services also profited at the peasants' expense. The owners of rural grist mills are an example. Usually, one miller ground all the grain for a village or group of villages. As payment, the miller received a percentage of grain or flour from each *mann* (6.54 pounds) of wheat. The actual amount varied between 10 and 20 *misqāls*[36] (1.635 and 3.27 ounces) per *mann*. In the larger villages where a miller each day ground at least 1 *kharvār* (654.6 pounds), his minimum earnings averaged between 10 and 20 pounds of wheat a day. Generally, this was more than sufficient to provide for the daily family requirements. The surplus was accumulated over time and used for loans in kind to the peasants during the winter. Sometimes, a miller sold his extra grain in the nearest market center, keeping a portion of the cash in order to make money loans to the peasants. Like other rural creditors, the miller practiced short-term, high-interest lending.[37]

In certain areas, *khwushnishin*s, known as *gāvband*s, benefited from their monopoly ownership of cattle.[38] Since ploughing was (and still is) largely dependent upon animal power, and especially the ox (*gāv*), possession of an ox, or preferably a team, was considered one of the five important factors of agricultural production.[39] Indeed, the ability to provide oxen was virtually a prerequisite to obtaining cultivation rights. If a peasant could not afford to buy and maintain an ox, it was necessary for him to rent one during the ploughing season. *Gavband*s were the chief rentiers of work cattle in certain districts. A *gāvband* who provided a team generally received 20 percent of the total harvest from the area ploughed by his oxen.

A *gavband* who owned sufficient oxen to provide all the plough teams required in a village usually obtained one-fifth of the annual winter crops (wheat and barley) and 10 percent of the summer crops. His share of the important grain harvest exceeded that of any cultivating peasant. Like the miller, a *gavband* generally accumulated a grain surplus. Sometimes the extra grain was used for seed. Contributing seed as well as oxen to the production cycle enabled a *gāvband* to claim up to 40 percent of the total harvest before its division between landlord and peasant.[40] *Gāvband*s were also credit sources, extending both cash and kind loans to the peasants. Like other rural lenders, *gāvband*s preferred granting loans on a short-term basis, repayment coinciding with the harvest. Monthly interest rates were rarely below 3 percent, often higher.

*Gāvband*s, millers, and the various tradesmen all profited from their economic dealings with the peasants. Although they were not landowners and did not engage in cultivation, these entrepreneurs and traders were beneficiaries in the villages of agricultural production. They obtained much of that portion of the annual harvest not reserved for landlords due to their control over the rural economic transactions. This control was maintained through credit practices which kept a majority of peasants impoverished and perpetually indebted. Landlords acquiesced in this economic exploitation of the peasants for two reasons. First, the political, social, and economic interests of landowners were in the towns where they lived, rather than the villages which they owned. Second, as long as the peasants remained poor and burdened with debt, they had no opportunities to improve their economic circumstances and thus gain a bargaining position from which to challenge the sharecropping arrangements.

Naturally, the possibility that a landlord, for whatever motives, would support one or more peasants against rural creditors always existed. Thus, it was expedient to cultivate the good will of landowners. Shopkeepers, for example, permitted owners to purchase goods on credit without interest. In the case of those absentee landlords who visited their villages only rarely, shopkeepers neither requested nor expected payment for "credit purchases." Other favors included free grain grinding by millers and gifts of produce from *gāvband*s. These various material concessions were considered necessary in order to encourage the noninterference of landowners in village economic relationships.

The fact that village tradesmen and entrepreneurs felt obligated to grant material favors to landlords served to emphasize their position in rural Iran. They definitely held inferior status vis à vis landowners. However, as long as they deferred to superior rank, landlords were willing to sanction practices which enabled these middlemen to elevate themselves above the mass of peasants. Thus, these people may be said to have constituted a distinct group intermediate in terms of power and influence between landlords and peasants.

THE PEASANTS

In rural Iran, a distinction was made between villagers who had customary rights to cultivate the land of absentee owners and those who did not. The latter were referred to as *khwushnishins*. Several terms were employed to designate the former; generally the terms indicated such differences as whether the cultivator provided only labor or also contributed other productive factors such as seeds, water, and especially plough animals. Regardless of the specific type of cultivator an individual might be, all cultivators shared in common the right to farm land and to receive a portion of its harvest. This right of cultivation was known as *nasaq*. The term *peasant* will be used in this book to denote any villager who possessed a *nasaq*. The first effort to determine precisely what percentage of villagers actually were peasants was not undertaken until 1960. An extensive agriculture survey conducted by what was then known as the General Department of Statistics estimated that of 3,218,460 rural households, only 60 percent (1,934,160 households) were *nasaq* holders; the remaining 40 percent (1,284,300 households) were *khwushnishins*.[41] While peasants thus constituted an absolute majority of all villagers, it is reasonable to assume, given the size of the population without cultivation rights, that possession of a *nasaq* was a valuable asset.

The *nasaq* conferred upon its holder the right to cultivate a portion of an owner's land and to use village water sufficient to irrigate the area sown. A peasant was considered to have earned a *nasaq* after working as a sharecropper for about two consecutive agricultural seasons.[42] Once he had acquired a *nasaq*, a peasant was not normally denied the privilege of participating in cultivation and retained his *nasaq* as long as he was able to perform all the work associated with production. However, if the landowner became dissatisfied, he could repossess the *nasaq* by purchasing the peasant's rights. Naturally there were abuses, but generally landlords honored the custom of compensation. Peasants realized that if a landlord wished to reclaim a *nasaq* and not pay for it, there was no real redress. Thus, peasants generally refrained from actions which would provoke landlords. In theory, cultivation rights were not inheritable. In practice, however, an older peasant was generally permitted to transfer his *nasaq* to one of his grown sons, or, if he had no male children, to a son-in-law or nephew. The new holder's rights were confirmed after he had cultivated some land for two or three seasons.

It is important to understand that a *nasaq* was not tied to any specific plot of land. It was only a privilege to cultivate some land, the owner retaining all authority over the assignment of plots. Indeed, it was common practice throughout the country for cultivable land in each village to be redistributed annually among the peasants. This procedure discouraged the growing of trees, grapevines, or perennial crops such as alfalfa. Since the roots of these plants remained alive for several years, Islamic law recognized that individuals cultivating them had certain rights to the soil while their plants continued to grow. (Such rights were known as *haqq-i risheh*.) Owners were generally opposed to the peasants acquiring any claims on the land and used the regular redistribution of plots to prevent this development.

The peasant holding a *nasaq* usually did not work an assigned plot of land alone. Rather, it was typical for the arable land of a village to be organized into units farmed cooperatively by teams of sharecroppers. These teams known as *bunehs*, were structures in which members had clearly defined roles. The *buneh*'s main function was the efficient exploitation of productive land; however, since village life and agriculture were so intimately intertwined, *buneh*s necessarily affected all aspects of rural society. Membership in a *buneh*, for example, gave social status to a peasant, while his actual position within the *buneh* determined the relative degree of influence he could exert in village affairs.[43]

Many factors determined the size and number of *buneh*s in each village: the amount of irrigation water, the extent of cultivable land, the number of adult male peasants, and the availability of draught animals for ploughing.[44] If, for example, a village had water sufficient to irrigate a certain quantity of land, this land would be divided up so that each area would receive an equal amount of water. In the case of a crop such as wheat, which, it will be recalled, needs one twenty-four-hour period of watering every twelfth day, the sown land could be divided into twelve sections with the irrigation schedule rotating daily among them. If there were also twelve *buneh*s in the village, each would be assigned one of the sections; more or less *buneh*s would require a fractional subdivision of the twelve areas.

The sown area assigned to a *buneh* consisted of one or more ploughlands. Since ploughlands were measured in terms of the amount of land which an oxen team (*juft-i gāv*) could plough in one day,[45] *buneh*s were described as having one, two, or more *juft-i gāv*s. Often, however, the number of ploughlands exceeded the available oxen teams or water supply; in these cases, some land would be left fallow (*āyish*) each season.

One peasant was necessary to manage each oxen team. Thus, a *buneh* of three *juft*s needed at least three men. Additionally, each *buneh* contained peasants who did not have specific responsibility for the oxen teams, but rather exercised a general supervision over all matters relating to cultivation. A typical three-*juft buneh*, for example, might consist of five men. In any one village, all *buneh*s (normally) were equal in terms of ploughlands, peasant members, and oxen teams, although the composition of *buneh*s displayed considerable variety from one village to the next. In smaller villages, *buneh*s had as few as three members, while up to fourteen men per *buneh* could be found in some larger settlements.[46] Usually, however, *buneh*s had from four to seven members.

The basic structure of *buneh*s was fairly uniform throughout rural Iran. Each *buneh* was under the charge of one peasant known as the *sarbuneh*.[47] All *sarbuneh*s were chosen by the landlords, who expected them to be fully responsible for the work on and production of the land assigned to *buneh*s. Naturally, experience and demonstrated expertise in agricultural affairs were necessary qualifications of *sarbuneh*s. Normally, competent peasants who were appointed *sarbuneh*s retained their positions for life. As *sarbuneh*s became elderly, it was common for them to prepare adult sons to take over their work. Although the occuaption of *sarbuneh* was not formally hereditary, landlords often did choose recommended sons to replace their fathers.[48]

As supervisors, *sarbuneh*s had considerably easier work than other peasants.[49] At the beginning of each agricultural year—autumn in most areas—all the *sarbuneh*s of a village gathered to decide how the fields should be distributed among the *buneh*s, which ploughlands would be planted, and which would remain fallow, and by what schedule irrigation would commence.[50] Once these basic decisions had been made, the *sarbuneh*s and the peasants mutually determined which *nasaq* holders would be members of which *buneh*s during the current season. After the *buneh*s were constituted, the important tasks of each *sarbuneh* included marking off the boundaries of his *buneh*'s fields and plots and helping with the planting of crops.[51] Sowing seed like wheat and barley was accomplished at the approximate rate of one hectare per day, the *sarbuneh* walking over the fields spreading the seeds by hand, while the other peasants followed behind him covering them up.[52] It was not customary for the *sarbuneh* to assist with the difficult tasks of ploughing, breaking up of the soil, weeding, irrigation, and harvesting. He did, however, inspect this work, since his own economic welfare was tied up with the productive success of his *buneh*.

The heads of larger *buneh*s had one or more assistants, whom *sarbuneh*s generally chose from among their friends and kinsmen.

The assistants helped supervise the work of *buneh*s, a relatively important responsibility, since the several ploughlands in each *buneh* were typically noncontiguous. Thus, while a *sarbuneh* was busy in one field, he could dispatch his assistants to attend to matters in the others. In their supervisory capacity, assistants often were exempted from performing some of the difficult labor of the *buneh*s.[53]

The foundation of the *buneh* structure was the peasant. From the initial autumn ploughing for winter wheat and barley to the final harvest of summer fruits and vegetables some ten to eleven months later, the peasants were responsible for performing most of the labor of the *buneh*s. Their days included tedious chores and many long hours. Their most important task was to work with and take care of the oxen teams. Usually, each peasant was in charge of one team.[54] The oxen were yoked together and harnessed to a single wooden nail plough.[55] The peasant drove the plough and oxen over the fields in preparation for planting crops, often ploughing the same field several times in order to properly prepare the soil. The process was time-consuming, often requiring one full day to plough about 2 hectares (5 acres).[56]

Generally, all the peasants of a *buneh* worked together in doing the other work. First the earth clods turned up by the ploughing had to be smoothed.[57] After the seeds were planted, there was a slack period in the winter. Spring brought a feverish revival of activity. Earthen channels and barriers for conducting and diverting irrigation water had to be constructed. Ploughing and sowing for summer crops, spreading manure for fertilizer, and weeding all took time. During harvest, peasants were expected to transport the cut grain from the fields to the threshing area on their backs.[58] Although all the preceding jobs were important, they constituted only part of the duties.[59] They have been mentioned to illustrate a significant feature of *buneh*s, i.e., the unequal nature of the division of labor.

The inequitable distribution of a *buneh*'s work was replicated in the division of its harvest. The allocation of shares followed a basic pattern which nonetheless displayed considerable variation from village to village. As a unit, each *buneh* divided its harvest with the landowner. In theory, the five productive factors—land, water, seed, labor, and draught animals—were assigned equal value, the contributor of each receiving one-fifth of the crop.[60] Thus, owners automatically took 20 percent of the harvest in recompense for the use of their land. Since most landlords had made the initial investment in a *qanāt* or paid for its repair, they could claim an additional one-fifth share for having made water available. Some landlords also provided seed and even the oxen teams. Thus, it was possible for a landowner to claim four-fifths of the crop. Only in a relatively few villages, however, did landlords actually take 80 percent of the harvest. In practice, many other fractional measurements were employed; nevertheless, landlords were the chief beneficiaries of the harvest.[61]

The share of the crop left for the *buneh* varied from one-fifth to one-half of the total. Before this could be subdivided among the *buneh* members, however, certain dues had to be deducted. These represented payments to various individuals, such as the local carpenter and blacksmith, for services rendered to the *buneh* in the previous nine months.[62] The amount remaining was the *buneh's* "profit." In some villages it was customary for each *buneh* to divide this equally among all members.[63] More typically, however, the division within the *buneh* was an unequal one. The *sarbuneh*s usually received a higher percentage than other members. In some areas, as much as 30 percent of each *buneh's* share of the crop went to the *sarbuneh.*[64] The *sarbuneh's* assistants sometimes received a slightly greater share also. Whatever the methods of crop division for the *buneh* of any particular village, everywhere the actual share of the members amounted to only a fraction of the harvest;[65] often this was sufficient only to maintain bare subsistence.

The economic position of the *sarbuneh* was slightly more favorable than that of other *buneh* members. In addition to enjoying a larger share of the crop, each *sarbuneh* usually received a bonus from the landlord. Often this was several kilograms of grain from the landlord's share of the harvest; sometimes a cash reward.[66] This extra income enabled the *sarbuneh*s to live, at least by village standards, a relatively comfortable life. For most *sarbuneh*s, "a comfortable life" meant being able to live at subsistence without borrowing; in an exceptionally good harvest year, there might be some surplus to invest in an ox or a luxury.

As a group, the *sarbuneh*s constituted the "upper class" of peasants. Their slightly more advantageous economic situation, their role as supervisors of agricultural production, and the favor shown them by landowners enabled *sarbuneh*s to maintain a relatively privileged position within rural society. Other villagers tended to regard them as part of the informal leadership known as *rish sefid*s (literally "the white beards").[67] Their ascribed status permitted them to exercise some political influence, although the nature of authority in villages necessarily circumscribed the scope of that influence.

The most important field in which *sarbuneh*s could make decisions relatively independently was dispute arbitration. Peasants brought their disputes, the majority of which concerned water rights, before the *sarbuneh*s for settlement. The *sarbuneh*s of a village generally met as a group to take up the merits of each case. If they found a peasant guilty of siphoning onto his own field water which rightfully belonged to another, or failing to prevent his animals from destroying his neighbor's crops, the *sarbuneh*s could demand that the offender restore the losses from his own resources. The *sarbuneh*s' decisions in such cases were normally accepted.[68]

The influential role of *sarbuneh*s depended heavily upon their landlords' good will. Their informal authority derived from the privileges accorded them by landowners. Thus, if an individual *sarbuneh* desired to retain his position, he had to execute his landlord's desires concerning which crops to cultivate, when to clean *qanāt*s, etc. If, for any reason, a landlord was dissatisfied with a *sarbuneh*, he simply dismissed him; worse, he could even abrogate a *sarbuneh*'s cultivation rights. *Sarbuneh*s were well aware of the relationship between their status and their landlord's benevolence. Therefore, they strived to please owners in their own work, and more importantly, since unacceptable behavior on the part of peasants could also jeopardize their status, *sarbuneh*s used their influence to encourage peasant submission to the prevailing agricultural regime.

Although peasants normally concluded that their own interests were best served by compliance with the advice of *sarbuneh*s, it was probably inevitable that there should exist some resentment against their privileged position. Peasants were especially dissatisfied with the distribution of labor and the harvest among *buneh* members. However, since serious evidence of noncooperation could result in a loss of *nasaq*, peasants were generally unwilling to challenge their *sarbuneh*s. Nevertheless, discontent remained and often found expression in the form of quarrels between *buneh* members, feuds among *buneh*s, and sometimes tense relations between peasants and *sarbuneh*s.

Despite the potential for conflict, there were some checks upon its development. Mutual interest in outwitting the landlord naturally encouraged a spirit of cooperation. Equally important, the existence of close family relationships among members of most *buneh*s tended to militate against friction. In this respect, it was not uncommon for fathers to head *buneh*s composed of sons and sons-in-law. Eldest brothers, uncles, and cousins as *sarbuneh*s generally received considerable respect on account of their kinship ties to other members.[69]

Although family bonds imbued some *buneh*s with group solidarity and long-term membership stability, they did not materially affect the customary way *buneh*s operated nor the attendant consequences. Thus, whatever the character of their relations with *sar-bunehs*, other members remained responsible for performing the hardest field work and received the smallest portion of the harvest. Since their shares were insufficient to support their families adequately, peasants were compelled to contract loans in order to make good the deficits. These loans, usually in kind, bore exorbitant interest rates which resulted in further impoverishment. In time, indebtedness, as well as poverty, became a permanent feature in the lives of most peasants.

Generally speaking, all peasants were victims of extortion and oppression against which they had little, if any, protection. Debts kept them tied to the land. Organized opposition was effectively stifled by the fear of losing cultivation rights. The consequences of being without *nasaq*s were very real to the peasants. In most villages a large minority of the population did not have *nasaq*s and lived in even more precarious and wretched conditions than did the peasants. Since such villagers did not have any privileges of cultivating land, they had few secure means of earning their livelihoods. The peasants considered them inferior and wanted above all to avoid joining their ranks. It is now appropriate to examine this lowest strata of rural society.

THE KHWUSHNISHINS

It has already been mentioned that *khwushnishin*s comprised about 40 percent of Iran's rural population in 1960. However, *khwushnishin*s were not evenly distributed among all villages. Generally, a greater percentage of the population were *khwushnishin*s in the larger villages and a lesser percentage in smaller villages. Indeed, in villages with populations in excess of 1,000, *khwushnishin*s often accounted for one-half or more of all families. Among *khwushnishin*s, the only common bond was the very basis upon which they were differentiated from peasants, that is, their lack of cultivation rights. Otherwise, *khwushnishin*s were a heterogeneous collectivity. As stated in the section on village shopkeepers and related positions, there were three distinct groups of *khwushnishin*s. The village tradesmen, whose socioeconomic status was superior to that of both peasants and other *khwushnishin*s, do not need further discussion. Therefore, the rest of this chapter will be devoted to explaining the characteristics of the two remaining *khwushnishin* groups, those in nonagricultural occupations and the agricultural workers. These two groups included over 90 percent of all *khwushnishin*s.

Those villagers engaged in essentially nonagricultural occupations probably represented only 10 percent of all *khwushnishin* households.[70] Nevertheless, their occupations were quite varied. Barbers, bathhouse attendants (*hammāmis*), blacksmiths, carpenters, coppersmiths, shoemakers, and religious functionaries (mullahs) were among the more common examples of villagers who provided specialized services and products for the peasants. Generally, social distinctions were made between *khwushnishins* who rendered personal services and those who made artifacts. For example, blacksmiths and carpenters invariably were considered to rank higher in status than barbers or bathhouse attendants.

The basis upon which villagers judged the status of various *khwushnishins* was often ambiguous.[71] This is best illustrated with respect to religious persons who were called mullahs. In general, the rural population used the term *mullah* to refer to a man who had acquired some training at an urban religious school and earned his livelihood by ministering to spiritual needs. In this sense, mullahs were different from *shaykhs* who also lived in the villages. While *shaykhs* were esteemed for their religious knowledge, literacy, and (often) reputed descent from the Prophet, and while they also were expected to perform religious functions, usually they had not received a formal religious education and they supported their families from small landholdings or by engaging in trade; consequently, *shaykhs* were considered to be either petty landowners or tradesmen, albeit deserving of special respect. In contrast, mullahs were clearly identified as among the second category of *khwushnishins*. However, whether villagers regarded mullahs as the most prestigious or least prestigious of nonagricultural *khwushnishins* was much less clear. On the one hand, mullahs generally were admired for their ability to read and write, their knowledge of the Qur'ān and principles of Islamic law, and their presumed piety. On the other hand, they were considered to be rather ignorant about practical affairs, especially agricultural matters which were of paramount concern to most villagers, and too solicitous of the welfare of landlords and their agents. In addition, peasants resented having to help support mullahs through levies upon their share of the crop. At the very least, one can conclude that village attitudes toward mullahs was ambivalent.[72]

In any discussion of mullahs, it needs to be emphasized that they were not a significant element in rural social structure. They were resident in only 10 to 12 percent of all villages, perhaps even less. In the villages with fewer than 500 inhabitants—85 percent of the total—mullahs were virtually nonexistent. Mullahs did not commonly live in the medium-sized (population 500–1,000) villages either. Their presence was restricted primarily to the larger villages, the same communities which tended to have a diversified *khwush-nishin* population. Given the high level of rural poverty in the twentieth century, it is probable that such villages were the only ones with sufficient resources to support mullahs. However, since mullahs rarely were of peasant origins and had spent at least a few years in an essentially urban environment for the purposes of religious instruction, it is possible that they preferred larger villages which had some of the social characteristics of small towns. Whatever the reasons for the general absence of mullahs in rural areas may have been, the consequence was that a majority of villagers had no regular contact with them.

In contrast to mullahs, various rural craftsmen were much more ubiquitous. These *khwushnishins* manufactured virtually all the nonfood products utilized by villagers. Two groups, the blacksmiths and the carpenters, had important, albeit indirect, roles in agriculture. Blacksmiths, for example, forged all the various metal implements needed by peasants in order to farm successfully.[73] The typical products included shoes for work oxen, the iron parts of yokes, ploughshares, spades, and threshing blades. Carpenters fashioned the wooden parts of agricultural tools.[74] Oxen yokes, shovel handles, plough, harrow and threshing beams, irrigation channel scoops, and winnowing forks were all common items made by village carpenters.[75]

Since blacksmiths and carpenters produced the tools necessary for successful agriculture, their relationship with the peasants tended to be more complex than that of other village artisans. Unlike coppersmiths and shoemakers, for example, blacksmiths and carpenters generally did not charge a fee for each finished product; instead, their practice was to outfit oxen teams with whatever implements were required in return for one annual payment.[76] The actual amount of compensation depended upon the number of teams which had been serviced, computed at the rate of x pounds of wheat and barley per pair of oxen.[77] At harvest time, each *buneh* determined how much was due the blacksmith and carpenter who had worked for it; the total was deducted from the *buneh*'s share of the crop before the division among its members took place.

Generally, blacksmiths and carpenters were better off economically than other craftsmen, although their living standards rarely were higher than the subsistence levels of the peasants.[78] Artisans such as coppersmiths, shoemakers, and potters were less advantageously situated. They did not have arrangements with *bunehs*, but rather made products on demand and expected to receive payment at the time patrons took possession. Handmade goods had no standard values; the worth of any particular item depended upon a peasant's perceived need, the unavailability of substitutes, and the bargaining skill of the manufacturer. The most expensive artifacts were canvas work shoes and copper pots used for cooking rice. In some areas it was necessary to barter up to 10 *manns* (65.5 pounds) of wheat to obtain one good pair of shoes or a large pot in the early 1960's.[79]

The position of all *khwushnishin* workers who provided personal services to the villagers was lower than that of any artisans. Barbers and bath attendants constituted the overwhelming majority of workers in this category. Typically, they received one annual payment from each peasant. Barbers, for example, shaved beards and cut hair for the men on a regular basis, such as once every two or three weeks. In some villages barbers received an equal payment from each peasant, while in others each peasant determined individually what amount would be appropriate. The payments were in kind, deducted by the peasants from their share of the harvest. In areas where per acre yields were high, barbers received as much as 5 *manns* (32.7 pounds) of wheat from each peasant; in the poorest villages, they received as little as 1 *mann* (6.5 pounds). Throughout the year barbers collected additional small fees from villagers for performing circumcisions, extracting teeth, and dressing wounds.[80]

Communal bathhouses were located in about one-third of all villages containing 50 or more families. Peasants frequented the simple Turkish-style baths as often as desired, compensating the bathkeeper (*hammāmi*) for his services at harvest time. In prosperous villages, bathkeepers received up to 4 *manns* (26.2 pounds) of wheat from each peasant. *Khwushnishins* and peasants from other villages paid the bathkeeper after each use. Traditionally, payment took the form of a loaf of flat, unleavened whole-wheat bread. In larger villages, however, a cash fee varying from one to five *riāls* per person was common.[81]

The peasants did not consider bathkeepers and barbers to have much social status. Their low prestige was intimately related to their occupations. Peasants thought their work was degrading. There were two essential reasons for this attitude: first, bath attendants and barbers served other people, and second, they were in constant contact with materials such as body dirt, hair, and blood, which were believed to be religiously unclean (*najes*). Despite this negative evaluation of their work, peasants did not view barbers and bath attendants as "untouchables." A caste system such as prevails in India did not exist in Iranian villages. Thus, it was acceptable for peasants to socialize freely with those they judged to be their inferiors.[82] Generally, barbers and bath attendants were considered equal, but some peasants felt bath attendants were slightly "better" since their work had a noble purpose, i.e., to cleanse the body for prayer.[83]

Although bath attendants and barbers were among the lowest-status individuals of all nonagricultural workers, they did not rank at the bottom of rural society. Since they had definite occupations, their social and economic position was superior to that of the third group of *khwushnishin*s, villagers who did not have regular jobs. These latter primarily were agricultural laborers whose livelihoods depended upon the seasonal availability of work. Their poverty was more extreme than that of any other group. Significantly, agricultural laborers and their families were more numerous than all the nonagricultural workers and their families combined, accounting for at least 80 percent of the entire *khwushnishin* population. In most villages, they comprised 25 to 40 percent of all residents.[84] Throughout Iran the percentage of this group of *khwushnishin*s had been increasing throughout the twentieth century. Indeed, it is possible that prior to the end of the nineteenth century before the rural population began increasing significantly, the *khwushnishin*s had been comprised primarily of village tradesmen and artisans.[85]

Since agricultural laborers neither possessed cultivation rights nor plied any trade, economic insecurity was a constant feature of their lives. Agriculture was virtually the only activity in which they could find employment.[86] Opportunities, however, were limited, since agriculture in most of the country was seasonal and the peasants did most of the work themselves. Nevertheless, laborers were hired to help out with various tasks, such as weeding crops, tending sheep, threshing grain, and picking cotton. More importantly, peasants relied upon agricultural laborers to do most of the grain harvesting.

The principal crops of wheat and barley usually were harvested during May and June. Reaping the grain was an arduous task accomplished with simple hand sickles. The fastest workers could cut only a maximum 2,000 square meters (one-half acre) a day. At such a rate, harvesting was a slow process. For example, if a five-member *buneh* which cultivated twenty acres assigned all its manpower to reaping the fields, it would take at least eight full days for the quintet to cut all the grain; if the *sarbuneh* preferred not to take sickle in hand (as was typically the case), reaping would last ten days or more. Since harvest time coincided with a generally busy period in the agricultural cycle, a week or more devoted exclusively to one activity meant that other crops would be neglected. Therefore, in order to attend to all work efficiently, peasants generally found it expedient to hire laborers to cut their grain.

Depending upon local practice, *buneh*s or individual peasants contracted with agricultural laborers to harvest some or all of their fields of wheat and barley. Reapers were compensated for the actual amount of land which they cut. The best workers could earn up to eight *tumān*s ($1.05), or the rough equivalent in kind, each day.[87] In addition to wages, it was customary for laborers to receive free lunches from the peasants during the harvest.[88]

Some laborers remained employed as reapers for an entire month. Since not all villages had large *khwushnishin* populations, laborers traveled around the countryside at harvest time and offered their services in those places where local manpower was insufficient. Thus, it was possible to work for ten days in one village, a week in another, etc. Usually, seasonal migrations were confined to districts located within a few day's walking distance of each laborer's home village. However, there were some agricultural workers in poor areas who banded together in groups and traveled 200 kilometers (120 miles) or more each season in order to find work.[89]

Once the grain harvest was completed, the demand for agricultural laborers declined sharply. The possibilities for relatively steady summer field work existed only in those few areas where summer crops were as important as wheat and barley. Usually, laborers had to depend upon whatever odd jobs became available from time to time. Those who succeeded in obtaining some work for 100 or more days each year were more fortunate than other laborers in the sense that they had fewer days of hunger with which to contend. Poverty, malnutrition, and disease were the perpetual lot of all *khwushnishin* laborers.

Although most agricultural laborers tended to be resigned to their conditions, some still hoped for some improvement. A few migrated seasonally or permanently to the towns, where they worked at various unskilled jobs. Others dreamed of acquiring *nasaq*s and becoming cultivating peasants. The possibility of rising in status actually did present itself to some agricultural laborers. If, for example, a landowner was displeased with a peasant, he might buy or usurp his *nasaq* rights and offer them to a *khwushnishin*. Also, landlords sometimes brought previously untilled land under cultivation and invited laborers to assume the *nasaq* rights. However, those who did become peasants represented only a tiny percentage of all agricultural workers.

The presence of large numbers of agricultural laborers had an effect on relations between landlords and peasants. From the owner's viewpoint, *khwushnishin* workers constituted a source of cheap surplus labor to draw upon at harvest time and for whatever maintenance jobs might need to be undertaken on the land. More importantly, owners could use them against the peasants in order to increase their own advantages. It was easier, for example, to impose sharecropping agreements whereby landlords received as much as four-fifths of the harvest as long as there were impoverished laborers willing to accept any terms the peasants considered unjust. For their part, peasants realized that their bargaining position was considerably weakened wherever a sizable population of laborers existed. Challenges to the inequalities of crop distribution and the arbitrariness of authority were futile and economically disastrous, since landlords could always transfer the *nasaq* rights of unruly peasants to more submissive agricultural laborers.

CONCLUSION

The preceding description of the hierarchical strata which existed in rural Iran during the twentieth century has been necessarily detailed in order to provide insight into the nature of agrarian society. It would be reasonable to assume that the majority of villages were dissatisfied with the prevailing land tenure and crop sharing patterns in the early 1960's. However, there was a notable lack of widespread peasant rebellion or even organized protest.[90] There was one major reason for this: the absence of any social group which can be identified as a "middle peasantry." As defined in the scholarly literature about peasants, "Middle peasantry refers to a peasant population which has secure access to land of its own and cultivates it with family labor . . . and possession of their own resources provides their holders with the minimal tactical freedom required to challenge their overlord."[91] Obviously, such a group was not present in Iran. As we have seen, the majority of the rural population consisted of poor peasants and landless laborers. Their relationship to landlords was similar to that described in other countries. "The poor peasant . . . who depends on a landlord for the largest part of his livelihood, or the totality of it, has no tactical power: he is completely within the power domain of his employer, without sufficient resources of his own to serve him as resources in a power struggle."[92] If we accept this perspective, then we can assume that for a typical Iranian peasant assessing his situation, the rational choice would be to avoid behavior which seemed likely to worsen his condition.[93] The whole system may be hated, but awareness of powerlessness and the consequences of revolt combined to induce general acquiescence.

3. The Origins of Land Reform

The impetus for changing the patterns of rural landownership de-scribed in Chapter 2 was to come not as a result of any revolutionary activity on the part of the peasantry but rather as a result of con-scious policy on the part of urban political elites. Essentially, land reform became one of several issues in the major political debate of twentieth-century Iran: what was the most effective way to preserve the integrity of the country in the face of political and economic challenges from a more powerful West? Broadly speaking, one can identify two opposing views in this debate. One was that domestic economic, political, and social reforms, designed to transform Iran into a society similar to those of Europe, were necessary in order to strengthen the country and secure its independence. The other was that Iran was not inferior and therefore that no fundamental changes were required; the best ways to safeguard the country were either to exploit politically the rivalries among the Western powers (a strategy advocates of reform often supported) or to keep diplomatic relation-ships at a minimum level in order to discourage interference. In gen-eral, the reformist view tended to dominate the government after the establishment of the Pahlavi dynasty in 1925. However, the re-formers did not succeed in developing a consensus among them-selves as to the types, extent, and pace of reform policies. In particu-lar, there was serious division over the question of whether political democratization or economic development should be accorded pri-ority. This conflict was not resolved, and inevitably there emerged among the reformers mutually antagonistic political factions which sought tactical alliances with groups opposing various reforms.

The conflict over the political nature of the government (i.e., a constitutional or authoritarian monarchy) was sufficiently intense during the 1941–1961 period to prevent the implementation of any substantive reforms. Yet, it was in this very period that land re-distribution became widely accepted among reformers as a prerequisite for a general program of economic development. Landowners obviously were not in favor of any scheme affecting their properties. Nevertheless, their interests were relatively protected during these years because the monarchy viewed them as allies in its own struggle with politicians determined to limit royal power. However, by the early 1960's the shah had consolidated a temporary victory over the democratic opposition, thus enabling the bureaucracy to turn its attention to economic and social policies. Some of the reformers coopted into the government were staunch advocates of land redistribution; eventually they succeeded in convincing the shah and key officials that land reform was an essential program for the country's overall economic development (and even political stability). Thus, an idea articulated by urban intellectuals for fifty years was to become a rural reality. In this chapter we shall trace the gradual acceptance of the concept of land redistribution by the political elite.

EARLY BACKGROUND

Land reform was advocated publicly as early as the Constitutional Revolution of 1905–1911. Land redistribution was one of the platforms of the Democratic Party, organized in 1909 by reform minded deputies of the Second Majlis.[1] However, the Democrats were only a minority party within the *majlis*; thus, opportunities to test their numerous ideas for reform were limited. Furthermore, they were distracted from developing any legislative program for land reform by more pressing political problems resulting from the intervention of Great Britain and Tsarist Russia in Iran's affairs. After the forced dissolution of the Second Majlis and the occupation of Azarbayjan Province by Russian troops in December 1911, the Democrats became absorbed with the nationalist cause, i.e., the eradication of foreign influence from domestic affairs; the party itself gradually disintegrated as its more influential spokesmen were drawn off into exile or into other political groups.[2]

The legislative failure of the Democrats was perhaps inevitable, due to Iran's precarious political situation immediately before and during World War I. It is curious, though, that the party leadership was composed mostly of intellectuals, yet they failed to draw up an analytical or philosophical basis for the land reform they advocated. This apparent lack of interest in developing such a set of ideas seems partially explicable if redistribution per se was not their primary goal, but was only one of several social and economic means to achieve and maintain a specific political objective: an ideal of democracy through constitutional government. In this sense redistribution would deprive the privileged aristocracy of some of it power and thus serve as a check upon arbitrary authority. The Democrats did believe genuinely in the necessity for reforms, but most of them considered constitutionalism, not land redistribution or any other specific reform, as the solution to their country's manifold problems.

Although the Democratic Party did not achieve any of its stated goals, certain individual Democrats were successful, at least temporarily, in carrying out their beliefs during World War I. For the duration of the war, most of Iran was under British (the south), Ottoman (the west), and Russian (the north) military occupation, despite its officially proclaimed neutrality. Democrats helped to organize various resistance efforts, including a major guerrilla campaign against the Russians in the province of Gilan. This force became known as the Jangali movement because it used the dense forests (*jangal*) of the Alburz Mountains as a cover.[3] The Jangalis are particularly interesting for this study because of their close involvement with and activities on behalf of the peasants. As noted in the best English-language study of the movement, "They increased the share cropper's portion of the harvest, lightened labor services, abolished dues in kind, investigated complaints against landowners, recruited peasants into their bands, paid for the food they obtained in the villages, and even forced wealthy collaborators to distribute some of their estates among the peasantry."[4]

Although Democrats among the Jangalis were the leading proponents of rural reforms, it is important to note that the movement was a coalition of diverse forces. The most prominent Jangali, indeed the founder of the movement, was Mirzā Kuchek Khān. As a *majlis* deputy, he had been associated with the Moderates, the faction which had opposed many of the reform ideas of the Democrats. The willingness of Mirzā Kuchek Khān and the Democrats to cooperate in the Jangali movement derived from their common opposition to foreign intervention, and in particular the Russian occupation of Gilan. That there also was agreement about the proclamation of certain agrarian reforms between 1916 and 1919 may have been due to mutually shared views. It is also plausible, however, that Mirzā Kuchek Khān may have seen the reforms as politically expedient since peasants were the primary recruits for the Jangali forces.

While Mirzā Kuchek Khān did support reforms aimed at improving the condition of the peasants, he seemed to have opposed any general concept of land redistribution. This issue became a major source of political conflict in 1920, after the Jangalis joined with a new Communist Party (formed by Iranians recently returned from the Caucasus provinces of Russia where they had worked for several years, primarily in the Baku oil fields) in creating a Gilan Soviet Socialist Republic. Strongly influenced by the revolutionary experiences they had witnessed in Russia, the Communists were determined to implement radical changes quickly and soon proclaimed the expropriation for redistribution of all large estates in the province. Mirzā Kuchek Khān refused to sanction what he considered to be an attack on private property.[5] The increasing tension between the Communists and their allies (including some Democrats) and the Jangalis and their supporters eventually erupted in open warfare (1921).[6] While this struggle was in progress, forces of the central government, which was at odds with the Jangalis over the question of their separatism, entered Gilan in order to reassert authority. The whole Jangali movement was suppressed (with Mirzā Kuchek Khān's decapitated head sent to Tehran for public display—and warning), and most of the rural reforms it had instituted were undone.

The "hero" of the suppression of the Jangalis was Reza Khān, the commander of the government's principal military force, the Cossack Brigade. Although he was to become the first shah of the new Pahlavi dynasty within five years, in 1921 Reza Khān was just beginning to emerge from relative obscurity to political prominence. In February of that year he had collaborated with a group of reformers under the leadership of Sayyid Ziā al-Din Tabātabā'i in a successful coup d'état. Their common goal was to establish a strong central government since they believed that the weak and decentralized nature of state authority was a major reason for the ease of foreign interference in the country. However, Reza Khān and Sayyid Ziā apparently had not discussed a program of reforms prior to the coup and were unable to agree upon appropriate measures afterward. After only three months in office, Sayyid Ziā was forced to resign as prime minister and went into exile.[7] Reza Khān then gradually consolidated power until he was in a position to have the Qājār monarchy deposed and himself proclaimed shah.

While several specific policies became a source of friction between Sayyid Ziā and Reza Khān, their political struggle basically was one over power. Nevertheless, it is interesting to note that the two men had very different approaches to the question of economic reform. Sayyid Ziā was convinced that healthy agriculture was an important key to the restoration of the country's prosperity and strength. To revitalize this sector, he proposed programs which were quite radical for a government in 1921: limited land redistribution and modifications in sharecropping arrangements in favor of the peasants. In particular, he planned to have all the state lands (*khāli-*

seh) transferred to the cultivators. Sayyid Ziā believed these measures would raise both overall productivity and rural living standards.[8] Reza Khān did not share Sayyid Ziā's concerns about agriculture; consequently, when the latter left the government, his plans departed with him.

Reza Khān's economic interests were focused upon industry. Indeed, after becoming shah (henceforth Reza Shah), he developed various policies for transforming the country into an industrialized state on the European model.[9] In contrast to the resources expanded upon industrialization, agriculture was virtually neglected during his reign. It is true that a few minor laws were passed to facilitate agricultural development, but these all benefited the large landowners.[10] There was even a program to sell certain unprofitable state lands to the peasants, but most of these properties actually were acquired by absentee landlords.[11] Policies dealing with broader issues of land tenure and the nature of owner-cultivator relations were never formulated. In fact, it was unlikely tht Reza Shah would be concerned with such matters, due to his own personal interests; by the time he abdicated in 1941, he had acquired, through both legal and extralegal means, more than 2,000 whole or partial villages— over 100 per year—as personal estates, effectively becoming the largest single absentee landlord in the country.[12]

LAND REFORM AND THE INTELLECTUALS

Even though the strong and authoritarian government established by Reza Shah was scarcely interested in agriculture, the ideas about agrarian reform propagated by various political activists in the 1909–1921 period did take root among a growing number of intellectuals. A major inspiration for the development of their ideas came from Europe, as an ever larger number of young men received some education in Berlin, London, Paris, Geneva, and other centers of learning after 1925. Several were attracted to the idea of rural reform. Some were genuinely appalled by the poverty of the peasants; for most, however, the agrarian situation was viewed as a primary cause of Iran's backwardness in comparison to Europe. The nature of landlord-peasant relations was considered to be essentially "feudal." If Iran were to develop and prosper as a modern nation, then the "feudal" aspects of its society would have to be eliminated.

Socialist and Marxist concepts were especially influential in the formation of reform ideas among European-educated Iranians. The individual who played the most prominent role introducing these concepts to his fellow countrymen was Taghi Arani.[13] Arani accepted the Marxist interpretation of society while studying in Berlin during the 1920's. He and his close followers actively disseminated Marxist ideas among students with whom they came in contact in Europe, and continued their educative efforts, albeit clandestinely, in Iran in the 1930's. Arani and a number of his friends were arrested in 1937 and charged with violation of a 1931 law proscribing the propagation of Marxist ideas. Arani himself died (1940) in prison, but most of his followers were released during the general political amnesty following the abdication of Reza Shah in September 1941. Immediately some of them set about to perpetuate Arani's ideas by organizing a Marxist political party, the Tudeh (Masses).[14]

The Tudeh naturally was not exclusively, or even primarily, interested in rural reforms. Although the party did organize some agricultural unions, its strength was in the cities and its rank and file membership consisted of urban workers. Nevertheless, the party did adopt some pro-peasant positions which Tudeh parliamentary representatives presented before the *majlis*. Specifically, these measures included demands that all *khāliseh* land be given to the peasants; that the government purchase the largest private estates for redistribution; and that a new crop-sharing law which protected the interests of the peasants be drafted.[15]

With the exception of some parliamentary seats and three cabinet posts in a brief coalition government (August–October 1946), the Tudeh Party was never in a position to exercise real political power. Thus, its professed dedication to the cause of rural reform was never put to a test. However, one Marxist group which had a rather tenuous relationship with the Tudeh did rule for a year in Azarbayjan. The Firqah-i Dimukrat-i Azarbayjan (Democratic Party of Azarbayjan) was organized in the fall of 1945 by communists who had participated in the Jangali movement.[16] They were disenchanted with the Tudeh, which they felt had no sympathy for provincial interests. In November and December of 1945, the party seized control of local governments and set up an autonomous regime in Tabriz.[17] In April 1946, the Firqah-i Dimukrat government adopted a land reform law which provided for the distribution of *khāliseh* and confiscated property to the peasants. Although several thousand peasants benefited from this measure, Firqah-i Dimukrat leaders actually cooperated with local landlords, confiscating only those estates (687 out of more than 7,000 villages) which belonged to non-Azarbayjani owners.[18] The party's rather cautious approach was deliberate. Determined not to repeat what they believed were causes for the failure of the Jangali movement—radical reform policies which alienated urban interests—the leaders made a conscious effort to cooperate with nonrevolutionary, but reform-oriented, groups which shared their political grievances against the central government.[19] These latter problems were never resolved. Despite several attempts to negotiate differences, Tehran was unwilling to accept the demands for provincial autonomy. Eventually, the army was dispatched to Azarbayjan and the Firqah-i Dimukrat was suppressed in December 1946. Subsequently, their land reform legislation was abrogated, although the memories of their policies could not be expunged.[20]

Even though the Tudeh had not been involved in the Azarbayjan insurrection, public expressions of support for the Firqah-i Dimukrat regime tarnished the party's image. Many intellectuals, including independent Marxists and socialists, believed that events in Azarbayjan had been instigated by the Soviet Union. Those beliefs derived from the fact that Soviet occupation forces were in Azarbayjan when the Firqah-i Dimukrat seized power and in some cases actually intervened to prevent central government troops from resisting the takeover.[21] Since the Tudeh generally supported the USSR's foreign policy, its appeal was seriously weakened among those whose nationalistic ideas were imbued with distrust and even hostility toward Russia. Nevertheless, the Tudeh's setback was only temporary, and by 1948 the party seems to have regained its influence. Its publications enjoyed wide circulation and served to educate a whole generation of literate Iranians about existing social and economic inequalities.

The discussion and advocacy of land reform in the immediate postwar years bore evidence of Tudeh influence. Most intellectuals interested in this issue were either former party members or sympathetic to leftist ideologies. In the latter category was Hassan Arsanjani (1922–1969), the man destined to become chief architect of the Land Reform Law of 1962. Arsanjani was philosophically a socialist, although it does not seem from his writings that he ever developed any coherent analysis of socioeconomic problems. His concern about rural reform did not originate solely from ideology but also from a genuine dislike for an agrarian system he believed to be feudal. He became convinced that a reformation of the land tenure system was the necessary prerequisite for ending the poverty and exploitation of the peasantry. He presented his arguments in numerous articles in *Dāryā*, a newspaper which he edited intermittently between 1944 and 1952.

Arsanjani did not simply call for land redistribution but also suggested some practical ways for implementing such a program. In a January 15, 1951, article, for example, he called upon the shah to take the initiative by distributing his own personal estates to the peasants. The shah could request the largest landowners to imitate his example. Subsequently, the government could draw up a land reform bill to regulate the redistribution of other properties.[22] Several days later, Arsanjani advanced a more radical view that agricultural land belonged by right to the peasant who cultivated it and stated that it was proper that the government expropriate all absentee landowners and give their holdings to cultivating peasants.[23]

The direct influence of Arsanjani, the Tudeh, and other advocates of agrarian reform stimulated intellectual discussion and undoubtedly played a role in political initiatives during the 1950's. For example, in January 1951 the shah issued a royal decree (farmān) providing for the sale of his 2,000 villages to the peasants.[24] While this gesture had tremendous symbolic impact, its actual effects were not very dramatic. Distribution proceeded very gradually over a ten-year period, and fully one-third of the royal lands were sold to various wealthy favorites of the shah, rather than to peasants.[25] Nevertheless, two political consequences resulted from the policy: (1) the shah became associated with the growing land reform movement, while (2) major landlords, far from following his example, became very suspicious of the court's intentions.[26]

Although the shah's actions were opposed by a majority of large landowners, political developments which were perceived as threatening the interests of both royalty and landlords helped to maintain a degree of mutual cooperation during the 1950's. Specifically, the National Front movement and subsequent efforts to eradicate its influence were preoccupations of both the court and landed elites in those years. The National Front had emerged in 1949 under the leadership of Mohammed Musaddiq (ca. 1880–1967) as a loose coalition of nationalistic and reform-oriented groups.[27] It rapidly attracted support from urban middle and lower classes who, for a variety of reasons, were discontented with the government. By March 1951 the National Front had become a potent enough force politically to secure the appointment of Musaddiq as prime minister.

Although the international crisis resulting from nationalization of the Anglo-Iranian Oil Company was the dominant concern of the Musaddiq government, some reforms were attempted.[28] Two decrees issued in October 1952 are of interest for this study. The first stipulated that following division of the crop, 20 percent of the landlord's share was to be returned to the village; 10 percent would be distributed among the sharecropping peasants and 10 percent would be reserved for village developmental projects.[29] Additionally, there were provisions for the setting up of village and rural district councils to function as local governments.[30] The second decree abolished free labor service and all the various dues which landlords customarily levied upon their peasants.[31]

Musaddiq's decrees certainly represented an effort to improve the lot of villagers.[32] However, measured in terms of the kind of reform advocated in such publications as *Dāryā*, they appeared rather insubstantial.[33] Part of the reason for Musaddiq's failure to deal with the fundamental problem of rural Iran, i.e., redistribution of the large absentee-owned estates, lay in the very nature of his government. The National Front was an alliance of various progressive, moderate, conservative, and even some reactionary political groups; their only common bond was nationalism. Obviously, the formulation of a program of land redistribution acceptable to all factions could not be an easy task under the most ideal political conditions. To complicate matters, Iran became embroiled in a major international controversy because of its nationalization of its British-owned oil fields and refineries. Furthermore, this conflict precipitated a domestic economic crisis due to the effectiveness of a British-enforced boycott of Iran's petroleum. Under these circumstances it would have been virtually impossible for the Musaddiq government to devote serious attention to the substance of fundamental reform proposals even if previous agreement as to their general content had been reached.

The two decrees which the National Front government had issued were destined to remain unimplemented. In August 1953, Musaddiq was deposed in a coup d'état. The leaders of the coup included the court, many senior military officers, landlords, and some members of the clergy.[34] This domestic coalition had both the sympathy and the financial support of interested foreign powers, particularly the United States and Great Britain. Consequently, a primary goal of the new government was to normalize relations with these powers, especially Great Britain. There was little interest in even minor rural reforms. Indeed, the decrees of 1952 actually were voided. Possibly among the landlords there was also a hope that all the land-redistribution rhetoric of the previous decade would be curtailed.

TOWARD POLITICAL ACCEPTANCE OF LAND REFORM

The coup d'état was undertaken on behalf of the shah. Mohammed Reza Shah Pahlavi (1919–1980) had acceded to the throne in 1941, following his father's forced abdication in the wake of the joint Anglo-Soviet invasion of the country. The first twelve years of his reign had witnessed the reassertion of parliamentary authority and the reduction in the status of the shah to the role of constitutional monarch. However, after the coup d'état, the shah proved to be an adroit political manipulator and used his military support to re-establish the primacy of the monarchy, that is, essentially he set up a royal dictatorship.[35]

Once the shah had consolidated his position, he had two interrelated domestic objectives: politically, he hoped to secure his power by broadening the base of his support; and economically, he wanted to develop Iran according to a capitalist model.[36] Initially, the political objective was the top priority. This was perhaps inevitable given the fact that his credentials as a nationalist and a reformer were widely questioned by sympathizers of the National Front movement. Indeed, after 1953 many intellectuals believed the shah was merely a puppet of foreign governments, a traitor to his country. For such critics, virtually the only way the shah could redeem his honor was to return the political system to the status quo ante coup. But the surrender of his political power was the one action the shah was unwilling to undertake.

The shah apparently hoped he could obtain some measure of popular legitimacy by championing various social reforms which had been advocated by the National Front and others. As early as 1954 he actually called upon landlords to redistribute their lands among the peasantry, presumably imitating his own example begun in 1951. However, at this time the shah was still in the process of establishing his own power and was unsure of the degree to which he could rely upon the loyalty of the military, his main support, in a potential confrontation with a group as influential as landowners.[37] Therefore, once landed interests started criticizing suggestions that they sell their villages, the shah refrained from active pursuit of the issue.[38] Nevertheless, it was during the 1950's that the shah seems to have become convinced of the need for land reform. While a desire to improve his domestic image was a major factor in the development of his attitudes, his motives obviously were more complex. Other considerations which shaped his views included idealism; a hope for national economic progress; a distaste for a system perceived as backwards, rather than modern; sensitivity to world public opinion (as measured in various international periodicals); and hopes for foreign approval (diplomatic representatives of the United States in particular were encouraging him to initiate a variety of reforms).

The shah viewed land redistribution as a policy that would enhance the power of the central government, in addition to generating broad political support. In the rural areas government control was very weak in the 1950's. For the most part, power in the countryside was monopolized by the large absentee landlords, especially those who lived in the major provincial towns. A program aimed at redistributing their holdings would erode their power. With their power reduced, if not eliminated, the opportunities for landlords to exert any independent challenge to the extension of governmental power would be considerably diminished. Viewed in this perspective, the shah's support for land reform can be considered as one aspect of the struggle between a centralizing monarch and the groups seeking to limit his authority that characterized Iranian politics from the time of the Constitutional Revolution of 1905–1911 until the 1978–1979 revolution which ended the monarchy.

By 1959 the shah felt sufficiently confident of the loyalty of his security forces to consider greater experimentation with social and economic reforms.[39] Accordingly, he advised his prime minister to draft a land reform bill for presentation to the *majlis*. Naturally, landowners were opposed to the legislation, but since the government controlled the *majlis*, their only recourse was to amend the bill in such a way as to make its implementation virtually impossible. The final version, which passed both the *majlis* and the senate in May 1960, limited individual holdings to 400 hectares (988 acres) of irrigated or 800 hectares (1,976 acres) of dry-farmed land; excess holdings were to be sold to the peasants. However, since the customary practice was to measure land by the number of parts of villages owned, any reform based upon the size of holding by acreage would require an extensive cadastral survey preceding implementation.[40] This procedure alone could consume several years, sufficient time for landowners to plot their next move.[41] Before any action could be taken to begin implementing this law, domestic political developments would lead to its abandonment in favor of a more effective alternative.

The abortive 1960 law was very favorable to landowners—to the extent that any compulsory redistribution can be—and was an indication of just how ambiguous were the shah's ideas regarding the pace and nature of reform. Nevertheless, domestic and foreign political developments during the next two years provided the impetus for his support of a genuinely fundamental redistribution program. Specifically, within Iran the opposition, which had been suppressed since the overthrow of Musaddiq, had begun to reactivate itself. The shah thus became preoccupied with political crises which for several months threatened to undermine his government. This unrest resulted from some six years of press censorship, secret security police abuses, and a general suppression of personal liberties. Social discontent and economic recession fueled the mood of protest. Police intervention was often brutal and served to aggravate, rather than quell, the grievances. Parliamentary elections held during the summer of 1960 were so blatantly rigged that the shah was compelled to nullify the results and order a second round of voting early in 1961. Official interference in these elections was only slightly less obvious than six months previously and contributed to a general deterioration in the political situation.[42]

By May 1961, the shah realized that some concessions were inevitable and asked Ali Amini, a politician who had been highly critical of recent government actions, to form a new cabinet. Amini's image as a man who would not be subservient to the shah and his pledge to initiate a program of wide-ranging reforms were reassuring to many groups and contributed to a marked decline in public protest incidents.[43] At the same time, however, Amini was generally suspect in the eyes of Nationalists because he had served in the cabinet of General Fazlollah Zahedi following the overthrow of Musaddiq, and also had helped to negotiate the 1954 oil agreement with a consortium of European and American oil companies. The shah himself was even distrustful of Amini, believing his independent character a potential threat to the monarchy.[44] That he felt compelled to appoint Amini to the prime ministership was an indication of how threatened the shah felt over the ongoing political crisis.

The shah's choice of Amini as prime minister was significant for international political considerations, as well as domestic ones. Since his acceptance of United States support against Musaddiq in 1953, the shah had relied upon the United States as the primary source of economic and military aid for Iran. Thus, he could not be insensitive to the idea being espoused by the newly inaugurated Kennedy administration, that economic and social programs, especially land reform, were the best ways of insuring successful containment of a mutual enemy, the Soviet Union. Whatever his own convictions on this subject, the shah obviously could not afford to ignore American advice at a time when his own authority had been weakened by almost a year of political unrest. In this respect, Amini was not simply a major political figure advocating the need for various reforms, but significantly one who had served as ambassador in Washington in the mid-1950's and who was perceived as retaining ties to influential leaders there. Therefore, by selecting Amini to head his government, the shah hoped to demonstrate that his ideas and goals for Iran were similar to those of Iran's principal foreign ally. Furthermore, official United States policy in the spring of 1961 was to support

Amini for the post of prime minister, a view communicated to the shah by the United States ambassador.[45]

If Amini did not have the full blessing of the shah, his government at least began in a mood of political optimism occasioned by the neutrality of opposition groups within the country and the enthusiastic support of Iran's principal foreign patron. However, these seemingly good omens were not sufficient in themselves to ensure success in the formidable task of resolving the many political, social, and economic problems which confronted Iran in the early 1960's. The implementation of any substantive reform measures would require a government commanding broad political authority. As the political crisis of 1960–1961 had demonstrated, there were groups in the cities who challenged such authority. In the villages, governmental authority was practically nonexistent. A potential solution to both facets of the authority question gradually crystallized during 1961—land redistribution. A program of land reform could break the power of large absentee landlords to interfere with the government's rural policies. At the same time the government could present itself to its urban opponents as a progressive advocate of their own reform ideas, thus winning their support. And many side benefits were envisioned: economic development, social change, increased agricultural productivity; in short, Iran's modernization (read Westernization). Thus was land reform accepted as a desirable goal by the country's political elites. The actual program is the subject of the next chapter.

Village houses in south central Iran, 1978. Mud brick is the typical construction material in all areas except the Caspian littoral. Note grapes drying on roof in foreground. Piles of dirt on center roof will be mixed with water and straw to make a new layer on the roof. Photo by Mary Hooglund.

Elderly peasant couple sit in sun in front of their one-room mud-brick home in a village near Shiraz, winter 1978–1979. Photo by Mary Hooglund.

Author discussing *buneh*s with Iran's leading authority on them, Prof. Javad Safi-nezhad, Tehran, summer 1979. Photo by Mary Hooglund.

Sowing wheat by hand at a village near Shiraz, autumn 1978. Photo by Mary Hooglund.

After wheat is sown, an intricate irrigation network is laboriously constructed with simple hand-crafted tools at a village near Shiraz, autumn 1978. Photo by Mary Hooglund.

Reaping wheat by hand with sickles, south central Iran, summer 1979. Photo by Mary Hooglund.

Using winnowing screen to separate wheat from straw and hulls, south central Iran, summer 1979. When winnowing is done by hand, the process involves two stages, of which this is the second. Photo by Mary Hooglund.

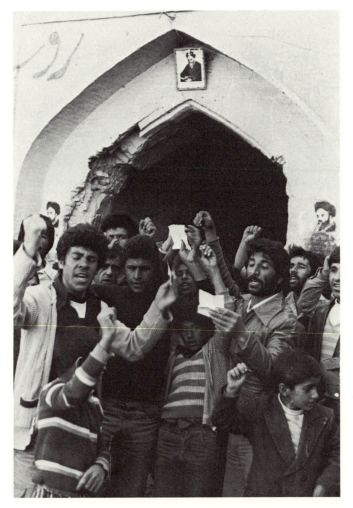

Villagers practicing anti-shah chants in preparation for a protest march through the village, south central Iran, winter 1978–1979. Photo by Mary Hooglund.

Peasants cleaning out the irrigation ditch following expropriation of absentee owners' land, south central Iran, autumn 1979. Photo by Mary Hooglund.

4. The Land Reform Program

On May 6, 1961, when Ali Amini agreed to form a new cabinet, few, if any, people suspected that his government's most important action would become the inauguration of a genuine land reform program. Indeed, Amini himself belonged to a large landowning family and probably had less interest in land redistribution than in more specifically urban economic and political problems. Nevertheless, the Amini government not only initiated a land reform program, but did so with such speed and energy that potential opposition was caught off guard. Gradually, however, landowning interests coalesced and successfully forced the adoption of measures which severely limited the transfer of land to peasants. Yet the effects in the villages of one year of relatively radical land reform activities were profound; eventually both the government and the landlords came to realize that the changes in peasant attitudes and expectations prevented any satisfactory containment of redistribution. Thus there was a reversion to the original goal of encouraging peasant proprietorship. As a result of official vacillation, one can distinguish three distinct stages in land reform policy during the decade in which the transfer of landownership took place. It is the purpose of this chapter to analyze these phases.

APPROACHES TO LAND REFORM

From the perspective of this study, the most important program of Prime Minister Amini's government was the Land Reform Law of 1962. The key factor behind its successful implementation was the attitude of the shah.[1] As indicated in the previous chapter, Mohammed Reza Pahlavi was interested in land reform for a variety of interwoven political and idealistic reasons. However, as late as 1960 his interest was still more passive than active due to his pressing concern to establish his personal authority and to guarantee his power through the support of loyal security forces. After successfully surviving the crisis of 1960–1961, the shah finally was prepared to champion land reform as a major objective of his regime. From his perspective there were at least four political advantages to be gained from such a policy, particularly if it were limited and controlled. First, if the large landowners who traditionally dominated the rural areas could be removed, then the central government could extend its own power into the villages. For a king interested in maximizing his own control over the apparatus of government, maximizing the power of that government was certainly perceived as an important goal. Second, since the shah was aware of his own unpopularity among most of the intelligentsia and urban middle classes, a program which cast him in the role of a reforming monarch who seemed to be interested in the welfare of his people could help improve his image vis-à-vis the very groups of the population who provided the main support of the opposition movement. Third, new bases of popular support for the monarchy could be created among the peasants, who would be grateful to the shah for giving them land. And, finally, redistribution would certainly appeal to the United States government of John Kennedy which was pushing land reform —despite the fact that the United States had never had a land reform experience of its own—with almost missionary zeal as a panacea to developmental problems in Asia and Latin America.

With the support of the shah for land reform seemingly firm, the Amini government included in the announcement of its proposed programs the intention of placing limitations on the size of landholdings. The man given responsibility for developing an appropriate policy was Hassan Arsanjani, who had propagated the cause of redistribution after 1945 (see Chapter 3). Arsanjani played a significant role in both the formulation and the implementation of the first phase of land reform.[2] Indeed, he claimed later that neither the government nor the shah gave much encouragement to land reform, and that he tricked both into supporting it.[3] Relations between Arsanjani and the shah became very strained after 1963, each trying to downplay the part of the other in the program. Whatever may have been the nature of their relationship prior to Arsanjani's forced elimination from land reform efforts in 1963, the significant fact is that he was accorded wide discretion initially, and utilized royal support to carry out a major redistribution of land.

Arsanjani's mandate as Minister of Agriculture was to implement the still unenforced Land Reform Law of 1960. However, he had little enthusiasm for this bill, the main provisions of which he regarded as unworkable. The law's major weakness was the hectare limitation on individual holdings. Such a provision seemed totally irrelevant for a country in which land was measured in terms of whole and / or parts of villages rather than the areal extent of cultivated fields.[4] Other points, such as the establishment of local land reform commissions to determine the price at which landowners would sell their surplus holdings and the creation of a council to allocate plots to the peasants, seemed devised for facilitating landlord evasion of the whole law.[5] Obviously, some fundamental alterations were necessary if the law was to be carried out with any hope of success.

In revising the 1960 law Arsanjani was guided by certain objectives which may be grouped into three basic areas: political, economic, and social.[6] The most important goal was the political one of breaking up the power of the large absentee landowners; only then could any social and economic progress be achieved. In order to redistribute the large estates quickly and easily, it was necessary to circumvent the cumbersome hectare limitation on individual holdings. Instead, Arsanjani proposed that maximum landownership be limited to one six-*dāng* village. All landlords with more than one village were required to sell their excess holdings to the government for a price to be determined by the value of the land as claimed for tax purposes. The government would then resell to each *nasaq*-holding peasant the plots which had been assigned to him during the most recent allocation of fields.

Socially, redistribution would create a class of peasant proprietors. These new cultivating landowners could emerge as an independent force capable of assuming responsibility for basic decisions affecting village welfare. The influence of absentee landlords would be drastically reduced and the negative social aspects of the sharecropping regime eliminated. These developments were necessary prerequisites for improving the health, education, and general living standards of the rural population.

Arsanjani's economic goal was for profit-oriented farming to replace subsistence agriculture. However, the nature of traditional rural credit would seriously handicap peasant initiatives to increase production. One solution to the problem of obtaining adequate long-term, low-interest loans could be a network of rural cooperative societies having access to government funds. The cooperatives could provide peasant members with sufficient credit to finance the types of investments that eventually would lead to higher productivity and some measure of prosperity.

The cooperatives were not to have purely economic functions, but political and social roles as well. Arsanjani envisaged the cooperatives as the primary institutions through which peasants could manage all village affairs.[7] Membership would be an obligatory condition for receiving any land under provisions of the land reform law. However, membership was to be limited only to those acquiring land in order to prevent control of the cooperatives by landlords, moneylenders, and others whose interests were opposed to those of peasants.[8] The development of effective, peasant-run associations also would discourage any tendency for government officials to replace the large landowners as arbiters of rural authority.[9]

The above ideas then constituted the main principles guiding Arsanjani's approach to revision of the 1960 land reform law. Basically his intention was to implement quickly a limited redistribution of the largest holdings to a new group of peasant proprietors with a minimum of social and economic disruption. On the surface such a program appears practical in view of the pattern of landownership in Iran in 1961. Upon deeper analysis, however, his approach raises some unresolved questions about the overall objectives of land reform. For example: Why did Arsanjani believe the creation of a class of peasant proprietors from only part of the sharecroppers would be beneficial? What would be the role of the remaining sharecropping peasants and all the rural landless? And how would land transfers according to *nasaq* rights be reconciled with the *buneh* system?

There are two possible explanations as to why these questions were not addressed. Arsanjani's own reason, offered after he had left government, was that he hoped to start a genuine revolution by "lighting land reform fires in the countryside . . . which would eventually become a conflagration."[10] That is, he expected that the example set by an initial redistribution of large estates would lead to the redistribution of all absentee-owned land, and consequently to a fundamental transformation of rural society. However, it is equally plausible that Arsanjani did not want to create rural revolution (at least not in 1961), but wanted to forestall its occurrence through reforms from above. To suggest this is not to deny his commitment to the cause of land reform. Arsanjani did feel a deep sense of moral outrage over the way landlords controlled villages and wanted to see their power destroyed. At the same time there is no evidence that his revulsion from feudalism led him to a more rigorous analysis of Iranian society and politics. To the contrary, Arsanjani's political activism both before and after 1953 was not in association with those groups advocating fundamental changes, but rather in association with aristocratic individuals like former prime minister Ahmad

Qavam and Amini (and even the shah) who supported only minor reforms. While Arsanjani's own reform ideas certainly were far more radical than those of his political patrons, his alliance with such men bears testimony to both his political ambitions and his ability to compromise ideals. If this interpretation is correct, then in 1961 Arsanjani was a man opposed not to the Iranian political and social system in general, but rather to its perceived injustices, foremost of which was his vision of feudalism. He was sufficiently politically as-tute to realize that his ideal of redistributing to the peasants all of the absentee-owned land would not be acceptable to his associates, so he settled for a more limited program which he could convince them to support. For Arsanjani, the most important goal was to curb the power of large landlords; other considerations were secondary.

THE LAND REFORM LAW

A land reform law incorporating Arsanjani's principal ideas was signed into law on January 9, 1962. Technically, this bill was merely an emendation of the 1960 law, but in actuality it was an entirely new one.[11] Major provisions were designed to effect the transfer of tenure with maximum ease.[12] Individual landownership was limited to one village; thus the law did not apply to small landowners. Land-lords whose property exceeded the permissible limit were required to sell their excess holdings to the government. They were allowed to choose which village to retain; instead of one complete village, a landowner could keep one *dāng* in each of six different villages, or any other combination which would equal six *dāng*s. These regu-lations obviated any need for cadastral surveys and would permit redistribution to take place speedily. Nevertheless, inevitable ine-qualities would result; more than half of all villages would not be covered by the law, while affected landowners could decide to re-tain the largest and/or most profitable villages. In addition, certain categories of land were exempted altogether; these included fruit orchards (*bāgh*s), tea plantations, woodlands, mechanized fields, and property which had been constituted as religious endowments (*vaqf*s).

The Ministry of Agriculture determined the purchase price of land upon the basis of taxes the owner paid on it up to January 9, 1962. The actual amount of assessed taxes was multiplied by a value coefficient which varied from area to area depending upon such fac-tors as irrigation practices, kinds of crops grown, and method of dis-tributing the harvest. Since it was customary for landlords to understate the income derived from their villages in order to pay as little tax as possible, this method of compensation resulted in the compulsory sale of many properties for considerably less than their real value. Procedures were established whereby any landowner could appeal the fixed sale price, but if his own tax dishonesty was the cause of an unfavorable settlement, the grounds for claiming an injustice were weak.[13]

After acquiring the land, the government immediately resold it to the peasants for the purchase price plus a maximum 10 percent surcharge to cover administrative costs. Payments were scheduled into fifteen equal installments due annually at harvest time following a one-year grace period. These payments usually consumed a smaller percentage of the harvest than had been taken by the landlords under sharecropping.[14] Indeed, the total cost of the land for most recipients was reasonable, thanks to the landlord penchant for evading taxes. Nevertheless, there was some resentment among peasants that they should have to pay anything at all for the land they received. Many would probably agree with the view of a peasant in the Khalkhal district: "Our fathers have worked this land for generations; it belongs to us and we should have it free of all burden."[15]

The basis upon which a peasant obtained land was the *nasaq*. With minor exceptions, only *nasaq*-holding peasants were eligible to receive land. In transferred villages, each *nasaq* holder acquired title to the land he was cultivating at the time the law became effective in his area. In instances where the land had been assigned to a *buneh*, rather than to the individual *nasaq* holder, the members would divide the *buneh*'s fields among themselves. Such an approach was advantageous to the peasants: the field layout whereby each peasant (or *buneh*) had equal access to the good, mediocre, and poor areas remained relatively intact, thus tending to equalize benefits to all recipients of a village. On the other hand, the land of most peasants was fragmented into several scattered plots; this would hamper efforts to farm efficiently.

The land reform law stipulated that, in addition to holding a *nasaq*, a peasant had to be a member of a cooperative society in order to receive land. The law did not, however, contain provisions for the establishment of cooperatives. Separate regulations for the setting up of cooperatives in each of the villages subject to reform were issued in June 1962. The cooperatives were to assist the peasants in obtaining credit, marketing crops, and purchasing agricultural supplies, and generally to facilitate the success of the land reform program. Every member would contribute to the capital of his cooperative by purchasing at least one fifty-*riāl* share. The government would add five times the amount subscribed by the members to the capital of each society.[16]

THE FIRST PHASE OF LAND REFORM

The implementation of the January 9, 1962, law is known as the first phase of land reform. Arsanjani's intention was to complete this stage within one year, then initiate a new program for the unaffected villages belonging to small landowners.[17] His "original strategy" for accomplishing this goal was speed.[18] He believed swift action was necessary in order to demonstrate the government's resolve and to catch anticipated landlord opposition off-guard. To generate popular support, he launched an extensive propaganda campaign deprecating the evils of absentee landownership and extolling the positive political, social, and economic aspects of land reform.[19]

The actual task of executing the law was the responsibility of the specially created Land Reform Organization. Initially the Land Reform Organization had a staff of only 20 trained officials, but within eighteen months personnel had increased to 1,184.[20] Although most of the officials were young and inexperienced, they displayed a high degree of competence and dedication.[21] There developed among them an *esprit de corps* for the common task of realizing the land reform ideal.[22] Their enthusiastic attitude both resulted from and contributed to the relatively successful implementation of the law during its first year of operation.

The limited number of land reform officials had one very important consequence for the program; that is, the law could not be applied simultaneously throughout the whole country. Instead, a district-by-district approach was adopted. Arsanjani deliberately selected the area around the city of Maragheh in East Azarbayjan province as the pilot case for implementation because of its high concentration of large absentee landowners.[23] Preparations for carrying out the redistribution were begun. even before the law had been signed. Thus, as early as March 1962, the shah was able to go to Maragheh to hand out personally the first series of title deeds to the peasants.[24]

The success in the villages around Maragheh encouraged the extension of the law to rural districts near the neighboring towns of Hashtrud, Mianduab, Shahindizh, and Tikab. Purchase of estates and their transfer to the peasants continued through the spring and summer. When this process was completed in September 1962, the Land Reform Organization reported that 1,047 villages in the districts of the Maragheh region had been wholly or partially affected. A total of 290 different landowners, including 40 small owners to whom the law did not apply, had sold their properties to the government. In addition, fifty-five cooperative societies had been set up.[25]

Meanwhile, the law was gradually being extended to other parts of the country. In May rural districts near the cities of Qazvin and Arak and villages in Gilan province were declared land reform areas. By autumn Ardebil and Ahar in East Azarbayjan and parts of Kermanshahan, Fars, and Kurdistan provinces were also brought under the scope of the law. At the end of September, a total of 7,500 whole and part villages were in the process of being purchased and redistributed.[26] Thus, although the Land Reform Organization still lacked adequate personnel, its accomplishments during the first seven months seemed impressive.

Although land reform was succeeding, the necessity of executing the law in one district at a time afforded landowners the opportunity to recover from the initial shock. By the end of the summer, opposition was beginning to organize. The largest owners, many of whom held high government positions, realized that a direct attack upon the principle of land reform was impractical as long as the shah supported the program. Therefore, they sought to undermine the law by questioning the wisdom of Arsanjani's hasty implementation. Since peasants in some villages unaffected by the law were refusing to hand over the landlord's customary share in anticipation of redistribution, this fact was seized upon as evidence that the present land reform program was not well planned and therefore was disruptive of rural society. Caution was advised; otherwise the reform from above could produce a revolution from below.

While the controversy over the speed of land reform's implementation was gathering momentum among members of the political elite, national political developments were occurring which ultimately would have profound consequences upon the direction of the program. Specifically, the shah, suspicious of Prime Minister Amini's ambitions, succeeded in forcing his resignation in July 1962. This incident did not have an immediate effect upon land redistribution—indeed, Arsanjani retained his post in the new cabinet. Its significance lay in the fact that it demonstrated that the shah had reestablished his position as the unchallenged political power in Iran. Henceforth he would assume an increasingly more active role in all policy formulation. This would be especially the case with respect to land reform. The early successes of the program and the favorable publicity it was generating would combine to help redistribution become one of the shah's pet projects.

Prior to the actual implementation of a law, the shah had supported the principle of land reform without giving serious thought to its consequences. However, once its effects started to become apparent, it was necessary to adopt some concrete policies to deal with the changes that were taking place. The shah's attitudes would be influenced by the fact that his own conception of the nature of land reform did not involve any idea of radical social or political change. Nevertheless, the very success of the limited redistribution under the 1962 Land Reform Law was creating conditions of potential political instability in rural areas. On the one hand, absentee landlords who were exempted from the law were nervous about its implications and wanted reassurances that the government would not also compel them to sell their agricultural holdings. On the other hand, a majority of peasants had heard about the program by the end of the summer and naturally were anxious—even expectant—that the benefits of landownership be extended to them. Particularly in villages that were proximate to redistributed ones, peasants tended to assume that their turn was close at hand, and some began withholding crops from their landlords. The belief that the government was compelling owners to leave served as a potent ideology to embolden previously docile peasants to defy landlords. To landowners accustomed to unquestioned obedience, the new mood was unsettling. From their point of view, the situation in the villages suggested the very instability the government was promising would not result. Since some owners were connected to various high government officials, it was inevitable that their concerns about stability would reach the shah. Indeed, the new prime minister, Asadullah Alam, was a prominent member of one of Iran's largest landowning families, and was sympathetic to their arguments. Significantly, Alam had always deferred to the shah, and unlike Amini he enjoyed the full confidence of the monarch. Thus, it is reasonable to assume that he used his close relationship with and easy access to the shah to impress upon the latter the inherent dangers to the political status quo of land reform as it was then being implemented.

Whatever the nature of Alam's arguments, after July 1962, the shah became convinced of the need for legislation that would stabilize the countryside by providing both security of ownership to landlords and security of cultivation rights to peasants. Arsanjani was delegated to undertake this task. During the fall he began preparing plans to deal with all those villages which had been exempted from redistribution under the January 9, 1962, law. His proposals were issued as five Additional Articles to the Land Reform Law on January 17, 1963.[27] Basically they provided that in all villages not subject to the original law landowners must choose between a cash rental agreement, sale, or division of the land with the sharecropping peasants. It is doubtful these moderate proposals represented Arsanjani's own ideas about the best approach to adopt. More likely these proposals were the result of concessions Arsanjani made to his ministerial colleagues in order to get their approval—and the shah's—for laws that would apply to all the villages. Perhaps he believed that in the process of implementation the regulations could be strengthened to benefit cultivators. However, he was not destined to implement these laws.

Arsanjani's demise was inevitable following a National Congress of Rural Cooperative Societies which he organized in Tehran in January 1963.[28] It was clearly demonstrated at that convention that he enjoyed enormous popularity and influence among the peasants.[29] At this point, the shah, who had continued to give Arsanjani critical support, became alarmed that his Minister of Agriculture was earning all the credit for land reform. The shah apparently resented the evidence of Arsanjani's widespread support and began to fear that Arsanjani could use his prestige to further his own political ambitions. The shah now became amenable to arguments that the changes occurring in the villages could easily go beyond the limits needed to maintain an authoritarian regime.[30] Thus, the shah rapidly turned against Arsanjani; in March 1963 Arsanjani resigned as Minister of Agriculture, presumably at the request of the shah. As he had been the guiding force behind the land reform program, Arsanjani's resignation had a demoralizing effect upon those officials who were enthusiastically executing the law and gave encouragement to those both in and out of government who desired a more leisurely rate of change.

As Amini's removal from office some eight months earlier had signaled the shah's determination to reassert his own primacy in all executive decision-making, likewise Arsanjani's removal signaled his intention to extend his personal authority over land reform. Already he had decided to make the program the symbol of his White Revolution, a policy of various social and economic reforms submitted to popular referendum at the end of January 1963. For the shah, the principal objective of the White Revolution was political: by taking the initiative with respect to reforms long advocated by opposition groups, he hoped to preserve the royal system of government, with himself virtually an absolute ruler. Thus the appeal of the opposition would be undermined and the shah could establish his image as a modern monarch sensitive to the needs of the people, seriously committed to reform, and thus deserving of support and loyalty.[31] It was perhaps natural that the shah viewed the year-old land reform program as a key element of the proposed White Revolution: the nearly 8,000 villages which so far had been affected provided healthy statistics for any propaganda campaign designed to generate enthusiasm for, and prove the genuineness of, the White Revolution.

The shah's goals of maintaining what amounted to a royal dictatorship while pursuing socioeconomic reforms were inherently contradictory, since real progress on the latter goals would necessarily erode the former. Nevertheless, the shah seemed convinced that, at least for the villages, changes could be introduced in such a carefully controlled manner that their results would be compatible with his overall political objectives. However, a prerequisite for the success of these aims was a strong governmental presence in the rural areas. Compelling the largest landowners to sell all but one of their villages had been an important step in the direction of strengthening the government's role, since it removed from the villages the very people with sufficient power and influence to challenge government agents at the local level. In a political sense, then, the aim of land reform became to substitute the authority of the central government for that of the landlord. Yet there was a realization that under Arsanjani this had not been happening. The ideals of the White Revolution notwithstanding, the shah apparently felt that it was time to halt the pace of redistribution in order to enable the government to extend and consolidate its authority in the countryside. Only after this had been achieved would additional reform measures be considered.

The shah's new mood toward land reform was clearly demonstrated by his choice of a military officer, General Isma'il Riahi, to succeed Arsanjani as Minister of Agriculture. The significance of such an appointment can be appreciated if one considers that since the 1953 coup d'état the shah had been relying heavily upon his security forces to maintain and consolidate his power. Riahi's appointment, together with the slow pace of redistribution over the next two years, suggests that priorities had changed and that, indeed, his primary responsibility was not so much the completion of the land reform program as it was consolidation of the central government's authority in the villages.

The new attitude encouraged opponents of land reform to avoid its intent. Especially in those villages not yet purchased for redistribution, landlords employed a number of subterfuges in order to evade selling villages to the government. They were helped in their efforts to retain their villages by rulings permitting wives and dependent children of landowners to hold separate title to one village each in their own names.[32] Thus, it became common to register villages in the names of wives and other relatives so that no single family member would "own" more than the maximum six-*dāng* limit. Some landowners purchased tractors, placed them in the fields, then declared that their land had been mechanized prior to enactment of the 1962 law and therefore was covered by the exemption provision for land worked by mechanical means.[33] In some areas, local government officials who were hostile to land reform cooperated with landowners to obstruct land reform agents' work.[34]

The slackening of government initiative prolonged the completion of the first phase of land reform by several years.[35] The official statistics of the Land Reform Organization are illustrative of this change in pace. By September 1963, a total of some 8,042 whole and partial villages had been purchased by the government and transferred to 271,026 peasants.[36] At that time it was estimated that at least half of the villages subject to the law had been affected.[37] Thus, it was necessary only to maintain the first year's settlement rate in order to conclude this phase expeditiously. However, the total progress during the last half of 1963 and all of 1964 and 1965 did not equal the results achieved during the first eighteen months of the program. By 1966, the number of purchased villages had reached 12,921, of which only 9,888 had been distributed; the number of peasant recipients had increased by 161,017 to 432,043.[38] Some of these results are summarized in Table 2.

After land reform was declared officially terminated in September 1971, the government reported that under the first phase it had purchased between one and six *dāngs* of 16,151 villages, in addition to 943 farms, for a total cost of 9,781,619,930 *riāls* ($128,283,540) and transferred them to 753,258 peasants.[39] The reader should be forewarned, however, not to accept any of the statistics (including those in Table 2) as wholly accurate. There are considerable discrepancies in figures in the various publications of the Land Reform Organization and Ministry of Agriculture with respect to number of villages per province and the numbers purchased under Phase 1. The only figures used with relative consistency are those for the number of peasant beneficiaries.

THE SECOND PHASE OF LAND REFORM

After Arsanjani's removal from the land reform program,[40] the government tried to regularize rather than to reform the existing land tenure system.[41] The shift in government policy was initiated

Table 2. Land Redistribution under Phase 1, 1962–1966

Province	Villages and Farms (Total)	Villages Affected by Phase 1			Peasants Receiving Land
		6-dāng	<6-dāng	Total	
East Azarbayjan	4,539	553	1,136	1,689	87,827
West Azarbayjan	2,905	166	330	496	18,236
Baluchistan and Sistan	2,295	26	2	28	335
Fars	5,506	165	1,220	1,385	26,639
Gilan	3,122	286	543	829	28,398
Gulf of Oman Area	667	5	13	18	218
Gurgan	791	0	6	6	65
Hamadan	1,494	107	565	672	23,125
Isfahan	6,811	31	321	352	16,643
Kerman	9,723	85	345	430	5,897
Kermanshahan	2,071	571	1,216	1,787	39,638
Khurasan	13,571	180	1,041	1,221	12,391
Khuzistan	1,830	221	954	1,175	61,256
Kurdistan	1,703	122	375	497	21,039
Luristan	2,400	62	428	490	13,163
Markezi (Tehran, Qazvin, Arak)	7,089	192	877	1,069	35,832
Mazandaran	2,413	65	583	648	37,746
Persian Gulf Area	568	37	46	83	3,515
Simnan	800	8	37	45	80
Totals	70,298	2,882	10,038	12,920	432,043

Source: Sāzamān-i islāhāt-i arzi, *Guzāresh-i sāl-i, 1345,* pp. 5–10.

by the shah. Three principal factors account for his attitudes after 1963. First, he feared rural political instability. On the one hand he apparently believed that land reform would lead to the creation of a class of peasant proprietors who would give him their support. On the other hand, he perceived an inherent threat to his regime by the creation of this same class which would be independent of the control of traditional rural authorities (i.e., landlords) who had been responsive to varying degrees of governmental manipulation. A second factor, which is closely related to the first, was the opportunity to assert central government control in the villages from which the power of large absentee landowners had been eliminated. And third, the shah had no appreciation for the socioeconomic problems of the villages, and thus no commitment to developing the kinds of agricultural programs required to assure the long-term success of land reform.

The change in governmental policy is clearly demonstrated by the second phase of land reform. Originally, this stage was to be inaugurated by the implementation of the Additional Articles prepared by Arsanjani. However, for two years no effort was undertaken to execute them. In this period parliamentary elections were held (1963) and the Additional Articles were submitted to the new *majlis*, which, with government acquiescence, amended them substantially. Ironically, 69 percent of the deputies were government employees, virtually all of whom had been land reform officials.[42] Nevertheless, their final version, approved in July 1964, represented a virtual retreat from the goal of land redistribution.

The *majlis'* version of the Additional Articles constituted the basis for the second phase of land reform. These laws provided for all land cultivated by sharecroppers to be settled according to one of five options: (1) the contraction of written rental agreements between peasants and owners; (2) owner sale of land to the peasants; (3) the division of the land between landlords and peasants; (4) the establishment of owner-cultivator joint stock farm corporations; or (5) the purchase by landlords of peasants' cultivation rights.[43] Landowners had complete discretion to choose whichever alternative they preferred. Thus the landlords would determine what, if any, land was to be redistributed among the peasants.

The first option permitted landowners under the Additional Articles was to conclude tenancy agreements with the peasants. Each tenancy would last for thirty years, the unexpired term passing to heirs in the event of a tenant's death. The owner would receive an annual cash rent. This was to be equivalent to the average income earned from the owner's share of the harvest during the 1961–1962,

1962–1963, and 1963–1964 seasons.[44] All religiously endowed properties (*vaqfs*) were to be settled by tenancies. However, in *vaqf* villages, agreements would remain in force for ninety-nine years and rents could be reviewed every five years.[45]

The landowners' second possible choice was to sell their land to the peasants. The price was to be determined by mutual agreement between the two parties. In contrast to the first phase, the role of the government in such transactions would be limited. Specifically, the government would neither request sale nor buy any estates for transfer. However, a government bank was authorized to provide each peasant with a long-term, low-interest loan equal to one-third of the value (at maximum) of the purchased land. Arrangements for the payment of the remaining two-thirds had to be worked out between individual landlords and peasants. Before any of these sales could be completed, land reform officials were required to certify that the prospective purchasers were actually *nasaq* holders, since the sale of plots to other than peasants was prohibited.[46]

The division of land between landlord and peasants was the third method of settlement under the Additional Articles. Division in any village was to be on the same basis as the customary division of the crop. Thus, if a landlord traditionally received two-thirds of the harvest, he could elect to keep two-thirds of the land and allow the other one-third to be divided among all the *nasaq* holders. Peasants were required to pay for the land, although the cost was to be only two-fifths of the total value of the land. They could obtain loans from a government bank to finance one-third of the compensation price, the remainder was payable to the owner in ten equal annual installments.[47]

A fourth choice provided landowners the opportunity, with peasant agreement, of constituting each village into a shareholding agricultural unit. Each member's number of shares in the unit would be in proportion to his share of the unit's assets, taking into consideration land, livestock, and tools. Profits from the sale of crops would be distributed according to shares. Supervision of each agricultural unit would be entrusted to a managing committee composed of one representative of the landowner(s), one representative of the peasants, and a third person chosen by mutual agreement.[48]

The fifth and final option permitted certain owners whose cultivated land did not exceed a specified maximum to buy the cultivation rights of *nasaq*-holding peasants. The maximum amount varied from region to region as follows: 20 hectares (49 acres) for rice land in Gilan and Mazandaran; 30 hectares (74 acres) for cultivated land in the suburbs of Tehran, including Varamin, Karaj, and Damavand;

40 hectares (99 acres) in the province of Gurgan and in the Dasht-i Mughan region of East Azarbayjan, and for all agricultural land other than rice land in Gilan and Mazandaran; 50 hectares (124 acres) in the suburbs of provincial capitals, except the cities of Kerman, Sanandaj, and Zahidan; 150 hectares (371 acres) in Khuzistan, Baluchistan, and Sistan; and 100 hectares (247 acres) in all other areas.[49] The peasants' agreement was necessary if the owner wished to buy their rights. Disputes between peasants and landowners over the proper amount of compensation were to be referred to the Land Reform Organization; decisions of that body would be final.[50]

These five methods of settlement applied to sharecropped land only. An owner could exempt 500 hectares (1,235 acres) from the provisions of the Additional Articles if he used a tractor to plough it and hired wage laborers to cultivate it. Although 500 hectares was, theoretically, the maximum limit for exemption, if an owner could establish that anything over that amount was land he had developed and worked with machinery, this also would be exempted. In effect, this meant there would be no limitation on the amount of mechanized land one individual could own.[51]

The implementation of the Additional Articles began in February 1965. A total of 54,032 villages, including at least 12,542 partially settled under the first stage, and 21,912 farms were subject to their provisions; these properties were owned by nearly 300,000 small holders and cultivated by approximately 1.7 million sharecroppers.[52] Government statistics claimed that within one year about 80 percent of all villages had been settled, and most of the rest by the end of 1967. Only 57,164 peasants obtained land as a result of sales by landowners; 156,279 peasants acquired land through the provisions governing division of land between owner and cultivator. However, 80 percent of peasants had their crop-sharing arrangements transferred to tenancies (1,246,652 thirty-year leases plus 172,103 *vaqf* leases). Another 83,267 peasants received shares in agricultural corporations, while only 17,157 peasants agreed to sell their rights.[53] The statistics for redistribution under the second phase are summarized in Table 3.

This sudden burst of activity in land reform activities appears very impressive on paper. However, one must be wary of the statistics, which don't necessarily provide an accurate account of what was taking place in the villages. I was in Iran during the implementation of the Additional Articles and knew several young men who were responsible for effecting settlements under this second phase of the program. From their experiences, as well as from interviews in subsequent years with other participants—peasants, landlords, for-

Table 3. *Land Reform Options under Phase 2 (through 1972)*

Option	Villages Affected in Whole or in Part	Owners Choosing Option	Peasants Affected
99-year *vaqf* leases	12,052	16,278	172,103
30-year tenancies	40,000 (est.)	227,490	1,246,652
Owner sale of land	[a]	3,275	57,164
Owner-peasant division of land	[a]	22,646	156,279
Owner-peasant joint stock corporations	3,977	41,774	83,267
Owner purchase of cultivation rights	15,024	8,989	17,157

[a] Figures are unavailable.
Source: Sāzamān-i islāhāt-i arzi, *Guzāresh-i sāl-i, 1350.*

mer government officials—it is possible to draw some general conclusions about the manner in which the Additional Articles were
executed. First, it seems to have been general practice for the Land
Reform Organization of the Ministry of Agriculture to rely upon sec-
onded personnel from other government agencies, including the
military, to aid in the implementation efforts; many of these officials
were ill informed about the provisions of the law, had little interest
in the peasants, and often viewed their trips to the villages more as
social outings than as serious work. There were, of course, notable
exceptions of dedicated and enthusiastic individuals; however, the
general attitudes were not supportive of such persons.

Second, it seems to have been a fairly common practice to send
teams out to designated villages without any prior preparation.
Teams frequently were given lists of villages in the morning and in-
structed to have them all settled by evening. This involved traveling
to villages which had received no advance notification, rounding up
as many peasants as could be found, reading the options available
(often without benefit of translation if villagers didn't speak Farsi),
and insisting upon immediate decisions. The ultimate choice almost always lay with the landowners, with the peasants being pressured to sign documents which they could not read. Indeed, I know
of many cases in which the status of villages actually was decided
in town among landowners and officials; then at a later date the documents were taken to the affected peasants for their signatures.

Again, it is important to point out that there were officials opposed to such tactics who honestly tried to explain the provisions and available options to the peasants and supported them, sometimes even against landowners, in selecting the choice most in their interests. Nevertheless, such individuals often had to deal with an unsympathetic bureaucracy. One notable example was related to me by a Kurdish-speaking friend who worked on settlement teams while serving in the army's Extension and Development Corps. He was in the habit of translating the Additional Articles into Kurdish for villagers in the Mahabad area. After helping peasants in a village owned by one of the region's major landowners, he was summoned before his superior officers, severely reprimanded, placed in jail for ten days, then transferred to a base far removed from Kurdistan; he was not assigned to any more land reform teams for the duration of his military service.

A third conclusion regarding the way the Additional Articles were carried out was the impact upon the villagers themselves. The practices just described obviously did not inspire much peasant confidence in government officials. The trust and rapport that had developed in 1962–1963 was rapidly dissipated after 1965 as thousands of peasants began to experience unpleasant encounters with agents representing Tehran. Their suspicions were reinforced by general unhappiness over the second phase of the program: expecting to acquire ownership to the land they tilled, they discovered that none of the options now presented appeared satisfactory. The peasants felt that these unacceptable "choices" were being forced upon them by often arrogant and insensitive officials; this only increased their feelings of disappointment in, and resentment toward, the central government.

Finally, it is necessary to inquire why the Additional Articles were implemented in such a manner. The apparent lack of genuine official concern for the welfare of the peasants is closely related to the nature of the land reform program as perceived by the shah and his close advisors. After 1963 the purpose of land reform was to establish and preserve Tehran's vision of an appropriate political status quo in the villages. The first phase had neutralized the large absentee landlords who were believed capable of interfering with, even obstructing, governmental authority in the villages. The objective of the second phase was to regularize the situation in a way that would provide for both central government political control and rural political stability. The latter aim could best be achieved by "reforming" the agricultural production system in a way that would abolish sharecropping practices that were considered "feudal" in favor of secure, long-term rental agreements between landowners and land cultivators. The government decided to complete this "reform" quickly in order to lay to rest the insecurity which had developed as a result of the initial redistribution. Naturally, the government's intention of transforming sharecroppers into tenants was welcomed by the landowners.

The reason for the popularity of tenancies—from the point of view of landlords—was obvious: the preservation of their property rights. Essentially, tenancy agreements represented the substitution of written, legally binding contracts for verbal sharecropping arrangements. Of course, there were other attractive aspects to tenancies. For example, cash rents assured owners a fixed annual income from their land. Also, all responsibility for capital investments in agriculture, protection of the crops, and marketing the harvest could be shifted to the peasants.

From the perspective of peasants, however, tenancies afforded few advantages and brought unwelcomed liabilities. The only clearly positive aspect was the security of tenure provided by the thirty-year leases. The obligation to pay cash rents constituted the chief burden of tenancies. The majority of peasants did not normally participate in a cash economy; distances from markets and inadequate transportation networks, as well as the necessity to move and sell crops quickly would hamper a transition from barter to monetary transactions.[54] The fixed nature of the rents posed other potentially serious problems. Given the unpredictability of rainfall throughout most of the country, the possibilities of poor harvests and even crop failures were quite real; since the law permitted a landowner to abrogate a tenant's lease whenever the latter fell more than three months in default on payment of the stipulated rent, mass evictions could occur whenever peasants fell in arrears.

Generally, peasants were not satisfied with tenancy agreements. Both government propaganda and the actual redistribution of considerable amounts of land during 1962 and 1963 had prepared a majority of them to expect that they would soon receive ownership of the fields they cultivated. Thus, there was naturally widespread peasant disappointment with the results of the second stage of land reform. Tenants in those villages which had been partially settled under the first phase were especially frustrated, since their situation was so obviously unfavorable in comparison with that of their friends, neighbors, and relatives who had become peasant proprietors. As discontent grew, it was directed against landlords, who were believed to have cheated the peasants by circumventing the law. Peasants commonly expressed the view that tenancy agreements had been illegally forced upon them by their landlords. A frequent allegation was that landlords had succeeded in having the good land reform officials replaced by others who were "in the pockets of the landlords"; these "corrupt" officials had cooperated with owners to prevent peasants from acquiring the land.[55] Peasants demonstrated their increasing mistrust and hostility through withholding rents, destroying landlord property, and participating in lesser forms of resistance and defiance.

During 1967 and 1968 peasant discontent continued to spread. In several districts owners had to enlist the aid of the gendarmerie to quell disturbances and to compel recalcitrant tenants to pay rents. A typical example was the village of Javadabad, near Tehran. In 1965 the two owners had divided the village with seventy peasants. The peasants were convinced that the half they obtained was the poorest land in terms of soil fertility and access to water. In 1967 mounting peasant anger erupted in a village uprising during which the recently mechanized fields of the former owners were "expropriated" and the owners and their representatives were prevented from entering the village. The situation was not normalized until the peasants were forcibly suppressed by the gendarmerie.[56]

THE THIRD PHASE OF LAND REFORM

The growing dissatisfaction with the second phase tenancy "reform" began to filter back to Tehran at a time when the government was becoming interested in formulating various agricultural development policies. The level of agricultural production was a special concern of the shah and his economic advisors during the late 1960's as it became obvious that land reform was not contributing to growth. Consequently, the government began considering a third phase of land reform, specifically aimed at improving agricultural productivity. There is no evidence, however, that either the shah or those officials involved with agricultural policy planning ever seriously studied any comprehensive, well-thought-out developmental plan. Rather, policy seemed to be guided by an attraction toward the capitalist model of agricultural development which stressed widespread mechanization and large financial investments.[57] The government's role in the establishment of farm corporations constituted the new initial stage of Phase 3 of land reform and will be discussed in Chapter 5. The focus in the remainder of this chapter will be upon the second stage of the third phase, the regulations to terminate tenancies.

Government planners who were concerned about the low levels of agricultural productivity tended to attribute lack of growth to "backwardness," i.e., the generally sparse use of mechanization in the production process.[58] Furthermore, they believed that one impediment to greater mechanization was the fact that a majority of peasants were tenants farming land which was owned largely by urbanites. Such officials reasoned that if the cultivating peasants were to become owners, then this change in status would provide sufficient incentive for them to be more receptive to the "modernization" of agricultural methods. This bureaucratic perception coincided with the developing consensus among owners that government intervention to convert tenancies to sales would be an acceptable solution to their own problems with the peasants. Thus, the stage was set for a final government initiative which would complete the land reform program.

Guidelines for terminating tenancy agreements were set forth in a January 13, 1969, amendment to the Land Reform Law. This provided for the sale to tenants of all land held on thirty-year leases.[59] The purchase price would be equivalent to twelve years of rent, with payment arrangements worked out by mutual agreement between owner and leasee. The government guaranteed to reimburse landlords if peasants defaulted.[60] Also, any non-leased land in dispute could be divided between owners and cultivators in the same manner that the harvest was customarily shared.[61] The law did not apply to the land in villages constituting *vaqf* property (leased for ninety-nine years), nor did it affect any of the exemptions in force for mechanized land.[62] It should be pointed out that Phase 2 was not completely abrogated by this law; owners could still elect to divide land with peasants or buy their rights. Also, the new regulations regarding the establishment of farm corporations permitted at least some of the larger owners effectively to usurp peasant rights (see Chapter 5 for more details).

The successful execution of the 1969 law would have resulted in virtually all peasants obtaining the land they cultivated. However, in this phase, unlike the earlier ones, the government's role was limited. Essentially, the government established the general procedures to be followed in sale negotiations, but avoided any involvement in the actual process of transferring landownership. This attitude also extended to the dissemination of information, and thus no concerted effort was undertaken to educate the peasants about the law and its contents. Under such circumstances, it was not impossible for unscrupulous landlords to interpret the law to their own advantage or delay its application. In addition, the assignation of land reform responsibilities among several equal and competing bureau-cracies was an important factor enabling landlords to subvert the law's provisions.[63]

Implementation of the law was begun in the spring of 1969. It was terminated nearly two and one-half years later, on September 23, 1971, when it was officially announced that the land reform program had been completed. In actuality, however, the law was never vigorously enforced. Government policy was to persuade owners to sell voluntarily to their tenants.[64] This permitted landlords to con-clude sale agreements at their own convenience. Generally, smaller owners, who had the most serious difficulties with peasants, were less reluctant to sell their holdings. Owners of whole villages, on the other hand, tended to ignore the law. At least a few of the larger and more influential landlords who did sell to the peasants successfully negotiated higher sale prices than legally permitted. For example, peasants in a village in Fars related this incident to me in the sum-mer of 1970: At the beginning of that year their landlord had caused a shallow well to be dug in the village. A few days later officials from the local land reform office came to the village and marveled at the "depth" of the new well. It was agreed, despite peasant protest, that the increased benefit of this well to the farmers necessitated an up-ward revision of the rents. Thus, all tenancy agreements were re-written to reflect an annual rent increase of 26 to 83 percent, and these new terms became the basis upon which the land was then sold to the peasants. The peasants alleged that their complaints were met with the answer that they would get no land at all if they per-sisted in "making trouble."

As late as 1980, it remains unclear just how many of the 1.25 million original tenants holding thirty-year leases benefited from the third-phase terms. Land Reform Organization statistics indicate some 738,119 peasants had purchased their tenancies by the end of 1972; in addition, 61,805 others acquired land as a result of owners choosing to divide their land with peasants.[65] Despite a wealth of publications after 1972, I have failed to find any later statistics. Nor have requests to explain the discrepancy between the 1.25 million officially enumerated holders of thirty-year leases under Phase 2 and the 738,119 conversions under Phase 3 elicited satisfactory re-sponses.[66] I do know that settlements under all three phases con-tinued unofficially after land reform's official termination in 1971. It is possible that several thousand additional thirty-year tenancies were converted during the 1970's. However, as late as 1978, one would occasionally encounter villages in which most of the agricultural land was farmed by tenants for either a cash rent or a share of the crop.

The relatively slow pace at which tenancies were converted to sales can be attributed to the government's ambiguous attitudes. The 1969 amendment was basically an expedient for defusing widespread rural discontent which some officials feared would result in serious economic and social problems. Selective implementation of the law in villages experiencing intense landlord-peasant conflict combined with the use of coercion against peasant leaders demonstrated that the situation could be managed effectively. This containment of unrest reinforced the views of those in government who believed that land reform did not necessarily imply that all peasants should own land, but rather that it should provide the basis for improved agricultural productivity. Throughout the 1970's small-scale peasant operations were to be viewed increasingly as impediments to such a goal. Thus, official reluctance to support peasant proprietorship in positive ways would intensify.

CONCLUSION

The shah proclaimed the official completion of the Land Reform Program on September 23, 1971, with the bold declaration: "There is no longer any farmer in the country who does not own his own land."[67] While this statement fell several hundred thousand peasants short of the truth, nevertheless a major redistribution of land ownership had taken place since January 1962. The first phase of the program was initiated by the 1962 Land Reform Law which required all landlords to sell their holdings in excess of one village. The redistribution of purchased properties among the peasants who traditionally had cultivated the land as sharecroppers served one of the government's primary reform motives: to limit the political power exercised by large absentee owners in rural areas. This policy aroused hope of similar benefits among unaffected peasants and apprehension about the future among small landowners. However, in the early 1960's, the government had no intention of carrying out a general redistribution until the increasing uncertainty in the countryside necessitated some action. Consequently, a second phase of land reform was inaugurated with enactment of the Additional Articles of July 1964. These provided peasants with security of tenure for the land they cultivated and guaranteed security of ownership to the landlords. The peasants, who had been anticipating the opportunity

Table 4. *Land Redistribution Summary, 1962–1971*

Total peasants with *haqq-i nasaq*, 1962	2,100,028
Peasants acquiring land	
Under Phase 1	753,258
Under Phase 2	
Owner sale to peasants	57,164
Owner division with peasants	156,279
Under Phase 3	
Purchase of 30-year tenancies	738,119
Owner division with peasants	61,805
Total	1,766,625
Peasants holding 99-year *vaqf* leases	172,103
Total beneficiaries of land redistribution	1,938,728
Peasants not obtaining land	161,300
Percentage of *nasaq* holders obtaining land	92%

NOTE: Each *nasaq* holder was a head of household. Iranian rural demographers assumed each village household averaged five members. Thus, if family members are included in the totals, actual beneficiaries numbered 9,693,640.

Sources: Compiled from statistics in Sāzamān-i islāhāt-i arzi, *Guzāresh-i sāl-i, 1346, 1347, 1348, 1350.*

to acquire land, generally were disappointed with the thirty-year tenancy agreements which replaced the customary sharecropping arrangements. The second-phase adjustments of the law did not quiet peasant dissatisfaction and hostility toward landlords, and violence against their property became common in various districts. After 1965, this growing instability forced both owners and the government to reappraise their negative attitudes toward further redistribution. Finally, in 1969, the government decided to introduce a third phase of land reform under which tenants were afforded the opportunity of directly purchasing the land they rented from the owners.

The results of ten years of land reform are impressive. In early 1962, before any redistribution had taken place, an estimated maximum of 2.1 million peasants held *nasaq* rights. Over 750,000 of these sharecroppers—one-third of the total—acquired land by virtue of living in villages which were subject to the 1962 Land Reform Law. Although the second phase sought to legitimize absentee ownership, approximately 200,000 more peasants received land under the provisions of options 2 and 3 of the Additional Articles. During the third phase, almost 800,000 tenants were able to obtain land. Thus, within ten years after initiation of the land reform program, approximately 92 percent of former sharecroppers had become peasant proprietors (see Table 4).

This chapter has examined only the legal framework for the transfer of land ownership. There are, however, important aspects of redistribution which must be considered in order to evaluate the significance of the land reform program. Specifically, what was the average size of peasant holdings? How much land remained under the control of absentee owners? And what was the position of villagers who didn't receive any land? The answers to these and other questions can provide clues to the nature of the new economic, social, and political relationships which evolved in rural Iran up to 1980.

PART II. THE EFFECTS OF LAND REFORM

5. Land Tenure after Redistribution

Now that the mechanics of land reform's implementation have been reviewed, we can examine the program's practical effect upon land ownership patterns. It has been demonstrated that virtually all of Iran's 16.6 million hectares (41 million acres) of arable land was owned by absentee landlords in 1962. This land was cultivated by approximately 2.1 million peasants, who received a share of the crop in return for their labor. If all of this land were redistributed equitably among the peasants holding traditional cultivation rights (*nasaqs*), then each peasant would acquire 7.9 hectares (19.5 acres). This figure is significant because it approximates the 7 hectares accepted by Iranian agronomists and rural sociologists as the minimum average amount of land required to support one village family of five members at a basic subsistence level for one year.[1] That is, taking into consideration that annually about one-half of the crop land is left fallow, a family cultivating 3.5 hectares ideally could sow 2 hectares in wheat, which would be sufficient normally to provide a twelve-month supply of flour for the dietary staple of whole-grain bread, and plant the remainder in fodder and cash crops to trade for necessities such as cloth, tea, and sugar.[2] However, as explained in Chapter 5, only part of the absentee-owned land actually was redistributed among the peasants. Consequently, the average size of holdings which peasants acquired was notably less than the 7 hectares considered to be adequate for subsistence farming. This fact has had significant implications for peasants, agricultural productivity, and the general process of agrarian reform.

The peasants and absentee owners were not the only elements of rural society affected by land redistribution. The approximately 1.4 million *khwushnishin* families had been specifically excluded as beneficiaries of land under all three phases of the reform. With the notable exception of a minority group of traders, *khwushnishin*s historically had comprised the lowest stratum in villages. Realistically, one could argue that their inclusion in the program was not practical since the land which was redistributed was inadequate to provide sufficient land to all the peasants. However, if the objective of an agrarian reform program is to improve rural living standards, then obviously some policies designed to deal in a positive manner with the conditions of most *khwushnishin*s would be essential. As we have seen, social and economic change was not a goal of land reform. Therefore, the government did not direct serious attention to the plight of the *khwushnishin*s, villagers whose situation was to be affected adversely as a result of redistribution.

The inquiry which follows will focus upon the impact of land reform on the three principal social classes in rural society: (1) large absentee and resident landlords; (2) *nasaq*-holding peasants who acquired ownership under the provisions of the law; and (3) the *khwushnishin*s. The discussion will demonstrate that in terms of its redistribution impact, the Iranian land reform was actually a very conservative program which in the long term provided most villagers with few positive advantages.

LAND REFORM AND THE LANDLORDS

It is very important to understand that the land reform program did not eliminate absentee ownership of agricultural land.[3] Indeed, this had never been one of the government's intentions. As previously explained, Tehran's objective with respect to landlords was to reduce their power and influence in the villages so that central control could be extended to the countryside.[4] Officials believed this goal could be achieved effectively by limiting the amount of land any individual might own. Once this aim had been accomplished (Phase 1), the government actually sought to protect the interests of the small and medium-scale absentee owners (Phases 2 and 3). As a consequence, tens of thousands of absentee owners still remained after 1971, although the great and powerful landlords had virtually disappeared.

There are no precise statistics on the number of absentee landowners after completion of land reform. Official publications between 1972 and 1976 variously list between 354,000 and 408,000 individuals as registered owners of land in the size classifications from 10 to 500 hectares; the higher figures tend to occur more frequently in later years (perhaps an indication of more efficient land registration procedures?). I have arrived at an estimate of 200,000 absentee owners by assuming that all holdings over 20 hectares belong to the absentees (a total of 194,000 to 208,000 persons, depending upon the source consulted). This assumption is based upon personal observation, although there are some properties over 20 hectares which are farmed by their owners. Also, some proportion of the 200,000 medium owners (11–20 hectares) are really absentees, although, again based upon personal observation, well below 10 percent.[5]

An estimate of 200,000 absentee owners during the 1970's may represent only one-half of the number of non-cultivating owners before redistribution began.[6] However, it will be recalled from the previous chapter that the owners most likely to have sold their land under Phases 2 and 3 were the smaller ones, particularly those whose holdings were under 20 hectares. Thus, absentees retaining land tended to possess relatively large tracts which could be exploited profitably. Inevitably, their properties were among the most fertile, had the best access to sources of irrigation water, and, as will be shown later, became the objects of continual resentment to the new peasant proprietors.

The amount of crop land owned by absentees following redistribution was about 50 percent of the country's total of 16.6 million hectares. However, there is considerable inconsistency in official statistics for the aggregate hectares in holdings of at least 20 hectares. The lowest figures are 6.5 million hectares (ca. 40 percent); the highest, 9.5 million hectares (ca. 60 percent).[7] These figures do not take into consideration absentee ownership of orchards and pastures, categories of land which were exempted from redistribution in all phases of land reform. Indeed, I have yet to locate any statistics which correlate orchard and pasture ownership with the size of other agricultural properties. On the basis of my observations in various regions of the country, it seems reasonable to assume that absentees own a proportionally higher percentage of orchards and pastures than they do of crop land. With specific reference to orchards, which occupy an estimated 300,000–400,000 hectares (741,000–988,000 acres), I found between 65 and 80 percent of all orchards to be absentee owned in sample villages in Azarbayjan and Fars provinces.

Despite the fact that such a significant amount of land remained under the control of a relatively small group, the nature of absentee landownership was transformed after 1962. Most obvious was the elimination of the large estate embracing several villages. A more fundamental change was the erosion of the traditional landlord-peasant relationship which once permeated village society. This relationship had been based upon almost total peasant subservience to the authority and prerogatives of landlords. When peasants acquired ownership of land, they automatically were freed of the various dues and obligations which had accompanied their status as share-croppers. Landlords who retained part of their agricultural holdings had to adapt to the new situation of independent, and sometimes even defiant, peasant proprietors in their midst. The new relationship was not, of course, one of equals, since the poverty of most peasants in contrast to the wealth of most absentee owners meant that the former were economically dependent, a fact which circumscribed their abilities to initiate autonomous activities. Nevertheless, by the 1970's, the typical absentee landlord could no longer view "his village" as a personal fief; rather, "his village" became more the locale where he owned some of the land, which, unlike peasant owners, he did not personally cultivate.

One must not assume, however, that absentee owners lost all their influence. Even though they no longer exercised absolute power, their continued possession of substantial landholdings enabled them to maintain an influential role in village affairs. This position was usually reinforced by their political connections with the regional, provincial, and, in some cases, national elite. Since the status of absentee owners did remain important in rural Iran, it is appropriate to examine the structure of large landownership in greater detail. To facilitate such an analysis, the properties under consideration can be divided into three subgroups based upon the particular form of ownership: (1) the endowed or *vaqf* land, (2) private holdings, and (3) corporate enterprises.

Vaqf Holdings

The absentee properties which have been the least contentious from the point of view of owner-cultivator relations have been the agricultural lands which form part of the real estate perpetually endowed for charitable purposes under Islamic law. In 1965, some 40,000 such holdings were registered as *vaqf*.[8] These included some whole villages, but most were fractional parts of villages, in some cases single orchards. *Vaqf* properties were found throughout the country, although the most extensive holdings were located in Khurasan, where considerable land had been endowed for the benefit of the *shi'i* shrine of Imām Reza in Mashhad.[9] All *vaqf* cultivated lands were subjected to the provisions of the second phase of land reform which required the conclusion of ninety-nine-year tenancy agreements between the *vaqf* administrators and *nasaq*-holding peasants. For most of the more than 170,000 peasants affected, the annual rent, at least during the initial five years, was lower than the value of the share of the harvest they owed prior to the reform.[10]

Although *vaqf* afforded the leaseholders lifetime tenure security, they were not devoid of potential controversy. Specifically, all
agreements provided for a review, and possible upward revision, of
rent payments at five-year intervals. Inevitably, the perceptions of
vaqf administrators and peasants regarding what amount consti-
tutes an equitable rent for the land have differed. Informants have
reported that considerable bargaining took place in the majority of
rent discussions between the two parties in 1970–1971, while the
1975–1976 revisions resulted in much acrimony on both sides.[11]
Significantly, the next regular review of rents took place during
1980–1981. While information about rental negotiations is unavailable, we can assume that the clergy-dominated government of
postrevolutionary Iran probably would make a more serious effort to
protect the interests of the *vaqf*s than did its secular predecessor.[12]

Private Land

The property remaining in the possession of pre-reform landlords was much more extensive than *vaqf* property. After 1971 some
200,000 persons owned at least 6.5 million hectares of agricultural
land, in holdings varying in size from 20 to 500 hectares (ca. 50 to
1,235 acres). At least 90 percent of these owners were small scale
(20–100 hectares), their holdings located in approximately eight out
of every ten villages.[13] Not all of these owners were absentees in a
strictly residential sense, since no less than one-third and possibly
as many as 40 percent actually lived in the villages. In such cases, it
was common for them to participate in some agricultural work, although normally in a supervisory capacity. However, whether they
were country or town dwellers, small-scale absentees tended to rely
upon two methods for the exploitation of their land: leasing it out
for a rent or employing wage laborers.

Typically, absentee-owned land was leased to peasant cultivators on a seasonal basis for a fixed rent, payable either in advance or
after the harvest. In some cases, especially orchards and certain
summer crops such as melons, the rent might be calculated as a
fixed share of the produce or as a share of the total sale price of the
marketed crop. Under lease agreements, it was common for the
cultivator to decide which crops to grow and to assume complete responsibility for all production costs. However, a variety of more
complex arrangements also existed. For example, some rentiers
would agree to finance certain aspects of production, normally irrigation, in return for a share of the harvest in addition to the land
rent.

When queried during 1971–1972 about the value of rents, most owners insisted that payments for leases were not as profitable as farming their land with hired labor would be. This belief may explain the increasing trend throughout the 1970's for small-scale absentee owners to employ workers to cultivate under their own personal supervision or that of a full-time agricultural expert. In such cases, the owners assumed overall responsibility for the production process, invested in machinery and other agricultural inputs, and generally sought to maximize the profitability of their holdings.

A special variety of small-scale absentee owner began to appear during the mid-1970's. This was the land speculator who bought and sold agricultural tracts in villages within a 30–50 kilometer (ca. 20–30 mile) radius of large cities in hopes of making substantial profits from potential resale for industrial or suburban developmental purposes. The practice was to buy land cheaply from indebted peasants who had decided to seek employment in the cities. Previously such peasants had rented their holdings to kinsmen or neighbors whenever they ceased cultivation, thus keeping the land productive. Urban speculators, however, were not interested in the agricultural potential of their purchases. While a few of them were willing to lease such land to farmers pending its ultimate disposition, many more simply enclosed the land and left it to weeds. In this way, much valuable crop land was taken out of production in the environs of Tehran, Isfahan, Mashhad, Tabriz, Shiraz, Kermanshah, and many smaller cities.

The enclosures were the source of much resentment in the affected villages. For example, in the village of 'Aliabad, located about 35 kilometers northwest of Shiraz, peasants complained that speculators had acquired not only some of the best land, but also the water rights to it. Much of this land subsequently was converted into factory sites and weekend house lots for wealthy urbanites. The country homes were especially irritating to the peasants, who believed the consumption of water for swimming pools, flower gardens, and car washing represented an unconscionable waste of a very scarce resource. Furthermore, they alleged that the amount of water available for irrigation purposes had decreased dramatically between 1975 and 1978. Significantly, since the revolution, peasants in 'Aliabad and many similar villages have expropriated enclosed lands for reconversion to cultivation. During the agricultural year 1979–1980, the general practice was to farm such lands communally until such time as a government policy regarding their fate could be formulated.

After 1971, truly large-scale private ownership (100–500 hectares) was limited to approximately seven thousand individuals.[14]

Their holdings were concentrated principally in three provinces: Gurgan, Khurasan, and Khuzistan. The lands were managed as commercial farms, and their owners behaved as agricultural entrepreneurs.[15] Production generally was based upon intensive specialization in cash crops, especially cotton and sugar cane. Wage labor, machinery, the latest seed varieties, and the most advanced agricultural techniques were all characteristic features. The owners tended to be very knowledgeable about all aspects of cultivation and often personally supervised some of the work. They employed agricultural experts, preferably persons trained at universities outside of Iran, and in a number of instances actually hired foreign technicians to assume overall managerial responsibility for their farms. Their primary objective was to obtain consistently high yields and big profits. Throughout the 1970's their operations were generally successful and served as role models to many smaller-scale owners.[16]

There are no reliable statistics regarding the number of villages whose fields were enclosed as part of commercial farms. My own experience has been limited to less than 1 percent of the total of such farms. Nevertheless, the patterns observed probably can be assumed to have general applicability. According to this assumption, the average commercial farm comprised at least 50 percent of the cultivated land of the village (or villages) near which it was located; in some cases the property embraced the entire village (especially true of smaller villages). Overall, as many as 10,000 villages may have been affected by the operations of commercial farms. While these farms did hire considerable numbers of villagers, generally relations between entrepreneurs and peasants were characterized by mutual suspicions and barely concealed hostility. This situation did not improve with time. Rather, by the mid-1970's, significant numbers of commercial farms had begun to hire Afghan laborers—usually illegally smuggled into the country—because the latter were much less troublesome.

The employment of Afghans for wages which generally were lower than Iranian villagers were willing to accept tended to aggravate rural resentment. Consequently, following the success of the revolution in February 1979, first the Afghans, whom peasants perceived as stealing job opportunities, then the large farm owners, whom peasants perceived as stealing land, experienced the accumulated wrath of villagers. The former were expelled forcibly from the absentee-owned properties where they lived in crude dormitory accommodations; deputized agents of various revolutionary committees then rounded up the aliens and compelled their return to Afghanistan. As for the commercial farm owners, in many villages their lands were expropriated by popular action.[17] In some areas, the Revolutionary Guards, civilian security forces formed after the revolution, have intervened in support of the peasants; however, in other villages they have sided with the owners in opposition to peasant efforts to take over land. As of 1981, the revolutionary government itself had yet to adopt a clear position with respect to rural property confiscations.[18] Interestingly, however, various officials of the ministry of agriculture have advocated the need for a redistribution of large farms to landless workers and poor peasants fairly consistently since the end of 1979. Nevertheless, the political instability which has characterized national politics since the revolution has thus far prevented the development of any policies to deal with the status of these controversial properties.

Corporate Land

The third category of large landownership was that controlled by government and private corporations. This was an entirely new form of landholding in rural Iran and had a profound impact upon tens of thousands of village families during the 1970's. For this reason, it is appropriate to examine these enterprises carefully. Government-managed operations are called farm corporations in the scholarly literature; the private ones are called agribusinesses. Separate laws setting forth the guidelines for the establishment of farm corporations and agribusinesses were approved by the *majlis* in 1967 and 1968. Together with the previously discussed regulations for the termination of tenancies, these laws comprised the third phase of the land reform program. The principal objective of these laws was to speed up the "modernization" of agriculture through the introduction of high rates of capital investment, mechanized production, and the specialized cultivation of cash crops, all of which was to be accomplished by concentrating fragmented individual holdings into vast corporate tracts. The spirit of these laws was, in effect, the negation of the original purpose of land redistribution.

The Law Governing Establishment of Companies for the Development of Lands Downstream of Dams (1968) resulted in the creation of fourteen agribusinesses, each occupying a minimum of 5,000 hectares (ca. 12,000 acres), between 1968 and 1978. Under the terms of this law, the government provided enormous incentives to private investors in the form of tax relief, low interest, long-term loans, cost sharing of major construction projects such as road and irrigation networks, and guarantees for the repatriation of profits to foreign countries.[19] Most importantly, the government undertook to acquire the necessary land from the peasants. For example, in the area of the Dez River Dam in Khuzistan province, the government compelled all the peasant owners of fifty-eight villages to sell their land, amounting to 67,000 hectares, and their homes at prices which the villagers believed were considerably lower than the fair market prices prevailing locally.[20] Subsequently, 55,000 persons were evicted, the villages were bulldozed out of existence, and the entire area leveled. Then the land was leased for thirty years to eleven specially created companies. The diverse stockholders of these enterprises included such multinational corporations as Hawaiian Agronomics, Dow Chemical, Mitchell Cotts, John Deere, Mitsui of Japan, and Shell Oil; a number of international banks also invested in these operations, including Bank of America, Chase Manhattan, and First National City.[21]

The total number of villagers displaced as a consequence of agribusiness development is not known; however, it would not be unreasonable to assume as many as 75,000 people were involved. This figure would include not only inhabitants of villages destroyed to facilitate the establishment of concerns under the terms of the 1968 law, but also those villages leveled to create some twenty-two smaller corporations (1,000–5,000 hectares), the shareholders of which were virtually all Iranians. While these latter technically were set up separately, in practice the provisions of the above law were applied liberally to their benefit. Thus, by 1978 there existed a total of thirty-six agribusinesses which controlled an aggregate of some 200,000 hectares (494,000 acres) of irrigated land. The government did have a policy to relocate the affected peasants to specially built new towns. Yet, the attention and resources devoted to this program were virtually nonexistent in comparison to official actions on behalf of the agribusinesses. Consequently, by the time of the revolution no more than 2,000 families—at most 10,000 out of 75,000 evictees—had been resettled.[22]

Agribusiness advocates have justified the adverse effect upon peasants as a necessary social cost that is outweighed by the overall national benefits that accrue from the creation of efficient and successful agriculture.[23] However, the performance of agribusinesses up through 1978 proved to be a "dismal failure."[24] There were four principal reasons for the general lack of success of these ventures. First was the motivation of the various investors: they were interested not in agricultural development, but primarily in obtaining high profits quickly, and secondarily in winning favor with the Iranian government "in order to smooth their way to bigger and better investments" in other sectors of the economy.[25] A second factor was mismanagement: the foreign managers of these enterprises all were ignorant of local agricultural conditions, the necessary skilled labor to run the machinery was inadequate, and there was a lack of coordination between the corporations and government agencies responsible for carrying out many of the construction projects.[26] Third, the technologically advanced machinery and methods that were introduced had been developed for use in specific climates, and their use in Iran had adverse effects on soil and productivity.[27] Finally, the size of these operations was too large for efficient management and production and burdened the units with very high overhead costs.[28] Between 1975 and 1978 the government had to intervene to rescue several of the agribusinesses with additional credits and concessions; in some cases, the government assumed control of the operations completely, managing them like farm corporations, enterprises which will now be discussed.

The farm corporations differed from the agribusiness corporations in three fundamental respects: (1) there was no private investment; (2) management was government-controlled by design; and, (3) the peasants were not dispossessed. Indeed, improving peasant welfare was, as stated in the articles of the 1967 Law Governing Establishment of Farm Corporations, to be as important an objective as raising agricultural productivity.[29] These goals were to be accomplished by concentrating all the landholdings of several adjacent villages into large single tracts. The individual peasant owners would turn over their land to the corporation in return for shares equivalent in value to the property contributed. The land then would be cultivated as a unit; peasants would obtain a portion of the corporation's annual profits based upon the number of shares held. Peasants also could supplement their incomes by working for the corporation for a daily wage. The decision as to which villages could be included with a farm corporation rested with the Ministry of Agriculture. Once a site had been selected, the law stipulated that the ministry had to obtain approval from 51 percent of eligible members before actually establishing the corporation. However, if a majority of peasants in a designated area did try to resist incorporation, various pressures were employed to compel their acceptance.[30] Once the corporation was set up, the Ministry of Agriculture appointed the managerial personnel from among specially trained civil servants.

By June 1978, a total of ninety-four farm corporations were operating in various parts of the country.[31] They encompassed some 850 separate villages with a population in excess of 300,000 and an aggregate area of 400,000 hectares. The typical farm corporation embraced 8–10 villages. However, two of them, Jonaghan near Shahr-i Kord and Rudpish near Fumin in Gilan, involved a single village each, while the extensive Jiroft Corporation included 45 villages in its boundaries. Inevitably, the incorporated villages included some of the most productive crop land in the country. The government especially was eager to establish corporations in those areas located downstream from the major dams it was constructing in the 1960's and 1970's. Thus eight corporations were set up in Khuzistan within the vicinity of the Dez River Dam, while eleven were located in the Mughan Plain of East Azarbayjan in order to benefit from the waters of the Aras River Dam. The largest concentration, however, was in Fars, especially the Marvdasht district, in which the Daryoush Kabir Dam was nearing completion in 1978.

The government's interest in the success of the farm corporations was high; it provided billions of *riāls* for investment purposes through low-interest, long-term loans and outright grants. Yet, despite the considerable financial and other resources invested in them right up to the fall of the monarchy, the farm corporations were not notably successful enterprises.[32] Their sheer size—each was several thousand hectares—tended to militate against efficient management. Also, worker productivity remained low. The establishment of farm corporations was not popular among affected peasants.[33] They tended to resent having to surrender their land to the government in return for a piece of paper; they did not believe the income from shares adequately compensated for the loss of land; they did not understand the purposes of the corporation; and they considered employment as daily wage laborers to be not an opportunity but a derogation in status.[34] Of course, the exact impact of peasant morale upon productivity is difficult to measure, but it is significant that by 1978 several corporations had reverted to sharecropping arrangements in order to encourage greater worker productivity.[35] Still others had to hire Afghan laborers due to the drain of villagers to cities and towns where they could earn higher daily wages.

The 300,000 villagers who were affected by the creation of farm corporations certainly did not experience anything similar to the trauma of peasants whose lands were expropriated by the agribusiness enterprises. Nevertheless, both groups shared a sense of injustice. Consequently, it is not surprising that they should be among the first people to take advantage of the revolution in order to rectify the situation. Thus, as early as the summer of 1979, attempts to alter the status quo had been undertaken in Khuzistan, Kurdistan, and Fars provinces. In the case of some agribusinesses, the lands have been expropriated and redistributed among former owners. On the farm corporations, the most typical action has been the expulsion of the managers; some corporations have reverted back to private holdings, while others are farmed collectively, the peasants themselves making the decisions about crops, planting schedules, work assignments, and distribution of profits. However, as with other postrevolutionary peasant initiatives, the legitimacy of these popularly implemented tenure changes must remain in abeyance pending the formation of an authoritative central government.

LAND REFORM AND THE PEASANTS

We have already learned that the overwhelming majority of peasants holding *nasaq*s on the eve of land reform's inception were able to acquire ownership rights during the decade after 1962. However, as discussed in the previous section, 200,000 absentee owners still retained half of all the crop land after the program had been completed. Effectively, this has meant that at maximum only 8 million hectares were redistributed among some 2 million peasants. Theoretically, this should have provided each beneficiary with 4 hectares (ca. 9.9 acres), not a particularly generous amount of land when one takes into consideration the official assumption that the average peasant family consisted of five members; that is, only .8 hectare (ca. 2 acres) per person actually was redistributed. In practice, however, it was not an objective of the land reform program to redistribute land equitably among *nasaq* holders; consequently, there were tremendous disparities in the amounts of land actually obtained both within and among villages. This fact has had significant implications with respect to the emergence of a new class of peasant proprietors: specifically, a class was created whose own interests were perceived differently according to the size of individual landholdings; and the resulting contradictions rendered any unity of purpose difficult to achieve. This development can be understood better by examining four interrelated aspects of redistribution's effect upon the peasantry: (1) the pattern of land ownership inequality, (2) the fragmentation of landholdings, (3) irrigation problems, and (4) the subsistence nature of farming.

Inequality of Holdings

The amount of land which individual peasants were able to acquire varied considerably. It is true that in some villages redistributed land was divided equally among all *nasaq* holders. This situation prevailed most typically in villages settled under the first phase of land reform, especially in those villages which were transferred under Arsanjani's tenure as Minister of Agriculture. A factor which played a key role in determining how most villages would be redistributed was the status of the *buneh* heads: in those villages where they had enjoyed no special privileges, it was more likely for all *nasaq* holders to obtain equal shares of the land. However, the more common pattern throughout the country was for a few peasants in any given village to acquire substantially larger acreages than did the majority.

Generally, former *kadkhudā*s and *buneh* leaders benefited from the inequitable redistribution.[36] Under the first phase, the government had delegated to them, as the village elders, extensive responsibility to apportion land according to the traditional field layout. In most villages it was natural for them to rely upon the *buneh* networks as bases for division. In effect, this meant that the typical peasant acquired a part of the fields most recently cultivated by the *buneh* of which he was a member. In villages where *buneh* leaders had been entitled to a preferential share of the *buneh*'s crop, they usually succeeded in obtaining an equally advantageous share of the *buneh*'s land.

Under the second and especially the third stages of land reform, the landlords tended to be much more actively involved in the redistribution process. Whether they sold all their holdings or opted to retain part of them, they usually showed favoritism toward their own agents and supporters in the villages. Thus, *kadkhudā*s and *buneh* leaders who had been cooperative in the past were permitted to purchase larger and better-quality lands than were other *nasaq* holders. Although peasants frequently protested to land reform officials, their complaints inevitably went unheeded because the landlords had influence among local bureaucrats while the peasants had none.

While a minority of peasants did acquire substantially more land than their fellow *nasaq* holders, it should not be assumed that the remaining land was distributed any more equitably. There were many villages in which this did occur; for example, one, two, or three peasants obtained at least 10 hectares each while all the rest obtained 5 hectares each. More typically, however, the pattern of redistribution was very complicated. *Kadkhudā*s and *buneh* leaders would try, sometimes successfully, to ensure that their own kinsmen and allies received preferential treatment in the acquisition of land. Also, the fact that peasants were required to pay for the land was an important factor contributing to inequitable redistribution.

Especially under the third phase, when government support for the peasants was virtually nonexistent, there was a tendency in some villages for land to go to the highest bidders among the tenants.

All of the foregoing practices resulted in the pattern of land-ownership among the peasants summarized in Table 5. This table dramatically illustrates the inequitable pattern of peasant proprietorship following the completion of the land reform program. It can be observed that less than 10 percent of all peasants acquired more than 10 hectares of land. (While some of these holdings were as large as 50 hectares, the majority were only 10–20 hectares.) At the opposite end of the scale, four times as many peasants (35 percent of the total) had holdings which were under 1 hectare (2.471 acres). Over 72 percent of all peasants obtained less than 6 hectares of land; thus, at least three-quarters of them did not own the 7 hectares minimum required for subsistence.

Land Fragmentation

The size of landholdings provides only partial insight into the nature of peasant proprietorship following redistribution. Of almost equal significance is the location of the landholdings. In this respect, it is important to point out that the holdings of a majority of peasants consisted of several noncontiguous plots scattered throughout the fields belonging to their respective villages. It will be recalled that under the *buneh* system of production, fields had been divided into areas judged to be of excellent, average, and poor soil fertility, and plots from each of these areas had been assigned to all the *buneh*s of a given village upon a relatively equitable basis. This same rationale was utilized to determine which land each peasant was eligible to acquire. In practice this meant that the plots for which an individual peasant had been responsible (or his share of the plots assigned to his *buneh*) at the time land reform took effect in his village were the ones he could purchase.

In those villages in which all the land was redistributed on a relatively equitable basis among all the *nasaq* holders, fragmenting the fields according to the above formula did not tend to present any serious hardships for the peasants. Indeed, in some of these villages, it was still the practice in the mid-1970's to divide up all the crop land in four areas consisting of fertile, average, poor, and fallow fields. These were then subdivided into numerous smaller plots and allocated upon the basis of random drawing until each peasant had drawn a number of plots whose aggregate area was equivalent to the total hectares to which he officially held title.[37] In contrast, fragmentation of holdings was more problematical in the majority of vil-

Table 5. *Peasant Landholdings, 1976*

Size of Holding (in Hectares)	Number of Peasant Owners (in Hundreds of Thousands)	Percentage of All Peasants
10.1–50	200	8.6
6–10	434	18.7
3–5.9	545	23.5
1–2.9	342	14.7
<1	801	34.5
Totals	2,322[a]	100.0

[a]An estimated 5–10 percent of this total are actually absentee owners distributed among all size-of-holding categories.
Source: Adapted from Khosrou Khosrovi, *Jām'eh-yi dehghāni dar Iran*, p. 96.

lages, in which peasant proprietorship was characterized by wide variations in the area of land owned. In most such villages, the best land was kept by the former landlord or sold to a few peasants, necessitating the reallocation of plots within the fields with the poorest soil; these tended to be far from the village and from water sources. Thus, it was not unusual for a peasant owning only 3 hectares to have his property dispersed in eight or more plots. Such fragmentation generally has made land management inefficient, and it has been the source of considerable bitterness on the part of the peasants (see Table 6).

Irrigation Problems

An original motive for land fragmentation had been to insure equitable access to fields of varying productive quality. A primary factor in determining soil fertility was the land's proximity to irrigation resources. Since Iran generally has a very arid climate, obtaining adequate water for crops is vitally important for agricultural production. Thus, for most peasants any redistribution of land without reference to its source of water would have been meaningless. Fortunately, most plots were redistributed along with their customary rights to a fixed amount of water at regular intervals. In villages which have depended upon a stream, river, or spring, traditional schedules have continued to be observed. However, water disputes have been common in villages which have been dependent upon wells or *qanāt*s for a significant part of their irrigation needs.

Even though some *qanāt*s have fallen under village control,

Table 6. Sample Survey of Peasant Land Fragmentation in Twelve Counties

Shahrestan (County)	A	B	C	D	E	F
Arak	266	256	96	9.9	16	.6
Bandar 'Abbas	118	95	81	5.2	4	1.3
Birjand	164	163	99	3.3	7	.5
Bujnurd	168	145	86	6.3	4	1.7
Darrah Gaz	36	31	86	9.7	5	1.9
Gonabad	35	32	91	2.5	10·	.3
Kashmar	59	40	68	16.7	5	3.3
Khalkhal	129	126	98	7.2	10	.7
Mashhad	324	243	75	14.5	6	2.4
Nishapur	198	187	94	11.8	11	1.1
Sabzavar	143	92	64	14.7	9	1.6
Turbat-i Jam	120	110	92	12.5	6	2.0
Totals	1,760	1,520	86	9.5	8	1.2

A: number of peasant owners interviewed.
B: number with fragmented land holdings.
C: percentage with fragmented land.
D: average size of holdings in hectares.
E: average number of plots.
F: average size of plots (in hectares).

Source: Adapted from Table 1, Section "H," Chapter 5, in Khosrou Khosrovi, *Jām'ehshināsi-yi rustā'i-yi Iran*, p. 168.

it has been more common for landlords to retain title to them, especially in those villages where land has been only partially redistributed. By keeping ownership of *qanāts*, absentee owners not only could insure adequate water for their fields and orchards, but also have surplus water to sell to local cultivators. In certain areas, most notably Kerman province, which is renowned for the length (several kilometers) of its *qanāts*, townspeople with surplus capital have traditionally regarded *qanāts* as profitable investments and since 1971 have demanded higher rents for water use than most peasants consider fair.[38]

Peasants who had to acquire their water needs from *qanāts* belonging to absentee owners generally were dissatisfied with arrangements that evolved. In the 1970's three grievances against *qanāt* owners were encountered with relative frequency: (1) The pre–land reform fixed amount of water allotted for each field had been substantially reduced because most of the flow was being reserved for new, water-thirsty cash crops growing on the land kept by the owners. (2) Fees for the use of *qanāt* water were arbitrarily determined and seemed to fluctuate at the owner's whim, as part of alleged intimidation efforts. (3) The cost of irrigation by *qanāts* had become prohibitive, averaging as much as one-quarter the total value of grain crops and more than one-third that of fruits and vegetables. Consequently, many peasants who felt unable to pay charges for water began to leave increasingly more of their land fallow each year, and to rely exclusively upon the uncertainties of rain, or rent out part of their land to the larger owners.[39]

Subsistence Agriculture

The irrigation problems discussed above illustrate the importance placed upon water in rural Iran. This importance derives directly from the simple fact that water resources are inadequate throughout most of the country for all the agricultural needs. This lack of water is the primary reason why approximately half of the total crop land is left fallow in any given year. Thus, if a peasant owns, for example, 7 hectares, in practical terms he can cultivate only 3.5 hectares (ca. 8.6 acres) annually; and even this land may be dispersed in eight or more separate plots.

The figure of 7 hectares was deliberately chosen as an example because that is the average amount of land, as discussed in the introduction to this chapter, a village family needs in order to grow adequate food for subsistence. However, it has already been demonstrated that at least 75 percent of all peasant proprietors acquired less than 7 hectares during land reform. That is, the majority of peasants did not obtain enough land to maintain their families at a basic subsistence standard of living. In effect, the land reform program created a class of peasant proprietors comprised of a small minority of profit-oriented farmers and a mass of poor peasants unable to support themselves from their holdings.

If such a large proportion of peasant holdings are below the subsistence level, how then have peasants survived throughout the 1970's? A supplementary means of support for peasants has been income earned from work on property other than their own. Irregular employment has been available in the fields both of peasants owning more than 7 hectares and of the absentee owners. For most peasants, however, such labor does not amount to more than several days' wages per year. Thus, it has been necessary to seek opportunities beyond the confines of villages. After 1971 this increasingly involved traveling to urban centers on a daily or seasonal basis; the permanent migration of some family members, particularly sons, also occurred. The level of need for outside income was directly related to the amount of land cultivated: those peasants who annually cultivated less than 2 hectares (probably 50 percent of all proprietors) were much more dependent upon wages earned from working for other persons than were those who farmed more than 2 hectares. Indeed, some of the smallest owners abandoned working their own land altogether; if they could not find renters, they left it barren and migrated to the towns.[40]

Anyone doing research in rural Iran in the 1970's could not avoid being impressed with the profound sense of disillusionment among the majority of subsistence peasants. Contrary to the view of the urban bureaucrats that peasants were stupid—a view often shared with their Western colleagues/advisors/educators and based upon the fallacious equation of illiteracy with ignorance—these villagers were well aware of the reasons for their fate. They were able to comprehend in a rather sophisticated manner the interconnection of economic and political influence. Nevertheless, they felt powerless to effect any change in the status quo, which they bitterly resented. When sure of not being overheard by government agents, they expressed considerable anger at being cheated out of land reform. Significantly, most subsistence peasants remained indifferent when the government was confronted by popular disturbances in 1978, and few of them shed any tears at the passing of the old regime.

LAND REFORM AND THE KHWUSHNISHINS

The third group in rural society affected by redistribution was the *khwushnishin*s. As noted earlier, they did not possess cultivation rights (*haqq-i nasaq*) prior to 1962, although they comprised 40 to 50 percent of total village population. *Khwushnishin*s engaged in a variety of rural occupations, but since the land reform specifically required that recipients of transferred land be *nasaq* holders, the *khwushnishin*s thus were excluded as beneficiaries of the program. Although in certain villages some of them did obtain land due to peasant initiatives in having them share in the redistribution, such instances were rare. On the whole, tenure transfers effectively were limited to former *nasaq* holders. Consequently, a dichotomy emerged between the new peasant proprietors and the landless villagers.

Even though all landless villagers are *khwushnishin*s, all

*khwushnishin*s are not equal in terms of their social and economic status. In Chapter 2, three distinct subgroups were identified: middlemen (traders and entrepreneurs); non-agricultural workers (artisans and service personnel); and agricultural laborers. Generally, the relative position of each group in village society did not change from the description presented earlier. However, the consequences of land reform have tended to reinforce the important role the first group traditionally had in the rural economy, and to aggravate the poverty of the other two.

The various middlemen probably account for only 6 percent of the entire *khwushnishin* population. They frequently ranked among the wealthiest of all villagers. The most common type of middleman was the village shopkeeper. The majority of shopkeepers succeeded in consolidating their economic position after land reform because they became the indirect beneficiaries of the share of the harvest which formerly belonged to the landlord. Once the peasants gained control over their crops, shrewd shopkeepers took advantage of the new situation by encouraging a number of practices which were to their own personal gain.[41] For example, they ceased limiting the amount of goods sold to peasants on credit (which was short-term and bore high monthly interest rates); they stocked their stores with various nonessential consumer items to entice more spending; they engaged in *salaf-khari*, the practice of purchasing the crops of the poorer peasants before the harvest at discount prices;[42] and they purchased small trucks in order to transport and sell produce for a fee during frequent trips to the city. Such efforts have not gone unrewarded; by the mid-1970's most shopkeepers were able to increase their business with peasants by 25–50 percent as compared with a decade earlier. In effect, the cash and kind (usually grain) they were receiving in exchange for merchandise and debt repayment represented a substantial part of whatever "surplus" crop the peasants had as a consequence of no longer sharing the harvest with the landlord.

Khwushnishin tradesmen have benefited from land reform primarily because an overwhelming majority of peasants received insufficient land for profitable farming and thus continued to depend upon credit advances to finance both basic consumption needs and agricultural expenses. Through various policies such as high-interest loans, food credits, and *salaf-khari*, traditional middlemen have kept a majority of the peasants perennially in debt and have siphoned off whatever surplus the peasants produced. The profitability of these relationships for the tradesmen was not unnoticed by the richer peasants. In several villages the latter built their own shops to rent out or run personally, and thus share in the gains of buying and selling.

Although the *khwushnishin* middlemen undoubtedly enhanced their position as a consequence of land reform, their influence in the rural economy was diluted after 1962 by government activities which undermined their former monopoly over capital and credit. For example, not only did rural cooperatives, the Agriculture Bank, and other institutions become new, alternative loan sources, but also their loans generally were long-term (one year) and bore low interest rates (6 percent annually).[43] As a result of this competition, loans extended by shopkeepers declined significantly as a percentage of total loans disbursed. Surveys of several villages in Arak, Birjand, Quchan, Turbat-i Haydari, and Turbat-i Jam have found that shopkeepers' loans accounted for, respectively, 37 percent, 39 percent, 50 percent, and 71 percent of the total in selected years.[44]

However, the overall impact of government-sponsored lending institutions was only to divert some potential loan candidates away from village creditors, rather than to pose any serious challenge to the creditors' position. Primarily, this was a result of official policy, which restricted borrowing to loans for agriculturally productive purposes. In effect, consumer credit was available only in the form of the traditional short-term, high-interest advances of the village moneylenders and shopkeepers. Yet the subsistence nature of farming forced a majority of peasants to remain dependent upon such credit in order to finance part of their essential consumption needs. Thus, even though *khwushnishin* middlemen no longer monopolized lending in general, their continued control over consumer credit enabled them to maintain a dominant role in the rural economy.

Although the position of various middlemen obviously was not adversely affected after 1962, the same cannot be said of the other groups, who account for 94 percent of all *khwushnishins*: i.e., the non-agricultural and agricultural workers. The deteriorating situation of the non-agricultural workers was not so much a consequence of land reform as it was a result of the greater availability of inexpensive manufactured goods which tended to undersell the handmade counterparts traditionally produced by village craftsmen. Such necessary items as shoes, clothing, copper utensils, earthenware, cutlery, wooden furniture, and agricultural tools are now mass-produced in factories and sold in the local markets and village shops at prices which often are lower than the cost of raw materials artisans must obtain in order to fashion similar goods. Thus, village blacksmiths, shoemakers, coppersmiths, carpenters, etc., have not been able to compete successfully with factory-made products and have experienced increasing difficulty earning livelihoods from their trades.[45]

The third category of *khwushnishin*s, the agricultural laborers, is, of all the groups and subgroups thus far discussed, the one which has been most adversely affected by the consequences of land reform. These *khwushnishin*s, whose numbers exceeded 1 million adult men by 1971, depended almost exclusively upon agricultural work for their livelihoods. However, they were intentionally excluded from acquiring land during all phases of the redistribution program. The effect of this policy was to create a class of peasant proprietors and a class of landless workers whose interests have been in mutual opposition. Of course, even prior to 1962, disparities had existed between the position of agricultural workers and peasants possessing *nasaq*s; but after the implementation of land reform, the position of the landless deteriorated vis-à-vis that of the villagers who obtained land. Consequently, relations between the two groups have been based upon an economic competition characterized by tension and even hostility.[46]

The situation of the *khwushnishin* laborers cannot be appreciated without reference to the majority of peasant proprietors who are subsistence farmers. First, these peasants own such small acreages that they can undertake all the work on their land, relying almost exclusively upon their own and their family's labor. This practice has eliminated work opportunities on as much as 25 percent of the land upon which agricultural laborers obtained seasonal employment prior to redistribution. And second, since subsistence farmers generally cannot support their families from their holdings, they have sought the jobs available in the fields of medium and large-scale peasant owners and on the property of absentee owners. Agricultural laborers are in direct competition with them for these jobs; their rivalry for the limited work available has helped to keep wages for agricultural work depressed.

Competition for work between *khwushnishin* laborers and poorer peasants also intensified throughout the 1970's due to the increasing mechanization of agricultural production. While Iranian farming techniques were still relatively labor-intensive by the time of the revolution nevertheless the use of machinery for major tasks such as ploughing and harvesting had become common on holdings over 10 hectares. The net result of this process was to reduce absolutely both the number of hired workers needed and the total work hours available for those employed. This further constricting of remunerative opportunities tended to aggravate *khwushnishin*-

peasant antagonism. Under these circumstances, landless laborers were virtually compelled to migrate away from their villages in search of work to support their families. After the completion of land reform, their migration was primarily toward the urban areas and eventually involved tens of thousands of them, chiefly the young. This movement helped, to some extent, to alleviate the pressures upon the landless who remained, although it could not affect their status as the poorest of all villagers.

CONCLUSION

This chapter has demonstrated that the practical effects of the land reform program were to confirm, albeit in a substantially limited form, absentee landownership, to enable sharecroppers to become peasant proprietors, and to reinforce the status of traditional agricultural workers as a landless rural proletariat. Land reform did not alter the basic character of the pre-redistribution agricultural regime—that is, a system under which a minority of owners derived profit from farming by exploiting the labor of a majority of villagers. Of course, the composition of the former group was modified as a direct consequence of the government's redistributive policies. Specifically, a number of former landlords were removed from the system altogether. Their position was taken over by the minority of peasants acquiring 10 or more hectares of land and the rural bourgeoisie (*khwushnishin* tradesmen); both of these latter subgroups should be considered part of the rural elite benefiting from exploitative relations with the majority of villagers comprised of subsistence peasant farmers and the landless proletariat.

It has already been established that it was not policy during the former shah's government to effect any radical restructuring of traditional relationships in rural areas. Thus, it should not be surprising that land reform did not do so. Yet, any program of land redistribution inevitably creates an image of fairly substantive change. Indeed, just such an image probably was one of the program's goals, even though in reality no serious alterations were to be permitted. The peasants responded to the image and initially hoped that land reform would lead to an improvement in their condition. For the majority, however, extreme poverty coupled with economic insecurity remained their lot. Consequently, they became disillusioned with and bitter toward the program, suspicious of the government, and resentful of the small group of absentee and peasant owners who did benefit from land reform.

The situation described above is the land reform legacy with which a postrevolutionary government of Iran must eventually deal. The fact that peasants in various regions of the country took advantage of the breakdown of central authority in 1979–1980 to seize an indeterminate number of private and corporate farms has made government intervention unavoidable. The inability of the government to respond to these peasant initiatives as late as the fall of 1981 means that it will become increasingly difficult to reinstate completely the ownership patterns which had existed at the beginning of 1979. If a sufficient number of expropriated farms are allowed to remain under the control of the peasants, this precedent could create pressures for additional land reform policies. One appealing policy which has advocates in Iran would be to redistribute all holdings in excess of 10 or 20 hectares on a relatively equitable basis. In the short term, any such program would certainly help to reduce village antagonisms generated by disparities in land ownership. For the long term, however, it is doubtful if such a policy would really resolve the problems attendant upon subsistence farming.

While the structure of land ownership is important, a more basic problem is the fact that Iran's rural population is excessive in relation to total arable land. Counting both peasants and *khwushnishins*, there are approximately 3.5 million families in the villages. If one assumes an equitable redistribution of the country's 16.6 million hectares of crop land among all of them, this provides each family with only 4.7 hectares (ca. 11.7 acres). Yet, we have learned that 7 hectares is considered to be the average minimum landholding for subsistence! Even when the 1.4 million landless *khwushnishin* families are excluded, the average amount per family comes only to 7.9 hectares; that is, bare subsistence. Thus, while the pattern of landownership certainly can be faulted for aggravating the poverty of the peasantry, reforming that pattern in a more equitable manner cannot of itself provide a solution to the economic problems of the villages. The country needs a comprehensive rural developmental program, of the type which land reform failed to provide.

6. Rural Socioeconomic Changes

The analysis thus far has demonstrated that land reform was an essentially conservative program. Nevertheless, even a restricted redistribution has inevitable economic, political, and social consequences. Now it is appropriate to examine some of these consequences in more detail. This chapter will describe the closely intertwined economic and social results of land redistribution and related policies; the political effects are discussed in Chapter 7. With respect to socioeconomic changes, the most obvious result was the transformation of sharecroppers into peasant proprietors. However, this rather fundamental change in landownership patterns failed to alter the traditional nature of agriculture, the primary characteristics of which were subsistence peasant farmers, a poor class of landless laborers, and a generally privileged class of absentee owners. Indeed, one can conclude that in social terms the results of land reform served to reinforce the relative positions of the three principal classes in village society. Economically, the overall consequences of land reform are not as readily apparent. However, the evidence presented below will show that the results of land reform were a major contributing factor to Iran's agricultural stagnation after 1970. This is ironic in view of the fact that a primary economic goal of the program was to increase agricultural production. Yet this outcome not only failed to happen, but more significantly the production of food crops actually declined during the 1970's.

The objective of this chapter is to try to understand why the land reform policies had such an adverse impact upon Iranian agriculture, despite the anticipation of beneficial effects. As will be seen, there is no simple explanation. However, it is possible to gain some insight into the problem through an evaluation of the multiple ways government agrarian programs affected key socioeconomic structures specifically and agricultural production more generally. In particular, it is useful to focus upon the role of *buneh*s and cooperatives after redistribution. Additionally, the reasons for the ineffectiveness of agrarian policies need to be studied carefully. After acquiring an appreciation for the complex factors which have contributed to relatively poor agricultural performance, we can examine the principal social manifestation of the lack of growth and development: the mass rural-to-urban migration of the 1970's.

THE BUNEHS AND REDISTRIBUTION

The decline in importance of the *buneh*s was a direct, albeit unintended, consequence of land reform. The reader will recall that *buneh*s had functioned as the primary economic units in most landlord villages. All aspects of agricultural production were managed through *buneh*s: manufacturing various tools and implements; ploughing, sowing, weeding, and irrigating the fields; harvesting the crops; and dividing up the harvest among *buneh* members and villagers who either worked for *buneh*s on a contractual basis or "sold" services to the members. Thus, *buneh*s functioned not only as means of organizing production but also as means of income distribution. The main beneficiaries of *buneh*s, other than absentee owners, were the peasant sharecroppers; membership in *buneh*s and the acquisition of cultivation rights (*haqq-i nasaq*s) actually were synonymous. Within each *buneh*, work was carried out as a group effort; there was individual responsibility for certain tasks, but not for specific plots of land.

The practical effect of redistribution was to divide the collectively worked ploughlands among *buneh* members.[1] The peasants who acquired private ownership of the land thus became free to decide whether they wished to continue farming their fields in cooperation with other proprietors or to cultivate alone. Since working together was a long-established tradition among peasants, there existed a strong tendency for *buneh*s to remain intact immediately following the implementation of reform.[2] However, there were changes in the terms under which *buneh*s operated; most importantly, the privileges, which had resulted in an inequitable distribution of both labor and the harvest, were eliminated.[3] This transformation of *buneh*s from essentially inegalitarian structures into partnerships of equals probably was a prerequisite for their initial maintenance. Yet, in the long run, the new independent cultivators were not satisfied with group farming arrangements. Consequently, participation in *buneh*s was gradually, but steadily, abandoned after 1965.[4]

The decline of *buneh*s has been thoroughly documented by

Table 7. Transformation of Bunehs in Talebabad after Land Reform

Agricultural Year	4-Member Bunehs	3-Member Bunehs	2-Member Bunehs	1 Person	Total Bunehs	Total Peasants	% in Bunehs
1965–1966	15	—	—	—	15	60	100
1966–1967	9	—	10	4	19	60	93
1967–1968	5	1	16	5	22	60	92
1968–1969	4	1	18	5	23	60	92
1969–1970	4	1	16	9	21	60	85
1970–1971	4	1	14	13	19	60	78
1971–1972	3	2	14	14	19	60	77
1972–1973	1	2	16	18	19	60	70
1973–1974	—	2	9	36	11	60	40
1974–1975	—	1	10	37	11	60	38
1975–1976	—	1	9	39	10	60	35

Source: Javad Safi-nezhad, *Buneh,* 3d ed., Table 30, p. 186 (original table is in Persian; I made some adaptations and added the last column on percentage of peasants in *bunehs*).

Iran's leading authority on the subject, Javad Safi-nezhad of the University of Tehran.[5] Between 1965 and 1978, he observed that their virtual dissolution in many villages followed a similar pattern. Initially, *buneh*s in a typical village were reconstituted in relatively the same size and number as had existed prior to redistribution. In successive seasons the number of *buneh*s actually increased as larger teams divided up into four-, three-, or even two-man units. Eventually, peasants began to work alone, leading to an absolute decline in *buneh*s. In a large but as yet indeterminate number of villages, this process ended with the complete disappearance, except in memory, of *buneh*s. However, in some villages *buneh*s have survived in the form of partnerships of at least two men farming their land jointly. An illustration of this pattern of *buneh* decline is provided for the village of Talebabad in Table 7.

Economic factors undoubtedly have been a primary cause for the decline of *buneh*s. In this respect the fact that some 75 percent of all peasant proprietors acquired less than the 7 hectares necessary for simple subsistence farming has had direct implications for the role of *buneh*s. First, since peasants typically cultivated only one-half of their holdings each season, the majority of them could normally manage their small plots adequately through the use of family labor; thus, there were no obvious advantages to be gained by cooperating with other peasants. Second, because peasant holdings in most villages were of unequal size, attempts to maintain *buneh*s readily led to friction over the amount of labor contributed by each partner and the methods for sharing the harvest.[6] And third, for the minority of peasants who did obtain sufficient land to exploit profitably, cooperation with subsistence peasants proved to be less practical than hiring daily wage workers. In sum, it seems reasonable to conclude that most peasants discontinued their participation in *buneh*s after calculating that their own interests were no longer best served through collective work efforts.

Despite the trend toward independent farming, certain factors have operated to preserve, at least partially, the *buneh* tradition. For example, in villages where close kinship bonds existed among members, *buneh*s often retained their essential pre−land reform structure for several successive seasons.[7] Significantly, even in those villages in which large *buneh*s have broken up into smaller teams of two or three men, it has been observed that the splits usually have been based upon family ties.[8] Of perhaps equal importance has been the necessity for continued cooperation in the management of water resources. Thus, in some villages which practice relatively intensive irrigation, *buneh*s have remained intact although each one functions only during the period of water allocation for the fields of its members; the end of the water cycle terminates the *buneh*'s work, and members perform all other tasks on their land independently.[9]

While *buneh*s have not disappeared completely from rural Iran, overall their decline has been dramatic. As early as 1972, *buneh*s had ceased to be the primary socioeconomic institutions they had been prior to the implementation of land reform. The basic reason for this development had been the reluctance of peasant proprietors to participate in *buneh*s due to the factors discussed above. Although these economic considerations have been important motivations for the peasants' attitudes, psychological factors should not be ignored. In this regard, we can refer to some of the literature about beneficiaries of land redistribution schemes in other areas. In countries as diverse as Bolivia, Egypt, Japan, Mexico, South Korea, and Taiwan, research has suggested that among new proprietors there is a strong preference for individual rather than collective initiatives in agriculture.[10]

While peasant proprietors generally may prefer to base their agricultural profits and losses upon their own personal initiatives, at least in the case of Iran, such tendencies were reinforced by the manner in which redistribution was implemented. That is, peasants acquired inequitably sized holdings, small enough to be farmed with family labor. Moreover, the decline of the *buneh*s was not due solely to peasant attitudes. At the time land reform policy was being formulated, government officials were unaware of the *buneh*'s role in the management of agricultural production. Consequently, no policies were formulated to take advantage of their existence to provide positive support for the land reform program. Ironically, officials believed peasants lacked sufficient managerial skills to farm successfully and were concerned about developing appropriate institutions to aid them. Even when the nature of *buneh*s became better understood after 1970 due to the research of Safi-nezhad and other Iranian scholars, among senior officials there still was little appreciation of their functions.[11] Thus, no policies were conceived which could help preserve, or even revitalize, the *buneh*s. Indeed, as the following discussion of cooperatives will demonstrate, the development of such policies would have been inconsistent with the paternalism and insensitivity to peasant needs which characterized the general approach of the urban bureaucracy to rural affairs.

RURAL COOPERATIVE SOCIETIES

A major concern of the architects of the original land reform law was to avoid serious dislocation in agriculture. Officials believed that landlords were the primary source of management and credit, and that their removal would deprive villages of resources that peasants could not replace for at least several years. To minimize the anticipated economic problems, they conceived of an extensive network of rural cooperative societies which would be supervised by specially trained agents and would serve as conduits for government-sponsored credit. To ensure the effectiveness of cooperatives, membership would be a prerequisite for receiving any redistributed land.

This assumption about the role of landlords was largely fallacious since they had provided little management and only a small fraction of credit. Indeed, the majority of landlords were absentee owners who had little interest in, or even knowledge of, agricultural affairs. The actual management of production, as has been shown, was undertaken by *buneh*s; even major capital expenditures such as *qanāt* construction and maintenance were usually financed by levies upon the harvest of *buneh*s. The officials in Tehran, however, were largely ignorant about the functions of *buneh*s; thus, not only were there no efforts to take advantage of the unique features of *buneh*s, but also it was widely believed that management and cooperation were somehow alien to the "nature" of peasants. This patronizing and naïve attitude about rural conditions unfortunately lay behind much of the government's conception of cooperatives.

These cooperatives were to be recognized as legal entities under Iranian law; thus, they could serve as purchasing agents for agricultural machinery, tools, fertilizers, pesticides, and other goods which were beyond the means of individual buyers. Also, cooperatives could organize facilities for the storage, transport, and marketing of their members' crops. But perhaps the most important activity of cooperatives would be the provision of reasonable credit in sufficient amounts so that peasants might avoid the traditionally extortionate loans of village moneylenders and also be able to make productive investments. If the cooperatives proved successful in these various undertakings, they could considerably aid peasants in their advance from subsistence to profit-oriented farming.

Unfortunately, from the very beginning the rural cooperative societies failed to measure up to their original ideal. Indeed, rather than helping the peasants in concrete ways, the cooperatives rapidly developed into the principal agencies through which the central government exercised its expanding control over villages after 1962. The way in which the societies were set up, the manner in which they were managed, and the type of activities in which they were permitted to engage were all strictly supervised by the bureaucracy. The extent of Tehran's role can be appreciated better by examining more closely the consequences of official policies in each of these three areas.

With respect to the establishment of rural cooperatives, initially government policy was to form several thousand societies throughout the country, each one serving between two and four villages. It was obligatory for peasants receiving land under the first phase of land reform to join cooperatives; however, this requirement was not enforced for peasants acquiring land under the second and third phases. By 1968 some 8,500 cooperatives had been set up—at least on paper—covering primarily villages redistributed under Phase 1 regulations. Subsequently, formation of new cooperatives was very gradual, although peasants were encouraged to join already existing societies. Thus, by 1972 only 8,800 of them had been formed; they served a total of 23,000 villages and had a membership of 1.5 million.[12] While these figures represented only about one-third of all villages and 70 percent of peasant proprietors, the actual number of cooperatives, each one relatively autonomous, proved unwieldy for the bureaucracy to control effectively. Thus, the government decided to consolidate the societies while at the same time including all peasant landowners as members. This action reduced the number of cooperatives after 1973 to about 3,000 "mother" societies (*sherkat-i mādar*) located in the largest villages. Membership was open to all proprietors in villages within a several-kilometer radius (distances varied from district to district). In some cases peasants in as many as twenty different villages were members of the same society. By 1978 government officials claimed that this supposedly more efficient arrangement served practically all villages and peasant proprietors.

While there is no evidence that any peasants had to forfeit membership in a cooperative as a result of the consolidation, some 6,000 villages did lose their functioning societies.[13] In practical terms, this meant that members lost what little independent decision-making authority they may have exercised with respect to their cooperative affairs. The new "mother" societies, with memberships inevitably exceeding 1,000, more easily fell under the influence of the largest shareholders, who also were the richer, large-scale peasant proprietors. This group of the rural elite usually allied themselves with government officials in order to enhance their own power in the villages. Their cooperation in this respect tended to reinforce the ability of the government to control the cooperative societies more directly.

The organizational structure of the cooperatives also facilitated effective control by the government.[14] The entire membership needed to meet in general assembly only once annually. This meeting elected the three-member executive council (each member serving a two-year term) which supervised the day-to-day affairs of the cooperatives.[15] The executive council chose a chairman from among its members, and a manager from the general assembly or even from outside the cooperative. Managers were the spokesmen for cooperatives in all official business with public and private organizations. Their responsibilities included the negotiation of loans from government lending agencies and working with supervisors from the Ministry of Cooperatives and Rural Affairs.

Although peasants predominated in the *de jure* structure of the rural cooperatives, the overall management of these societies effectively was undertaken from Tehran. A Central Organization for Rural Cooperation (CORC) had been established as a department within the Ministry of Agriculture as early as 1963. By 1972 various bureaucratic reorganizations had resulted in the attachment of this agency to an independent ministry which dealt primarily with policies affecting the cooperatives. CORC had a hierarchy of officials, known as *sarparast*s, who were responsible for supervising the activities of the cooperative societies. The district (*bakhsh*) *sarparast*s were the agents in charge of the cooperatives at the local level. They were required to visit the villages regularly in order to interpret government policy for the managers and executive councils and inspect progress toward implementation of previous official directives. *Sarparast*s were not expected to encourage any independent initiatives on the part of cooperatives in their districts; indeed, any projects which did originate with members had to be approved through the layers of the CORC bureaucracy.

This manner of management effectively turned the cooperative societies into tools of government policy. Indeed, the societies' own officers, who were chosen from among the membership, became de facto government agents in the sense that they had to cooperate, willingly or not, with the *sarparast*s, who in turn received their instructions from higher authorities. Thus, despite a continual stream of rhetoric extolling the value of cooperative work, Tehran did not allow the cooperatives to develop into independently run institutions for organizing communal efforts in agricultural undertakings.[16] Not surprisingly, during the entire seventeen-year period from the implementation of land reform until the fall of the Pahlavi monarchy, the government failed to devise any coherent policy for strengthening the role of the cooperatives; that is, there were no officially sanctioned attempts to encourage their involvement in an extensive range of appropriate productive activities.[17]

The types of activities in which Tehran did permit the cooperatives to engage were those which could be most easily supervised. Thus, important agricultural support services such as selling members' crops and purchasing machinery and supplies for collective use were virtually ignored, apparently because the government lacked adequate personnel to provide bureaucratic oversight.[18] Perhaps as many as half of all societies were permitted to establish cooperative stores, but their stocks were limited to commodities made available by various government agencies; primarily this meant kerosene, although the range of goods did become more diversified by the mid-1970's. Nevertheless, while some members benefited from lower prices on a very restricted range of consumer items, most lived in villages too distant from the locale of the store to be able to take advantage of it. The most significant business of cooperatives, however, was the provision of credit to members. Through its support for cooperative lending, the government was able to acquire considerable influence over village affairs. For this reason, cooperative credit needs to be more closely examined.

The importance of credit to the typical peasant proprietor cannot be overestimated. Since farming is a seasonal occupation, income is received only at the time the harvest is sold. Whatever is earned must be used both to provide for the family and to finance recurring agricultural expenses. However, due to the subsistence nature of farming, profits often are insufficient for both purposes. This compels the peasant to obtain credit to make up deficits. Prior to land reform, loans had been available through village shopkeepers, peddlers, and other moneylenders whose exorbitant interest charges served to worsen the peasant's situation. What was needed was long-term, low-interest credit in sufficient amounts to enable the peasant to make the kind of productive investments which would lead to improved yields, higher profits, and better living standards. If the cooperative societies were to supply such loans, this service could help the peasant in the struggle to break out of perpetual poverty and indebtedness.

The effectiveness of the cooperative societies in meeting the peasants' primary need—credit—would depend upon the availability of adequate capital resources out of which to finance lending. At the very outset, men like Arsanjani realized that the poverty of the peasants would severely limit their monetary contributions. Thus, it was decided that the government should assume a supportive role providing important credit reserves to the cooperatives. The basic source of funding would be the peasants themselves. Each member of a cooperative society was required to purchase at least one share, which had a nominal value of 50 *riāls*.[19] The income from the sale of shares was deposited in special trusts held by the government-controlled Agriculture Bank.[20] The bank was authorized to give each society credit equivalent to a maximum of ten times its subscribed capital. This credit, for which the cooperatives paid 4 percent interest per annum, could be used only for loans to members. Each member was entitled to contract a loan for up to 20,000 *riāls* or ten times his investment in the society, whichever was less; interest on cooperative loans was 6 percent a year.

If the cooperative societies were allowed to contract loans up to the maximum limits, the long-term effect upon the peasantry would be beneficial. However, such was not the case. From the beginning, obtaining adequate funds for lending purposes was a major problem of virtually all the rural cooperatives.[21] Even after the oil boom which began in 1974, the government failed to provide sufficient capital resources to meet the demand for cooperative credit. The Agriculture Bank, which in theory was supposed to make available to each cooperative credit equivalent to ten times its subscribed capital, in practice rarely extended to any society credit which exceeded more than four times the value of all its paid-up shares. Consequently, the amount of money cooperatives could borrow to re-lend to members was inadequate relative to the credit needs of most peasants. For example, in the period 1962–1963 to 1973–1974, cooperative loans averaged only 6,000 *riāls* per capita; this sum was the average expenditure required to produce a single hectare of dry-farmed winter wheat! While per capita loans increased steadily in successive seasons between 1974–1975 and 1978–1979, agricultural production costs increased at an even faster rate; that is, the average percentage of production financed through cooperative credit actually declined during the economic boom induced by large oil revenues.[22]

In addition to restricting the total amount of credit, the government's Agriculture Bank also adopted policies which tended to inhibit the flow of available credit. The most important was the requirement that cooperative loans be granted on the basis of *zanjiri*. This meant that all members of a cooperative society received their loans on the same day (usually March 21) and had to repay the principal and interest in full by a fixed date (usually the following January); if any peasant was in default, none of the other members could contract a second loan until the overdue debt had been repaid.[23] Thus, the practical effect of *zanjiri* was to assign collective responsibility for individual debts.[24] Given the very real financial difficulties of most peasants, some defaulting was inevitable, and consequently a majority of cooperatives were unable to extend loans on a regular (i.e., annual) basis. Even when repayment schedules were met, this often involved serious inconvenience for members. For example, it became common for some peasants to obtain high-interest private loans to use to repay their cooperative debts; then, when they received new credit from their societies, a substantial portion had to be reserved for repaying moneylenders.[25] The cumulative result of this practice was to increase peasant indebtedness and to reduce the amount of money available for productive investments and expenditures.

Another Agriculture Bank policy which limited the effectiveness of cooperative credit was a requirement that all loans be extended for maximum terms of twelve months. Because of the nature of Iranian agriculture—i.e., the principal crops of winter wheat and barley have nine-month growing cycles—this meant that loans contracted to finance production costs had to be repaid out of the income derived from the harvest. Thus, there was virtually no opportunity for peasants to accumulate profits, as would be the case if loan repayments were scheduled over several years. In such a situation, cooperative loans were used for annually recurring agricultural expenses, rather than for the productive investments which would help peasants to become economically self-reliant.

From the above discussion, one can conclude that the overall impact of inadequate loan amounts, *zanjiri*, and short terms was to restrict severely the potential value of cooperative credit. This is not to say that the economic role of cooperative societies was wholly insignificant. Their credit was important in the sense that it represented at least a partial alternative to usurious village moneylenders. Indeed, the total amount of borrowing from moneylenders was reduced in villages where cooperative loans were available. In some villages cooperative credit represented as much as 65 percent of the total; in others as little as 20 percent. For all villages, the average proportion of loans obtained through cooperatives may have been as high as 35 percent by the late 1970's.[26] Nevertheless, because their provision of credit was limited vis-à-vis the actual needs of the peasants, the cooperatives did not succeed in benefiting the majority of their members. Consequently, even with cooperative credit, most peasants still had to resort to temporary survival and/or production expedients such as obtaining additional loans at high interest rates from traditional sources; foreselling their harvests at disadvantageous prices; cutting back on certain production inputs, which then decreased overall yields; and leaving larger than normal amounts of land fallow. All such practices contributed to reducing total income from agriculture, and thus worsening the status of affected peasants.

The failure of the cooperative societies to provide more than marginal benefits to the peasants was directly the result of government policy. That is, it was official policy which determined the Agriculture Bank's credit practices, and official policy which decided the proper activities cooperatives might pursue. While expressions of concern for the welfare of the peasantry became standard clichés for the shah and his advisors, in reality any program or project aimed at improving their condition was necessarily circumscribed by the implicit objective that any changes in the rural socioeconomic status quo be consistent with maintaining the national political status quo. Thus, the cooperatives were not allowed to develop into truly autonomous institutions; rather, they became for all practical purposes agencies of the central government, which utilized them to dispense certain limited benefits in a manner bureaucrats believed to be supportive of overall stability.

Officials in Tehran did not perceive the inability of the majority of peasants to increase either their production or their incomes as related in any way to the cooperative policies they decreed. To the contrary, there was a tendency to fault the peasants for virtually all problems of agricultural production.[27] This attitude was seemingly unaffected even by the International Labour Office's 1972 commissioned report which criticized the weaknesses of the cooperatives, and agricultural policies generally, for their negative impact upon production.[28] Thus, in planning strategies for agricultural development in the 1970's, no policies were formulated to reinvigorate the rural cooperative societies. Indeed, not only were the cooperatives ignored in terms of any substantial infusion of funds from the increasing oil revenues, but some of these policies actually contributed to a further worsening of the economic condition of the peasantry.

AGRICULTURAL POLICIES

It is beyond the scope of this chapter to provide a detailed examination of Iran's various agricultural development policies during the last seventeen years of the Pahlavi dynasty.[29] However, it would be useful to review the general impact of some of these programs upon village social classes. Especially after 1971, a variety of policies were implemented, innumerable studies commissioned, and billions of *riāl*s invested, all with the intent of aiding the peasants and improving production. Nevertheless, all these efforts were generally uncoordinated and ineffective in the long term. Indeed, the most striking aspect of Iran's agricultural policies in the post–land reform period was the absence of any comprehensive development plan.

The overall approach of the central government betrayed a lack of serious commitment to resolving the very real socioeconomic problems which constituted a major obstacle to developing the country's agriculture. This becomes clear when its specific economic policies are examined. Generally, virtually all of the latter may be classified into two broad categories of agricultural credits and commodity price supports. The net effect of these forms of government intervention was not to increase production but rather to reinforce the rural socioeconomic conditions which had emerged as a result of land redistribution.

The government's role in the provision of short-term credit through the cooperative societies has already been examined. Long-term credit was less readily available, representing an average of only 10 percent of government-sponsored lending in agriculture during the 1970's.[30] Moreover, with the exception of a few small projects primarily related to irrigation, the bulk of such credit was extended in the form of individual loans with a minimum value of 100,000 *riāl*s.[31] This amount automatically excluded subsistence farmers as potential borrowers, since all had annual incomes which at most were less than half this sum; yet their need for long-term, low-interest loans was desperate. In effect, most of the recipients were the largest owners and the farm corporations. Their virtually exclusive access to this highly favorable source of credit was an important factor encouraging the commercialization of large-scale agriculture; it also contributed to widening the income disparities between the minority of wealthy absentee landlords and the mass of peasant proprietors.

The government's long-term credit policies had a negative impact upon overall agricultural production as well. With their concessionary loans the commercial farmers invested in cultivating profitable cash crops such as cotton, sugar cane, and sugar beets; less and less of their land was planted in food crops such as wheat and rice. The subsistence-farming peasants did continue to grow primarily grains, but due to their lack of investment capital they were unable to increase yields substantially; in addition, they tended to consume most of their production. Consequently, the annual marketable surplus of staple grains fell relative to the annual increase in urban population. By the early 1970's the government had begun regular importation of some wheat and rice (as well as many other foods) in order to offset the domestic deficit in supply versus demand.

The government's price support policies were not any more enlightened. This was most dramatically illustrated by the effects of government intervention with respect to wheat.[32] This crop is the single most important one for Iranian agriculture; 60 percent of the annually cultivated land is sown in wheat; among all peasant proprietors, wheat accounts for an average 75 percent of total production. Additionally, wheat is the staple of the national diet. Thus, a primary objective of the government's wheat policy as early as the mid-1960's was to stabilize the wholesale price of this grain in order to benefit both the rural producer and the urban consumer. This goal was to be accomplished by setting a minimum price at which the government would purchase wheat directly from the farmer whenever the market prices fell below this minimum.

In practice the minimum-price policy for wheat failed to benefit the producers of this important food crop. This failure was due to the combined effects of several tactics employed by the government. First, the Ministry of Cooperatives and Rural Affairs agency responsible for wheat, the Cereals Organization, did not announce its minimum price for a given year earlier than the third week of June, which corresponded with the last half of the wheat harvest season for most areas of the country. By such a late date most growers, particularly the subsistence-level peasants, had felt pressured into signing purchase contracts with private wholesalers; in most years the free market prices in May and early June were lower than the official minimum price subsequently established.

A second negative tactic was the Cereals Organization's unwillingness to buy all the grain offered for sale by farmers. Indeed, its annual wheat purchases at its own minimum price accounted for an insignificant portion of total production.[33] Unable to sell their surpluses to the government, peasants were obliged to sell to wholesalers whose prices, more often than not, were below the official minimum. The lack of adequate transport and storage facilities served to increase most peasants' dependency upon buyers affiliated with the urban market network. Consequently, even when the Cereals Organization began to expand its purchases after 1975, the overwhelming majority of peasants had ceased to regard sales to it as a realistic alternative.

The problems which derived from the delay in setting minimum prices and the failure to buy a substantial amount of the wheat harvest were compounded by the lack of any rational basis for determining an appropriate floor price. Throughout the period under consideration, the variable levels of the minimum price bore no apparent relationship to actual production costs. Initially, in the early 1960's, the minimum price seems to have been set with reference to the then prevailing wholesale price. During the next decade, there were only minute changes despite wide fluctuations in wholesale prices. By 1974 wholesale prices were more than twice the government price, a fact which undoubtedly prompted the first significant increase—by two-thirds—in the minimum. However, production costs had risen during the same interval. Consequently, by the mid-1970's, the cost to the farmer of producing each ton of wheat exceeded the minimum price offered by the government for the same amount. The dramatic rise in the minimum price after 1974 succeeded only in narrowing this differential; for example, during the early summer of 1978, the minimum price was 12,000 *riāls* per ton for wheat, but the production costs to the farmer averaged 14,000–17,000 *riāls* per ton, depending upon the area and the type of inputs used. Under these conditions, one can conclude that the government's minimum price policy served more as a disincentive than as a support to agriculture.

It is perhaps natural to inquire into the motives for the poor management of government price policy. It is highly unlikely that malicious intent guided official thinking regarding the minimum prices. Rather, bureaucratic insensitivity and general ignorance probably provided the general context for the relevant decisions. In addition, the Cereals Organization perceived its responsibility as one of protecting the urban consumer from inflationary prices (for political, rather than altruistic reasons), not necessarily helping the rural producer. Indeed, most of its efforts between 1970 and 1978 were directed at purchasing wheat (or flour) in foreign markets, rather than domestically, in order to ensure an adequate supply of bread for the cities. For example, in 1974 the organization purchased only 85 tons of wheat from Iran's farmers (less than one-tenth of 1 percent of total production), but imported over 1.25 million tons from abroad.[34] Ironically, the imported wheat cost the government an average of 2,500 *riāls* more per ton than it paid its own producers.[35] The foreign grain was then subsidized by selling it to millers and bakers below cost.

RURAL MIGRATION

The discussion thus far has demonstrated that the overall effect of the government's various agricultural policies was to increase the difficulties most peasants experienced in trying to make a livelihood from their landholdings. In the first place, land redistribution itself did not materially benefit the majority of peasants in the sense that they acquired ownership only to plots of (at best) subsistence size. In addition, nearly half of the rural population—the agricultural laborers—had obtained no land at all. Thus, by 1971, when land reform was declared officially completed, the overwhelming majority of villagers were in no better economic situation than they had been prior to implementation of the program. Indeed, the evidence suggests that the relative economic position of thousands of rural families actually worsened during the "revolutionary" decade of land reform. Not surprisingly, the frustrations of trying to earn a living from agriculture encouraged villagers to consider improving their condition through migration. By the mid-1970's migration to the towns in search of work had assumed the proportions of a rural exodus which was to have significant implications for the economic, political, and social structure of villages.

Although rural-to-urban migration had been common in Iran at least since the 1940's, after 1970 this movement accelerated dramatically.[36] The greatest impact was upon the largest cities, especially Tehran, Isfahan, and Mashhad. However, virtually every town which had a population of at least 25,000 in the 1966 census experienced significant rural migration during the 1970's; the majority grew at average annual rates of 4–6 percent during the decade, in contrast to a yearly growth of less than 1 percent for the total rural population (see Table 8). In all cities squalid slums sprang up to accommodate the rural newcomers.[37] Typically, these quarters lacked services such as electricity, piped water, and sewerage disposal which had become basic features of more established urban residential areas by 1970. Nevertheless, since more than 90 percent of all villages lacked these amenities as late as 1980, their absence in the slums did not detract from the overall appeal of urban life: the opportunity for work.

The availability of jobs was the primary lure of the cities for the peasants. During the 1970's, when the rural economy was stagnant, Iran's urban areas were experiencing a general economic boom stimulated by steadily increasing oil revenues. The government utilized a substantial amount of these revenues to finance innumerable construction projects throughout the country. The construction industry accordingly underwent significant expansion, with employment increasing at an average annual rate of 6.7 percent between 1972 and 1977.[38] Construction was very labor-intensive and relied chiefly upon low-paid, unskilled workers. The overwhelming majority of employees were peasants who had recently migrated. At the height of the construction boom, from 1975 to 1977, more than a million men worked on building sites; they accounted for approximately 15 percent of the entire urban labor force, or one out of every six workers.[39]

Even though the construction industry provided employment for tens of thousands of rural migrants during the 1970's, in Iran it was not a trade which offered secure work.[40] Except for a minority of highly skilled (and highly paid) technicians of inevitably urban origins, most workers were hired on a daily wage basis and terminated as soon as their labor was no longer needed on a given project; they were left to their own resources with respect to finding new jobs, since there were no unions or even government agencies which represented their interests. Despite the amount of construction activity, obtaining jobs on construction sites was not necessarily easy for rural migrants. By 1976 they had to compete for such jobs with large numbers of Afghan workers imported, usually illegally, by contractors. The Afghans' presence not only restricted available jobs but also helped to keep wages for unskilled labor depressed. In addition, government efforts to deflate the economy in 1977 led to a gradual but steady slowdown within the construction industry between September 1977 and September 1978. The coming of the revolution affected construction even more adversely: many wealthy contractors fled the country with their capital, while the new government did not regard construction activities to be a major priority. Consequently, by the summer of 1979 many thousands of workers who had become accustomed to relatively regular, albeit short-term, jobs on building sites were no longer able to find employment.

Manufacturing was probably just as important as construction as a source of urban employment for villagers. This sector also experienced significant expansion as a result of the oil-induced boom of the 1970's. By 1977 some 2.5 million people were employed by manufacturing establishments. Although there are no countryside statistics which provide data on the origins of these workers, one 1963 survey of Tehran factories did reveal that 68 percent of workers had come from villages.[41] Undoubtedly the proportion would be higher for other cities, most of which began to experience major industrialization and immigration only during the boom. It is important to point out that while Iranian manufacturing had become quite diver-

Table 8. Migration to Selected Cities, 1966–1976

Rank	City	1976 Population (Thousands)	1966 Population (Thousands)	Absolute Increase (Thousands)	% Increase	% Increase Attributable to Migration
A	*Large cities*					
1	Tehran	4,496	2,719	1,777	65.4	52.5
2	Isfahan	671	423	248	58.6	47.1
3	Mashhad	670	409	261	63.8	51.3
4	Tabriz	598	404	194	48.0	35.6
5	Shiraz	416	269	147	54.6	43.5
6	Ahvaz	329	206	123	59.7	48.1
8	Kermanshah	290	187	103	55.1	43.7
9	Qumm	246	134	112	83.6	62.9
B	*Medium cities*					
13	Ardebil	147	83	64	77.1	59.4
16	Karaj	138	44	94	213.6	85.1
19	Arak	114	71	43	60.6	48.8
21	Khorramabad	104	59	45	76.3	60.0
24	Sanandaj	98	54	44	81.5	61.4
C	*Small cities*					
26	Bandar 'Abbas	89	34	55	161.8	80.7
31	Sari	70	44	26	59.1	47.7
36	Shahi	63	38	25	65.8	52.4
40	Bushehr	57	23	34	147.8	79.4
44	Mahabad	47	28	19	67.9	52.6

Source: Calculations derived from Iran Statistical Organization, *Preliminary Report of 1976 Census.* The natural population increase for Iran from 1966 to 1976 was at an average annual rate of 3.1 percent. For each city I calculated the natural increase assuming a 31 percent growth rate for the ten-year period. I subtracted this figure from the actual increase to determine the real increase attributable to immigration. I obtained the percentage attributable to migration by dividing the real increase attributable to migration by the absolute increase. For all cities except Tehran, we can assume that virtually all the increase due to immigration originated in rural areas. Tehran experienced considerable immigration from the smaller cities and towns as well as rural areas; however, at least half of Tehran's increase from migration came from villages.

sified by the mid-1970's, it was still essentially small-scale; enterprises employing less than ten persons accounted for more than 90 percent of all concerns and employed 72 percent of all workers in manufacturing.[42] Most of the factories, then, were actually small workshops, especially outside of Tehran. Such firms were major employers of rural migrants; wages were relatively low, and usually no specific skills were required since on-the-job training was provided as necessary. Generally, rural migrants who worked in manufacturing were in the less prestigious industries, such as textiles, leather, and food processing; they rarely obtained any of the better-paid positions in the more highly skilled industries. However, the less-skilled industries have been the ones least adversely affected by the revolutionary upheaval in Iran; consequently, there has been less unemployment among these workers than among those in larger factories and in construction.

Villagers also found employment in a wide variety of urban services. Some of the more common activities included work as domestic servants, porters, office tea boys, and street vendors. Jobs in the service sector of the economy generally were among the lowest paying and consequently were the least desirable. Rural migrants tended to regard such employment as temporary and changed jobs frequently in order to secure more remunerative work. Their dream was to get a construction or factory job. While there was considerable job mobility up through the revolution, there have been few prospects for better work since early 1979.

A more detailed discussion of the fate of rural migrants in cities, although an important topic, would unnecessarily divert attention from our main concern, the impact of migration upon the villages. With respect to this subject, it is first necessary to consider the effect of migration upon rural population trends. A comparison of the 1966 and 1976 census figures can help shed some light on this matter. Accepting the official definition of a village as any settlement with fewer than 5,000 inhabitants, the census figures reveal an increase in village population from 15.3 million in 1966 to 16 million in 1976; that is, an increase of only 5 percent in total village population for the ten-year period.[43] However, the population growth for all Iran averaged 3.1 percent annually, or 31 percent for the stated period. Assuming an absence of rural-to-urban migration and evenly distributed growth between censuses, the villages would have had a total natural increase of 4.7 million at a 3.1 percent annual growth rate. But the actual increase amounted to only 700,000. That village population in the absence of migration actually would have increased 3.1 percent annually is probably unlikely, given the significantly higher infant mortality rates and lower average life expectancies in rural areas; nevertheless, it can be concluded that at least 2 million villagers did migrate to the cities between 1966 and 1976.[44]

A second aspect of migration that needs to be considered is the age distribution.[45] In general, rural migrants included both sexes and all ages. However, a preponderant majority of them were young men in the age group fifteen to twenty-nine. Indeed, out-migration among this category was so extensive that many villages were virtually de-populated of their young men. Sample surveys suggest that about 70 percent of young men had migrated to urban centers by 1978. They tended to leave their villages prior to age twenty and while still single. They viewed their migration as permanent. Although those who did marry usually sought brides from their natal villages, they eventually brought them to the cities. In contrast, the less pervasive migration of older (thirty and above), married men tended to be seasonal; they left their families in the villages for weeks or months at a time, sending home money for them when possible.

The migration of such a high proportion of young men—the primary rural labor force—had profound consequences for the villages. For it was not just the sons of the landless *khwushnishin*s who left, but also those of the peasants. Thus, not only did surplus workers more or less voluntarily depart the countryside, but by the mid-1970's so did considerable numbers of essential workers. Naturally, not all villages were affected to the same degree; however, two general patterns were observed in data that I gathered during 1977 and 1978–1979. First there was a direct correlation between economic status and migration. Among the landless agricultural laborers, for example, virtually all the young males of many villages migrated to cities and towns; in addition, the movement of entire *khwushnishin* families became common after 1974. However, this migration did not significantly reduce the proportion of *khwushnishin*s in the rural population because the migration of young men of subsistence peasant families also was very extensive. Unable to support themselves from their holdings, young peasant men abandoned work on the land en masse in favor of urban jobs. Even among the minority of prosperous peasants, the young men tended to be disinclined toward farming and preferred to enter urban occupations, which they perceived as economically more rewarding.[46]

The second pattern related to village distances from the large cities (i.e., those with populations over 100,000). Generally, the more remote the village was from a large city, particularly at distances greater than 75 kilometers, the higher was the incidence of village out-migration. In isolated areas of Kurdistan and Fars, for example, as many as 90 percent of the young men of some villages had migrated to urban areas by 1977.[47] For closer villages (up to a 50-kilometer radius of Tehran and the five next largest cities; up to a 30-kilometer radius of cities having populations between 100,000 and 300,000), the rate of out-migration was usually lower, sometimes as low as 20 percent. However, even though a majority of young men in these villages did not migrate, they nevertheless worked in cities; that is, they commuted daily into nearby cities to jobs on construction sites or in factories.

The fact that Iran's population is so predominantly youthful—with more than two-thirds of the total under thirty years of age—has reinforced the inevitably adverse economic impact on the villages of the loss of a majority of males aged fifteen to twenty-nine. Their migration seriously depleted the labor force which comprised the backbone of peasant family farms. As more of the burden of cultivation fell upon children and older men, certain negative developments occurred with respect to subsistence farming: agricultural efficiency declined, the amount of sown cropland contracted, and the production of important food grains such as wheat and rice fell. While these developments generally were not applicable to the 25 percent of peasant holdings which constituted middle and large peasant farming, nor to the absentee-owned properties—foreigners, especially Afghans were "imported" to work on these lands—the overall result of the decline in production on peasant farms was to increase the demand for food grains both in the villages and in the cities.[48] This situation only aggravated the generally unfavorable economic status of poor peasants and *khwushnishin*s who remained in the villages. Thus, while persons leaving the villages for economic reasons *may* have experienced some improvement in their personal welfare, the overall affect of migration upon most villagers was to worsen living conditions already characterized by extreme poverty, indebtedness, and low resistance to diseases.

A final point about the consequences of rural-to-urban migration needs to be mentioned. That is, villagers with relatives in the cities generally did not benefit from "remittances," because the overwhelming majority of young men who migrated did not send money to their parents and siblings still in the villages. What surplus income they earned over expenses—and most were so poorly paid that their wages went to buy basic food, shelter, and clothing—was saved for marriage. In interviews, many older peasants complained about the lack of any financial support from offspring in the cities; however, some also insisted that it was not proper for children to support their parents. In villages close to cities, if young men lived at home but commuted into town to work, there was a greater tendency to contribute to overall household expenses. However, in virtually all such cases I encountered, there was a certain degree of acrimony between sons and parents over the appropriate amount of such contributions.

CONCLUSION

By the mid-1970's, researchers in the villages were encountering widespread frustration and pessimism. Most peasants seemed to despair of ever being able to support their families from their land and were resentful toward the minority of farmers and absentee owners who were actually prospering from their holdings. These latter were generally prepared to exploit the situation to their own advantage and made known their readiness to purchase land from peasants desiring to sell their holdings and go join sons in the cities. Many families decided to do just that: in certain districts as many as half of all subsistence owners sold their property and migrated; in fact, in remote areas, where potential purchasers were scarce, some peasants simply abandoned their land. In theory, the sale of fields acquired under land reform was illegal; however, a variety of subterfuges were employed to disguise the transactions, and the government seemed to turn a blind eye to the process. Overall, these land changes served to increase the disparities between the group of large owners and the rest of the villagers.

The land which changed ownership in the 1970's usually was then sown in profitable cash crops, or sometimes resold to urban land speculators. Previously, when cultivated by subsistence farmers, it had produced crops such as wheat, barley, and rice. Taking into consideration the previously discussed factors negatively affecting cultivation of these crops, it should not be surprising to learn that there was an absolute decline in the acreage planted in essential food grains. This resulted in a stagnation in the production of the country's commodities at the very time that consumer demand was increasing. Consequently, Iran became increasingly dependent upon foreign sources to supply part of its domestic food requirements. By 1977 food imports cost $2.6 billion per year; lacking any improvement in domestic production, they were expected to reach $4 billion in 1980.

By 1977 the stagnation of agricultural production and the increasing need to import greater amounts of foodstuffs began to concern high government officials, including the shah. Accordingly, a special conference of rural specialists was called to discuss the problems of agricultural development resulting from the virtual exodus of youth to the cities.[49] The shah's wife addressed this conference and encouraged the participants to criticize, albeit "constructively," past government policies affecting agriculture. Suggestions for programs aimed at discouraging further rural migration by making farming profitable and village living conditions equal to urban ones were accepted by the government. Subsequently, considerable rhetoric about rural reconstruction was issued from government information bureaus. Nevertheless, during the last eighteen months of the regime, no new policies were devised. In the final analysis, this is not surprising, given the previous record of government initiatives with respect to rural affairs.

While the effects of rural migration upon agricultural production were undoubtedly negative, Tehran tended to view the transformation of "marginal peasant producers" into urban workers as both positive and essential to the industrialization program which was its chief priority in the 1970's.[50] Officials believed that they knew what was "best" for the villages. After all, the government was informed about developments in every village. Its agents visited the villages regularly and reported on all activities. That is, for the government the most important consequence of land reform was not redistribution nor rural socioeconomic change, but the expansion of its own role in the villages. It is now appropriate to examine that role.

7. Caesar's Will

The real significance of the land reform program lay not in its redistribution of agricultural property, but rather in its role as a symbol of the determination of the shah's government to intervene in rural affairs. From 1962 until the revolution in 1979, the government's involvement in the villages increased steadily through a variety of economic, political, and social policies. The primary objective was to extend Tehran's control over the countryside. As suggested previously, the shah's motives for wishing to assert governmental authority in the villages were complex. However, the political goal of concentrating power at the center obviously was the paramount motive, at least after 1963. As this chapter will demonstrate, the penetration of central authority into rural Iran was achieved. Viewed from this perspective, the land reform program was successful in the short term. However, from a broader perspective, the results of redistribution were dubious. Even the political accomplishment of replacing landlord control by government control did not promise long-term stability, since the authoritarian nature, and arbitrary exercise, of power was resented in the villages. Nevertheless, so long as peasants did not perceive any alternative to the power of the central government, they generally obeyed its directives, a rational behavior given Tehran's monopoly over various and effective instruments of coercion. The shah and his bureaucrats misinterpreted this obedience as allegiance, and consequently were to be disappointed at the failure of the peasants to support the regime during the revolution.

The purpose of this chapter is to examine the process of central government penetration of the villages after the initiation of land redistribution. The analysis will attempt to demonstrate how Tehran utilized both (1) village elites and political institutions and (2) its own agents to consolidate its authority. The discussion will begin with a review of the evolution of village political patterns after 1962.

VILLAGE POLITICS

The most significant political consequence of the land reform program was the termination of the absolute power which landlords and their agents had exercised in villages. The redistribution of approximately half of all agricultural properties coupled with the abolition of all feudal dues and forms of peasant servitude deprived absentee owners of their monopolistic control over both land and labor. The immediate beneficiaries of these changes were the former sharecroppers who emerged as a new class of peasant proprietors. In the long term, however, the overall effects were less negative for absentees and less positive for peasants because of the different character of the relationships each group had with the ultimate beneficiary, the central government. Over time the dependency of both groups upon the government became stronger, but it was the class of absentee owners who were best situated to exploit political connections advantageously. Thus, even though they no longer possessed the means and prerogatives of local political authority, these large owners continued to wield considerable influence in the villages.

There were three reasons why the associations with government officials helped the absentee owners to maintain locally important political roles. First, peasants believed large owners had government support, especially in cases of conflict between peasants and absentees. In many areas this perception was reinforced by the publically observed social contact between large owners or their agents and various bureaucrats. In addition, such owners possessed the resources to influence decisions in their favor on the part of a government renowned for its agents' susceptibility to bribes. Second, large owners, especially if they actually resided in the villages, became the primary interpreters and enforcers of government policies for rural areas. And, third, absentee owners were able to serve as intermediaries between villagers and various bureaucratic agencies due to their relationships with provincial officials. As a result of these factors, peasants generally assumed that large landowners in their midst possessed substantial political influence. Consequently, even though such owners were no longer feared as in the past, most peasants commonly behaved deferentially toward them.

Although absentee owners continued to be very influential, their exercise of authority within the villages was circumscribed by the emergence of new political institutions and power relationships. That is, after 1962 local political authority was progressively diffused among several offices which ultimately were responsible to Tehran. Inevitably, villagers occupying these positions tended to be recruited from the minority group of "rich" peasants and "rich" *khwushnishin*s. Like absentee owners, they sought to control the villages in a manner that would preserve and expand their own interests.[1] However, this common purpose did not necessarily guarantee shared views between the two groups, primarily because the status of the wealthy peasants was maintained, at least in part, by continued encroachment upon the interests of the large owners. Thus, there was as much competition as cooperation among village elites with respect to the conduct of local politics. This potential rivalry between wealthy peasants and large owners served to check the extent of overall authority any individual could acquire in the villages. Even more significantly, however, the rivalry was exploited by the central government in order to consolidate its own power in the countryside.

The role of the ancient office of *kadkhudā* after land reform illustrates both the limitations of authoritative positions in the villages and the government's successful efforts to weaken and control them. It will be recalled that prior to redistribution *kadkhudā*s had been responsible to the landlords, who normally designated them. With the end of the sharecropping regime, each *kadkhudā* in theory became responsible to the villagers. For example, accession to office was now dependent upon election. However, since a primary function of the *kadkhudā* was to serve as intermediary between the government and the village, it was virtually mandatory that potential officeholders have a reputation for extensive contacts with provincial bureaucrats; that is, that they possess sufficient influence to facilitate transactions with the government.[2] Therefore, not surprisingly, most "elected" *kadkhudā*s were men who originally had been selected by the landlords. Even in villages where the unpopularity of former *kadkhudā*s resulted in new men being chosen for the office, such individuals inevitably were persons who had demonstrated a capacity for dealing effectively with governmental officials.

The functions of the *kadkhudā* were essentially duties assigned from Tehran. For example, *kadkhudā*s were provided with the official seals required for the validation of important documents such as birth, marriage, and death certificates. They also had the authority to summon gendarmerie aid to put down local disturbances and arrest villagers accused of various offenses. In addition, they were expected to cooperate with the secret police (SAVAK) in providing information relating to political security. And finally, they were permitted some discretion in determining which young men would be drafted into, and which exempted from, military service, although their role with respect to such decisions became progressively less significant throughout the 1970's.[3]

The role of *kadkhudā*s since land reform suggests that the nature of the office of village headman had not changed. That is, both before and after redistribution, the *kadkhudā*s were the de facto representatives of those wishing to control the villages. Thus, their authority was not based upon popular legitimacy, but rather derived from the implicit threat of coercion. The peasants correctly perceived the shift of power from the landlords to the government and understood the position of *kadkhudā*s under the new political regime. Thus, most did not really expect *kadkhudā*s to represent their interests; at best it was hoped the *kadkhudā*s would handle the new rulers with sufficient tact to mitigate the impact of policies regarded with much suspicion. Therefore, they preferred men of proven influence, thereby powerlessly acquiescing in a system which reinforced the government's ability to control the countryside.[4]

Although the central government used *kadkhudā*s to further its own political aims in rural areas, it was unwilling to strengthen their position by assigning responsibilities more substantive than those enumerated above. Thus, Tehran did not rely exclusively upon the *kadkhudā*s for the implementation of its various village oriented programs after 1962, but instead created several new institutions which shared authority with the *kadkhudā* in managing local affairs. Effectively this led to the development of rival power centers at the village level which paralleled the rival power centers at the national level. Just as the shah manipulated the rivalry among national political institutions to enhance his own power, so the central government exploited the political rivalry among village offices to entrench its own control over the villages.

The most important of these new institutions was the village council (*anjoman-i deh*). Although laws regulating the formation of village councils had been passed as early as 1952, the councils did not really become part of village political structure until the initiation of land reform.[5] Specifically, in 1963 a cabinet decree provided for the establishment of five-member councils in each village with a minimum population of 250. Election would be by secret ballot every three years. The councils were empowered to levy a 2 percent tax on the income of each family and to use this revenue for village improvement and development projects.[6] While there are no reliable statistics on the number of councils which had been established up to the time of the 1979 revolution, they probably existed in the overwhelming majority of targeted villages, as well as in many villages with less than 250 inhabitants.[7] Interestingly, few of the several thousand councils were formed as a result of village initiatives. Instead, the typical procedure was for specially appointed government representatives to organize each council.[8] Normally, these officials selected the five most prominent peasants to form a council; these men were then confirmed by village consensus since they were regarded as influential.[9]

The most important member of each village council was its president. It was his responsibility to assess the 2 percent general income tax levied upon each family. In theory, all net profit from farming was considered taxable income, but presidents had complete discretion in deciding what percentages of gross income constituted agricultural expense and profit. For example, by overestimating certain expenses and excluding some profits (e.g., livestock additions), council presidents could undervalue income, thus reducing the total amount upon which tax was computed. Obviously, this power gave them potential influence.[10]

In large and prosperous villages, the tax revenues might be substantial. In such cases membership on village councils assumed considerable importance because the councils determined how the monies would be expended. Decisions were made by consensus among the five members. Sometimes men from other prominent village families were consulted regarding major projects. Normally, however, the majority of peasants had no role in deciding how taxes were to be spent. Indeed, when queried regarding their opinions on how council revenues were utilized, most peasants were convinced that a large share of funds "were eaten" by the council members.[11] Nevertheless, certain development projects were undertaken. Typically these included constructing school buildings, communal bath houses, and mosques. Even during the 1970's, when significant oil revenues were available to the state, the majority of such development projects continued to be financed by village taxes since the government made only inconsequential contributions toward their costs.

The rural cooperative societies which were discussed in the previous chapter may be considered at least semipolitical institutions since their officers acquired influence in the villages by making credit decisions. Inevitably, the officers were the richer peasants. *Kadkhudā*s often were on the three-member executive councils, while the other members frequently served concurrently on the village councils of the villages in which the societies were headquartered. The executive council and the manager collectively had the authority to determine who would receive loans and how much. Theoretically, the amount of credit extended each member was based upon his ability to repay within one year, but decisions were basically subjective and could be arbitrary. In some cases managers reportedly accepted "commissions" from loan recipients in return for their favorable action on an application.[12] Nevertheless, serious abuse of power by the leadership of cooperative societies was probably minimal since the government *sarparast*s generally exercised close supervision over their activities.

Even if it is assumed that the majority of cooperative societies were run honestly and efficiently, still they benefited principally the wealthier peasants. Since credit policies were designed to favor members with the highest incomes, those farmers in least need of financial aid received the most generous loans. The minority of prosperous peasants thus were able to finance productive investments. The majority of poor peasants, on the other hand, had to use their insufficient loans for basic expenses, and were never able to improve their situation. Consequently, cooperatives helped to preserve the political as well as the socioeconomic status quo.

A final political institution to consider is the rural court (*khāneh-i insāf*). These courts were established after 1963 and functioned as local tribunals for the adjudication of disputes over such matters as water rights and property boundaries and the settlement of civil suits involving less than 5,000 *riāl*s (ca. $66). By September 1972, there were 6,479 rural courts, each one serving two to four separate villages.[13] I have been unable to locate authoritative statistics later than 1972, although the formation of rural courts continued right up to the 1979 revolution. There may have been as many as 11,000 by the end of 1978, serving nearly half of all the villages.

Each court consisted of three presiding judges and two alternates, all of whom were elected for three-year terms, supposedly by secret ballot; a presiding judge was required to disqualify himself in favor of an alternate judge in cases involving his relatives. In practice, judges were chosen by government officials who then presented the candidates to an assembled group of villagers for confirmation. The majority of judges were the same individuals who served on village councils or executive councils of cooperative societies; some also were *kadkhudā*s. Considering the performance of these persons in those offices, it is not surprising that during interviews peasants stated that the rural courts were controlled by the *rish sefid*s (i.e., the rich peasants) and that they had little confidence in their administration of justice.[14]

Peasant complaints about *rish sefid* control of the rural courts and other village institutions are illustrated dramatically by the results of a survey that I conducted during 1972. Out of a total of 128 officeholders in twenty sample villages on the plain stretching between Shahr-i Rayy and Varamin, none of the landowners had less

Table 9. *Land and Power in the Varamin Plain*

Size of Landholding	Number of Officeholders	% of All Officeholders
>20 hectares	7	5.5
15–20 hectares	46	35.9
10–15 hectares	55	43.0
7–10 hectares	11	8.6
Owners of capital (shopkeepers, *gāvbands*, etc.)	9	7.0
Totals	128	100.0

Source: Author survey, 1972.

than 7 hectares. The overwhelming majority (about 85 percent) owned 10 hectares or more (see Table 9). In contrast, two-thirds of all peasant proprietors in these villages own 5 hectares of land or less. Thus, one can infer that the largest peasant owners did indeed dominate the political life of the villages in the post–land reform period.

Not only did the richer peasants as a group control village politics, but among them there also tended to be a concentration of power in the hands of the most prominent families. In the study above, for example, it was found that the 128 officeholders actually occupied 166 separate positions; that is, 23 individuals held two or more offices apiece. Not untypical was the wealthiest peasant of Fardis, who served as *kadkhudā*, manager of the cooperative society, and member of the village council. An extreme case was Saveh, where the four largest farmers shared among themselves thirteen of the village's fifteen offices, an average of 3.5 per person.[15]

Even though the small peasant owners resented the domination of village affairs by their richer neighbors, they did share some mutual interests with the ruling village elites. Specifically, both poor and rich peasants tended to work together in generally successful efforts to exclude landless laborers from participation in all village institutions. In this respect, the most striking examples were the cooperative societies. Agricultural and other workers were barred from membership because they did not own any land; yet cooperatives were the only source of reasonable credit, a service desperately needed by these poor *khwushnishins*. Their exclusion from cooperatives especially, but other organizations too, emphasized the vicious cycle of poverty and impotence which afflicted this large rural minority group: because *khwushnishin* laborers were so poor, they had no influence; because they had no influence, they had no power; and because they had no power, they had no opportunity of access to institutions which could be used to help improve their position; and thus, their status did not change as long as they remained in the villages. The maintenance of the *khwushnishins'* social and political status was the common interest of all peasants regardless of the size of their holdings.

The rivalries between peasants and *khwushnishins* represented only one aspect of the contradictions which riddled village society. In addition to the contradictory interests of poor *khwushnishins* and poor peasants, poor peasants and rich peasants, as well as rich peasants and absentee owners, often had opposing interests. These various contradictions were serious impediments to any kind of unified or purposeful action. Even more significantly, the class divisions facilitated government control of the villages. That is, by co-opting the village elite through the judicious dispensation of influence and economic rewards, the government obtained the loyalty and cooperation of the group most determined to maintain the rural socioeconomic status quo. Since the maintenance of their privileged position depended essentially upon government support, including coercion as necessary, the village elite inevitably became little more than local representatives of an authority based in Tehran. If one leaves out of consideration the obvious—and very substantial—improvement in their economic status, then their political role after redistribution was similar to the more informal influence they had wielded under the landlords.

THE CENTRAL GOVERNMENT AND THE VILLAGES

The discussion of village politics had demonstrated that in the years following land reform the villages failed to gain any real autonomy in determining their own affairs. The central government progressively extended its authority into the rural areas after 1962. While its day-to-day control relied upon the village elites who emerged as a consequence of redistribution, the government also sought to penetrate the countryside more effectively and directly. This aim was achieved principally through two means. First, Tehran strengthened the bureaucratic and security apparatus supervising village affairs. At the same time, the government also stationed in villages various agents charged with responsibility for the direction of several programs designed to bring about officially sanctioned changes.

Bureaucratic supervision of villages was rather complex under the monarchy. To begin with, all policy decisions affecting villages originated in the cabinet. They were then transmitted to the appropriate ministries and agencies for the implementation process which moved down through the national, provincial, county, and district bureaucracies to the villages. The place in the chain of authority at which control over individual villages began was the county government. In the period 1962–1979, there were approximately 130 counties (*shahrestān*s) in Iran, averaging 4,892 square miles in area. Every county was divided into two or three districts (*bakhsh*s) each of which in turn was subdivided into at least two *dehestān*s; normally, *dehestān*s ranged between 200 and 600 square miles in area and contained a minimum of thirty villages.

The county, on behalf of the central government, maintained control over rural affairs through direct supervision of the village institutions discussed above: *kadkhudā*s, village councils, cooperative societies, and rural courts. The position which received the closest attention was that of *kadkhudā*. The official view of the *kadkhudā* was that the village chief executive was the one individual responsible to the government for all matters which were considered relevant to local and national security. Although not paid a salary by the government—he was expected to collect any remuneration from the villagers—the *kadkhudā* was seen as the government's representative at the village level and had authority to act as both interpreter and enforcer of all laws.

Although the position of *kadkhudā* became formally elective in 1963, no villager could hold this office without at least tacit approval from county officials.[16] Potential *kadkhudā*s were introduced to *dehestān* and *bakhsh* authorities by prominent county figures such as former landlords or large absentee owners who maintained various business, personal, and family relationships with important members of the county, provincial, or even national bureaucracies. The recommendations of such well-connected persons were generally sufficient to inspire confidence in the loyalty of prospective *kadkhudā*s. Once individuals had been properly certified by the county establishment, an agent was deputized to arrange for elections, which were conducted by a public show of hands and without the nomination of opposition candidates or any debate.

The *kadkhudā*s' obligations to the government were manifold, as has already been described. It will be recalled that they were expected to cooperate continually with officials charged with implementing various programs in the villages. Also, they had to exercise general oversight of the activities of both individuals and institutions and report any improper political behavior to the appropriate authorities. *Kadkhudā*s were not empowered to initiate policies and ran the risk of dismissal if they attempted to act too independently of limits prescribed from Tehran. However, despite their effective subordination to the government, some officials were dissatisfied with this system. Thus, throughout the 1970's there was intermittent discussion of recruiting 60,000 high school graduates to be trained for special appointments as *kadkhudā*s under the Ministry of Interior. These would replace present *kadkhudā*s who were not part of the bureaucracy and, because of their status as peasant proprietors, were not always enthusiastic about programs and policies originating from Tehran. This program was never implemented prior to the revolution, although talk of it probably influenced incumbent *kadkhudā*s to be even more cooperative with government agents.

The government did not rely completely upon *kadkhudā*s to keep it informed of developments in the villages. Special officials, known as *dehyār*s, assisted village leaders in running local affairs. *Dehyār*s were *dehestān*-level employees of the Ministry of Interior; in the 1970's there were approximately four *dehyār*s for each *dehestān*, but the eventual goal was to have sufficient numbers so that each *dehyār* would be responsible for no more than ten villages. *Dehyār*s usually were charged with supervising *kadkhudā*, village council, and rural court elections. They served as the link between *kadkhudā*s and the county bureaucracy and oversaw the activities of village councils. In this latter regard, they certified the eligibility of peasants for council and court membership, i.e., ascertained that candidates were loyal supporters of the regime, and advised councils which projects would be appropriate for the expenditure of their tax revenues. In some villages, peasants alleged that *dehyār*s exercised an absolute veto over proposals which the councils planned on their own initiative.

Official supervision of the rural cooperative societies was discussed in Chapter 6. However, it might be pointed out here that their superintendence was not the responsibility of the Ministry of Interior bureaucracy as was the case for the other village institutions. Rather, the Ministry of Cooperatives and Rural Affairs was charged with their guidance. Although direction still originated in Tehran, *sarparast*s tended to be less paternalistic in their behavior toward peasants than their counterparts in the Interior Ministry. Nevertheless, on several occasions I observed that their presence seemed to stifle peasant initiatives.

The ultimate reason for supervision was to insure that village institutions operated according to predetermined expectations. If village officials for any reason did not cooperate, then they were speedily removed from their positions. Open defiance on the part of any villager was punished even more severely. In such cases, the government relied upon its principal coercive agent, the gendarmerie. This constabulary had headquarters in every *shahrestān* (county), with units stationed in each *bakhsh* and *dehestān*. Government officials and *kadkhudā*s could summon these units at any time to help maintain order. The gendarmerie had a reputation for brutality and the arbitrary use of power. Its methods included public physical punishment, arrest, and imprisonment. It was greatly feared and even hated by the peasants. Indeed, the relationship between the people and the gendarmes constituted a major rural social problem.[17] However, since the function of the gendarmerie was to defend the interests of the government, rather than the interests of villagers, officials naturally had little concern for this problem. Significantly, as the monarchy began to crumble in December 1978, gendarmes abandoned their posts en masse in apparent fear of peasant retribution.

Although the government's primary interest was to maintain rural political stability, this was not its only objective with respect to the villages. The shah, especially, was attracted by various proposals for rural development. As early as January 1963, he had inaugurated a broad social and economic development program which he called the White Revolution.[18] The land reform which had begun a year earlier was retroactively made the cornerstone of this program. Initially, there were five other "reforms" concerning such matters as the status of women, natural resources, industrialization, health, and education. Subsequently, more principles were added so that the total was sixteen by 1978.[19] Three of these principles which had the most direct relevance for the villages were the special Literacy, Health, and Extension and Development Corps established within the army for the specific purpose of directing government-sponsored change in rural areas. These corps were made up of young men and, beginning in 1969, women, draftees who had completed secondary school or some higher education. They were assigned for fifteen-month periods to live in the villages and undertake various educational, medical, and construction projects.

The Literacy Corps was the oldest and largest of the military service corps. Its personnel literally were known as the soldiers of knowledge, or *sepāh-i dānesh*. Between 1963 and 1978, some 100,000 *sepāhi*s were sent out into the villages. Although they were technically uniformed junior officers (second lieutenants), their work in the villages came under the authority of the Ministry of Education. Their primary responsibility was to serve as teachers for village children; an important secondary duty was to organize adult literacy classes. *Sepāhi*s also initiated school construction projects.[20]

The Health Corps (*sepāh-i behdāsht*) was set up in 1964 in order to provide some medical services in rural areas. In principle, all Health Corps members were supposed to be organized into units of four persons, one of whom had university training in the medical sciences; in practice, most units consisted of just two *sepāhi*s, and in a few cases only one. Up through 1972, a total of 2,830 units had been sent to various parts of the country.[21] Usually *sepāhi*s managed clinics in small towns (population 5,000–30,000), but they also took frequent trips to nearby villages as part of some five hundred mobile health care programs. Probably the most important aspect of their work was to immunize several hundred thousand villagers against formerly common and serious diseases.

The Extension and Development Corps (*sepāh-i tarvij va ābādāni*) was established in 1965 with the aim of sending educated young men out to the villages to advise peasants on new farming techniques and to help them build roads and bridges. By the end of 1972, a total of 18,874 of these *sepāhi*s had been assigned to rural areas.[22] Usually, they worked in teams and were responsible for a group of villages.

The purpose of all three corps was to implement quickly and uniformly various social and economic programs which the shah had decided to carry out in the rural areas. The use of the army as the executive agent was viewed as a convenient way to enlist the skills of the educated urban youth who normally would have no interest in working in villages. A basic assumption was that the peasants, given adequate resources, could not undertake these programs without direction from above.

The reaction of the peasants to the various *sepāhi*s was mixed. On the one hand they generally welcomed the provision of services which prior to 1963 had been unavailable. On the other hand, they tended to be suspicious of the corps members, whom they regarded as government agents. In those villages in which *sepāhi*s actually resided, peasants often had difficulty determining their precise status and role. Not only as government officials, but also as military officers, *sepāhi*s seemed to outrank local administrators; and some villagers behaved so as to indicate that they considered *sepāhi*s more authoritative, thus weakening the position of *kadkhudā*s and other leaders.[23]

The behavior of *sepāhi*s tended to reinforce peasant proclivities to view them as part of the local power structure. Typically, *sepāhis* were urban, middle-class, educated young adults who had no prior rural experience. The conditions and problems of villages thus were alien to their backgrounds, and often they were unable or unwilling to adjust to the standards of village society. Consequently, they usually acted in an authoritarian and patronizing manner when dealing with the peasants, whom they considered incapable of determining their own needs.[24]

The attitudes of *sepāhis* were important factors contributing to the generally unsatisfactory results of the government-sponsored rural development efforts undertaken after 1963.[25] Since the opinions of the peasants were not sought in either the formulation or the implementation of projects, it was difficult to enlist their active support for programs supposedly intended for their benefit.[26] Unfortunately, many *sepāhis* tended to attribute perceived peasant indifference to ignorance and behaved even more arrogantly as a result.[27] Consequently, there was progressively less inclination on both sides to cooperate. There were, of course, many notable examples of *sepāhis* who made genuine efforts to understand the villagers and consequently were effective as teachers and technicians. On the whole, however, most *sepāhis* resented their compulsory tours of duty in the villages, were not above exploiting the peasants, and generally left behind a negative impression of themselves and the government which had sent them.

In the final analysis, responsibility for the overall performance of the various development programs lay not with the agents, but with the government. In this respect it must be admitted that the government never committed sufficient resources to launch a major program of rural social development. Sending 10,000 *sepāhi* teachers out to the villages annually was really not an adequate response to the educational needs of the country's 67,000 villages. Consequently, by 1978, some fifteen years after the inauguration of the Literacy Corps, only 62 percent of Iran's rural youth of school age were enrolled in classes.[28] The internationally acclaimed adult literacy classes conducted by the corpsmen and corpswomen were equally unimpressive: in 1978 nearly 90 percent of all rural women over fifteen years of age were illiterate, as were at least 60 percent of adult men.[29] The achievements of the Health and the Extension and Development Corps were even more meagre, since the personnel of these services was only a fraction of those in the Literacy Corps.[30] Thus, on the eve of the revolution which toppled the monarchy, a majority of villagers had not been affected by the various development programs and still lacked access to such basic social services as education and health care. Unfortunately for the government, villagers now were keenly aware of their relative deprivation, since a combination of extensive rural-to-urban migration and the ubiquitous presence of agents served to bring into the villages knowledge about the various social amenities in the cities.

The government's poor performance with respect to the implementation of rural development programs eventually would be "rewarded" by a lack of interest on the part of villagers in whether or not the government survived the mass opposition movement which gathered momentum throughout 1978. Before turning to that subject, however, it is appropriate to inquire why the government's policies were so ineffective. The shah himself had frequently reaffirmed his commitment to the rural development goals proclaimed in his White Revolution program. Why, then did he not use his power, and the considerable oil revenues he controlled, to accomplish these goals? The primary reason, as has been seen, was political; that is, the principal objective of government policy toward the villages was to assert its own control. Consequently, those policies whose scope was basically socioeconomic had to accord with the overall political aim. Thus, even though the shah and his advisors probably believed in the necessity for rural development, their priorities focused upon the political, rather than the socioeconomic implications of all plans. Therefore, the activities of the various service corps became important primarily for their role in extending government control.

A secondary reason why the shah did not insist upon achieving rural development goals had to do with his own conception of development. The introduction of farm corporations and agribusinesses after 1968 was a clear indication that the shah no longer believed in the potential of a peasant proprietor class to be either a base of political support or a means through which to raise agricultural productivity. Thus, the best approach for modernization was not to perpetuate inefficient and backward villages, but to encourage villagers to leave. This would be achieved by establishing agricultural "poles" —farm corporations were one example—consisting of model villages in the most productive regions; the populations of "marginal" villages would be encouraged to migrate to the cities to work in the factories being built for the industrialization of Iran. While the shah probably believed sincerely that his visions for the future of rural society were in the best interests of the peasantry, obviously, such ideas were very remotely removed from the social and economic reality of Iranian villages during the 1970's.

The reality which the shah and his bureaucrats did not comprehend was well understood by the villagers. Generally, they desired to improve their living standards, which they realized were low in comparison to those of townspeople. They believed that the only way this could be achieved was through government help. Yet attitudes toward the government were ambivalent in the 1970's. On the one hand, peasants wanted the government to provide their villages with some of the basic urban amenities. On the other hand, their experiences with various government agents often were unpleasant and tended to cause many to wish for a simple life in preference to one which involved any contact with officials. These mixed feelings were summed up quite poignantly by one young Kurdish farmer during the course of an extended conversation:

> The *sepāhi* doesn't come here any longer. We had two before.
> The first boy was good. He built the school. I sent my son
> there for three years. And I went to the adult class, too. The
> other *sepāhi* was a bad example [for the children] and we were
> happy to see him go. Now we have a teacher from town. He
> comes every day. He always curses at the children and calls
> them stupid [*khar*]. And we have to pay for this teacher. But I
> can't. I know my son must learn if he is not to be a poor peas-
> ant like me. But where do I get the money? My family must
> have bread. So my son doesn't go to school any longer. And the
> doctors [*sepāh-i behdāsht*]! We also were told they were free.
> But those dog fathers [*pedār-sag*] sell everything to fill up their
> own pockets. I don't have any money. What good are all these,
> if we can't use them? Yes, we need schools and doctors, but
> they are just for the rich. I wish I didn't even know doctors
> existed. Before, we were ignorant, but now we know that pills
> and shots can help us. But we can't buy them, so we watch our
> children die from sickness as well as hunger. Before, the elders
> said that if a child died, it was the will of God [*dast-i khudā*],
> but now, I think that it's the will of the government [*dast-i
> dowlat*].[31]

8. Villages and the Revolution

The preceding analysis has demonstrated the most important consequence of land reform for Iranian villages: that the virtually absolute, and often arbitrary, political power which formerly had been the monopoly of the large landlords was assumed by the central government. The success of the program in attaining its political objective was attested to by the pervasiveness of governmental authority in the villages. Whereas in 1962 the overwhelming majority of the rural population had virtually no contact with government agents, by 1978 the reverse was true. Indeed, even remote and seemingly inaccessible villages had become subject to regular visits from various officials. Generally, villagers acquiesced in the establishment of bureaucratic rule. However, there is no evidence to suggest that they approved of their new "landlord."[1] The first real test of rural attitudes toward the role of the shah's government was to occur during the revolutionary upheaval of 1978–1979. As the power of the monarchy began to crumble rapidly under the pressure of an urban-based mass protest movement, the maintenance of authority in the villages became dependent upon popular support. This support failed to materialize in the crucial final three months of the regime.

The purpose of this chapter is to examine why village support for the shah was not forthcoming. No study of land reform would be complete without addressing this subject. While we can conclude that the actual benefits of the entire White Revolution were very limited, still it must be admitted that certain results were positive for a significant proportion of villagers. Most prominently, of course, was land redistribution which enabled approximately one-half of all village households to acquire ownership of land previously farmed under sharecropping arrangements. Leaving aside the problems associated with subsistence agriculture, one might expect the peasants, at least, to exhibit some gratitude toward the person whom all government officials and all textbooks presented as the sole innovator of land reform and the unequaled champion of rural interests. Nevertheless, it will be shown not only that most peasants were surprisingly indifferent to the fate of the monarchy, but also that many of them actively participated in political demonstrations which helped to topple it.

VILLAGE POLITICAL ATTITUDES

Village attitudes during the revolution can be classified according to orientations toward the shah and his government.[2] Generally, three distinct orientations were observable: (1) supportive; (2) anti-government; and (3) apolitical. As the revolution gathered momentum, the first two orientations began to be expressed through overt political activity in the villages. This resulted in the formation of a pro-shah group among villagers inclined to support the regime and an anti-shah (really, pro-Khomeini) group among those opposed to the government. Both groups competed for the allegiance of villagers who were predisposed toward a more or less neutral position vis-à-vis the developing confrontation.

Those villagers who supported the shah seem to have been a minority in virtually all villages. However, they were a very important minority. Predictably, the most enthusiastic defenders of governmental policies were those rich peasants who had benefited from land reform and subsequent programs. These included much of the ruling elite of the villages, that is, those men whom the government had chosen to serve as *kadkhudās*, village council members, and officers of the cooperative societies. As noted in the previous chapter, such village leaders were in practice local representatives of the central government. They and the government normally had a mutually satisfying relationship: in return for cooperating with Tehran in controlling the villages, they obtained local political influence and economic rewards. Understandably, there was a tendency for many of the wealthy peasants to identify their interests with those of the government. Furthermore, their attitudes were reinforced in contacts with absentee owners—rich peasants served as their agents in the villages—and other members of the provincial elite who tended to be supportive of the government.

Villagers who opposed the regime also seemed to be a minority. Since any active hostility had been quickly suppressed by the gendarmerie and other security forces in the past, awareness of the fate awaiting persons accused of anti-government behavior was a strong deterrent to any expression of opposition. Nevertheless, in most large villages, and many smaller ones as well, there were persons who intensely disliked the government, which they accused of being brutal and repressive, at least when not afraid of being overheard by those they suspected of being informers. In general, these villagers were motivated by what Barrington Moore has described as "moral outrage"; that is, a shared sense of anger against the perceived injustices of those in authority.[3] They were considerably emboldened by political developments during 1978 and gradually emerged as open opponents of the government. Indeed, many of them became political activists and organized anti-shah demonstrations in their villages.

Villagers opposed to the government included persons belonging to each of the rural social groups. However, members of two particular groups accounted for the majority of opponents; these were middle peasants and *khwushnishin* traders. In general, middle peasants may be defined as owners of 7–10 hectares of land. This size of holding—less than one-fifth of all holdings—normally was sufficient to provide a surplus above basic family consumption needs, although inadequate to permit the accumulation of wealth. A primary concern of middle peasants was to increase their crop yields (and profits) through the utilization of mechanical and chemical production inputs. Yet middle peasants lacked the resources to finance most of the costs involved, especially the costs of mechanized production. Typically, they believed that the government should aid them through the provision of reasonable credit and low prices for fertilizers and improved seed, the very kind of help it made available to larger-scale farmers. Middle peasants thus felt that government policies discriminated against them unfairly. Prior to the revolution, only a fraction of them had dared to express their grievances openly, but during 1978 middle peasants emerged as one of the village groups most antagonistic toward the shah.[4]

No less vocal in their condemnation of the shah were most of the *khwushnishin* traders. Their views of the regime were strongly influenced by the attitudes of urban retailers and wholesalers with whom they maintained extensive business relations. The town merchants owned small shops in the traditional covered market areas known as bazaars and hence were referred to as *bāzāris*. Beginning in 1975 the government decided to bring the relatively independent *bāzāris* more directly under its control. In addition to the initiation of policies which had adverse economic effects upon most *bāzāris*, there was official talk about plans which effectively would uproot them by "eradicating their 'wormridden shops,' bulldozing some of their districts to make way for major roads, and building a state-run market."[5] The government also tried to use the *bāzāris* as the main scapegoat for the spiraling inflation which was induced by the $20 billion per annum in oil revenues; some 8,000 *bāzāris* were jailed for being "profiteers," another 23,000 were exiled from their home towns, and as many as 200,000 were fined.[6] The main consequence of all these actions was to earn for the shah and his government the hatred of the *bāzāris*. Since many *khwushnishin* traders associated with *bāzāris* on a fairly regular basis, inevitably they were sympathetic to their plight. Thus they became early converts to a view of the regime as being an unjust tyranny.

Throughout much of 1978 the majority of villagers were neither supportive nor antagonistic, at least overtly, in their attitudes toward the government. Basically they were apolitical. That is, they avoided becoming involved in conversations about developments in the towns as reports of demonstrations filtered back to the rural areas. Their apparent indifference was important for two reasons. First, the general disinclination to defend the record of the shah during the evolving political crisis was an indication of the lack of any genuine or widespread loyalty to him or his regime in the villages. Second, the equally notable reluctance to oppose the government enabled Tehran to maintain its authority in the villages until very late in the revolution, approximately December 1978 in most rural areas.

It is appropriate to inquire into the motives for the apolitical attitude of most villagers. Indifference was especially characteristic of poor peasants and poor *khwushnishins*, the very groups which had benefited the least from land redistribution. Typically, they expressed intense cynicism about the role of any government. Most programs, including land reform itself, were regarded with considerable derision, even resentment. Whenever I asked in casual conversations what they thought was the principal function of government, apolitical villagers responded that they believed it was to serve rich people, especially those who lived in Tehran. Generally there was widespread mistrust of the government, but simultaneously an acceptance of its power to control events, especially opposition movements. Under these circumstances, most villagers concluded that it was in their best interests to accommodate the government whenever necessary in hopes that it would ignore them most of the time.

Given these village political attitudes, the next section will examine how these views were translated into purposeful action during the course of the revolution and, specifically, will analyze the process by which opponents of the shah organized their forces and succeeded in mobilizing the apolitical majority against the government. It will be shown that rural young men (aged eighteen to twenty-five) played an especially prominent role in bringing the revolution to their villages.

AGENTS OF REVOLUTION

The immediate antecedents of the Iranian revolution lay in the economic, political, and social developments of 1975–1977, and more distantly can be traced back to the consequences of the 1953 coup d'état.[7] The incident which inaugurated the revolution was the suppression of a religious demonstration in Qumm on January 9, 1978. The customary fortieth-day mourning ceremonies for the victims—officially only six, unofficially up to one hundred—of the Qumm disturbances were marked by demonstrations in several cities and in Tabriz resulted in several days of disorder during which there were several hundred casualties and millions of *riāl*s in property damage. This set in motion a cycle of mourning demonstrations, forceful dispersals, and deaths which continued at forty-day intervals throughout the spring and summer. By August the demonstrations had begun to assume genuinely mass proportions in Tehran, Isfahan, and Shiraz, especially, and were unambiguously directed at changing the dictatorial character of the government. In response to the political challenge, the shah imposed martial law upon eleven major and two minor cities. This action served only to shift the focus of the developing opposition from the largest cities to smaller urban centers. During October an average of five different towns each day were reporting disturbances which were suppressed with loss of life. The city of Amol (population ca. 70,000) near the Caspian Sea and the small city of Paveh (population ca. 9,000) in Kurdistan both witnessed exceptionally bloody confrontations extending over several days. Less destructive in terms of numbers killed but resulting in extensive property damage were major demonstrations in such cities as Dezful, Kerman, Rasht, Sanandaj, and Zanjan. In addition, during October the country's economy and bureaucracy were virtually paralyzed by mass strikes of civil servants, engineers, medical personnel, oil workers, shopkeepers, students, teachers, and technicians. The formation of a military government on November 6 and the use of increasingly brutal force in many areas only seemed to inflame the popular anger, which by then was centered upon a demand for the removal of the shah. The military proved ineffective in dealing with the revolutionary upheaval; in many instances junior officers refused to obey orders to quell demonstrations, while the draftees began to desert. Finally, the shah decided to go into voluntary exile on January 16, 1979; four weeks later the revolution succeeded.

The purpose of the above summary is to demonstrate that the revolution was not a political phenomenon restricted to the capital and the largest cities. It was a nationwide popular movement in which all of Iran's diverse social and ethnic groups participated. Between October 1978 and February 1979, each of Iran's 130-plus legally defined cities (settlements with at least 5,000 population) had at least one major anti-shah demonstration. Most of them had several, often resulting in serious confrontations with security forces. This character of the revolution is significant to this study for this reason: a majority of villages were accessible to a town in which there existed revolutionary ferment. Therefore, villages could not remain unaffected by political developments. Indeed, in some villages there were demonstrations—and confrontations—as frequently as there were in towns. A principal factor which seemed to influence village political activity was proximity to cities. Generally, those villages which were less than an hour's commuting distance from a city in which anti-shah activism was intense were most likely to be revolutionary; and those villages which were located more than an hour's commuting distance from an urban area tended to remain relatively calmer, the remoter villages experiencing hardly a single demonstration. Of course, the mere fact of physical proximity is insufficient in itself to account for urban influences on villages. These influences are possible only if the closeness facilitates the development of ties between cities and villages. This is precisely what happened in Iran during the 1970's. Significantly, thousands of young men living in villages near large cities did not migrate in search of work, but rather commuted daily to city jobs. By continuing to reside in the villages, they served as important agents of urban ideas, especially political ones.

A general study of village commuters has yet to be undertaken. However, I did conduct an extensive survey of them in the villages of the Shiraz area during 1978–1979.[8] The patterns which I observed are similar to those which Iranian colleagues have noted for such cities as Ahvaz, Arak, Isfahan, Karaj, Kermanshah, Mashhad, Qazvin, Shahr-i Rayy, and Tabriz. It appears, then, the village commuters in Shiraz are fairly representative of their counterparts in the vicinities of other major cities. For this reason, it is instructive to examine the case of Shiraz in some detail.

Shiraz is the historic administrative capital of Fars province. In 1978 its population was approximately 450,000, making it the country's fifth largest city. By any measure—commerce, education, industry, medicine, recreation—it is the preeminent city of south-central Iran. It is located in an especially fertile agricultural area. Since 1966 much productive land—with the corresponding villages —close to Shiraz has been urbanized; however, beyond a 10-kilometer radius from the city center, the countryside is essentially rural. At least fifty villages are within easy commuting distance (less than one hour by road). In these villages the percentage of young men (eighteen to twenty-five years old) who commuted daily to jobs in Shiraz varied between 49 and 90 percent of the total prior to the revolution. For all villages, a majority of young men were commuters, some 3,000 traveling to the city—or to the factories on its outskirts —each day.

The majority of village commuters were sons of poor peasants and poor *khwushnishins*. Generally, they lacked non-agricultural skills and had obtained only primary educations. Consequently, their jobs tended to be ones requiring little or no technical training and paid low wages. The numerous construction sites around Shiraz were a major source of employment. These commuters also worked in the small-scale manufacturing shops of the bazaar, in bakeries, and in unskilled positions in factories. A minority of village commuters were sons of middle-peasants and *khwushnishin* traders. As a group, they tended to be better educated than other commuters. Most of them had some high school education; a few had acquired secondary school diplomas. Thus, they were able to qualify for better-paying and higher-status jobs. Their occupations were quite diverse: they worked in factories, government offices (especially the Post, Telephone, and Telegraph Department and the Water and Power Authority), banks, and the city police; some even utilized family savings to set up their own businesses such as taxi services and small retail shops.

The commuters acquired political attitudes through their work and social experiences in Shiraz. A majority acknowledged ignorance about politics prior to 1978. Following the Oumm incident, interest in, and opposition to, government policies gradually developed. The significant politicizing event seems to have been the demonstrations in Shiraz on June 5; these were forcibly suppressed, resulting in numerous fatalities and arrests. Villagers noted that this occasion was the first time they had seen or heard the slogan "Death to the shah" (*marg bar shah*). While no commuter admitted to having participated in these demonstrations, many were in one of the areas where they took place and witnessed the police assaults; some had to flee for safety as a consequence of the indiscriminate use of clubs, firearms, and tear gas by security forces. The initial reaction to the suppression was one of shock. Recounting their feelings more than a year later, and after having participated in many more brutal experiences, villagers still typically would remark of June 5: "I had never seen anyone killed before."

There were periodic demonstrations, generally on a small scale, in Shiraz throughout the summer of 1978. The city, as well as two smaller towns in Fars, was among the urban areas placed under martial law on September 8. By this time village commuters were beginning to talk about the government at home. Already, a vocal minority of young men were expressing strong opposition to the shah's dictatorship. Surprisingly, these budding activists were not necessarily from families which traditionally had been anti-government; many of them were from apolitical families, while some of them had fathers and/or other close relatives who were firmly pro-regime. Thus, it was not the political views of their families which influenced their own attitudes, but clearly their experiences in Shiraz.

It was also during the summer that the commuters brought new interpretations of religion to their villages. The transformation of Shi'ā Islam from a religious ideology concerned primarily with regulating the believer's behavior on earth in preparation for the afterlife in paradise to a religio-political philosophy encouraging followers to struggle against earthly tyranny served to provide the opposition to the shah and his government with a powerful source of legitimacy. This politicization of religion was eagerly accepted by village youth. In this process they acquired a new interest in religious personalities and practices. This is significant because the experience of most young men with formal religion had been relatively limited prior to 1978. While it is true that living near Shiraz, which has several shrines and a theological college, afforded many opportunities for exposure to religious figures, still most villagers had no regular contact with the clergy. Indeed, like most other Shi'i villagers throughout the country, their attitudes toward the clergy were rather ambivalent. On the one hand, they respected the clergy for their perceived piety, spirituality, and learning. On the other hand, they mocked the clergy for their perceived ignorance of work, fun, and village customs. Part of the reason why Ayatollah Rouhollah Khomeini had such a charismatic appeal to these young men was that they believed he was not like the other members of the clergy. That is, they were convinced that he had suffered deprivations like themselves, and therefore really understood the troubles of the poor. Consequently, they embraced his interpretation of religion: to actively involve oneself in the just battle against the forces of oppression.

It was during the autumn of 1978 that the opposition movement against the shah became virtually synonymous with the movement in support of Ayatollah Khomeini. By now probably an absolute majority of village commuters identified with the anti-regime forces. When demonstrations resumed in Shiraz in October, following a four-week respite during which all groups were adjusting to the imposition of martial law, rural youth became active participants, some becoming casualties in the inevitable confrontations with the military. Initially, the villages afforded a sort of retreat from the heady political atmosphere of Shiraz's streets. However, it was not possible to avoid for long confrontations between the pro-shah elements who generally controlled the villages and the increasingly visible anti-shah activists. Ugly incidents between the two factions occurred as early as November in some villages. As in the past, the village elite relied upon the gendarmerie to deal with the "trouble makers." The rural police proved uncharacteristically ineffective; as central authority began to collapse, the government was unable to provide it the traditional and necessary support services. Gendarmerie personnel themselves became apprehensive about the future and began deserting their posts after mid-December, apparently fearful of retribution if the anti-shah people were to win the political struggle.

Revolutionary political activity gathered momentum in the villages in December. Most commuters now were going into Shiraz not to work, but to participate in demonstrations against the regime. Upon returning, they boldly organized meetings and marches in the villages. Without the gendarmerie, the army, or the secret police, the pro-shah elites were incapable of preventing their activities. The struggle between the two groups now intensified. However, a majority of the noncommuting villagers seemed indifferent. Efforts by the defenders of the shah to enlist the support of the "silent majority" would receive a polite hearing, but the only response was a nonchalant "What has he done for us?" Of course, it was true that many of these villagers were the parents of anti-shah activists. Nevertheless, they seemed equally unimpressed by the arguments of their sons; often they would reply to praise of Ayatollah Khomeini with a noncommittal phrase such as "But what is he going to do for us?"

Once it became clear that the power of the central government was really weakened, the villagers who had observed the anti-shah/pro-Khomeini struggle rather impassively began to assume a more serious interest in local political developments. Gradually, most of them abandoned their almost neutral stance in favor of support for the faction which seemed to be winning in late December and early January: the pro-Khomeini forces. The eventual success of the anti-shah revolution at the national level was vindication that they had foreseen the outcome of the political battle correctly.

The preceding case study has focused upon the role of village commuters in the Shiraz area. We may reasonably assume that their activities in the villages in the environs of other large cities was similar. However, such villages account for, at most, only 5 percent of all villages in the country. Consequently, the manner by which revolutionary ideas were introduced into these villages is not applicable generally. Nevertheless, urban agents still had an important influence in preparing a majority of the 60,000-plus other villages for the revolution. With respect to these latter, the principal interpreters of political developments during 1978–1979 were the villagers who had migrated to the cities. Since migrants played such a significant role, it is useful to examine them more closely.

It will be recalled from the discussion of rural-to-urban migration in Chapter 6 that at least 2 million villagers may have migrated to cities just in the decade 1966–1976. It is quite likely that not a single village remained unaffected by this migration. However, migration did not mean an "uprooting." Quite to the contrary, after settling in towns, most migrants maintained regular contacts with relatives in their natal villages. Indeed, many migrants were able to visit their villages as frequently as every month. These visits were facilitated by the fact that migrants to cities other than Tehran (which attracted villagers from all parts of the country) tended to originate in the hinterlands of the city to which they had moved; thus, travel time between an adopted city and the home village generally was less than five hours, an amount of time considered bearable, especially during a long weekend. Migrants from villages reachable within two hours returned to them as often as every Friday. This continued association of migrants and villagers served as an important means through which information about the city was disseminated in the villages.

As a group, migrants were more diverse than commuters. Migrants included all ages and both sexes. Some of them were relatively recent arrivals in the city, while others had resided in urban areas for a decade or more. They worked in a wide variety of jobs, most of which were classifiable as unskilled or semiskilled lower-class occupations. In general, migrants seem to have been rather apolitical prior to 1978; however, most of them were effectively mobilized during the revolution, providing the crowds for the mass demonstrations which took place in the major cities.[9] Among all migrants, the most politically active were the young men aged eighteen to twenty-five. In terms of background, values, and occupations, these men were similar to their village counterparts who commuted. Indeed, urban youths of village origins and rural youths who worked in cities during the daytime tended to share the same jobs, the same social interests, and the same entertainment activities. However, there were notable differences among them: politically conscious migrants became involved in opposition activities very early in 1978; they became political organizers in the poor and slum areas of the cities; and they emerged as group leaders during the demonstrations.

Only a minority of migrant youths were revolutionary political activists; however, a majority of them did participate in political activities beginning in October when the movement against the shah intensified. Meanwhile, visits to villages of origin continued amidst the political turmoil. These visits were occasions for former villagers to convey much information about the urban political developments which had begun to receive attention even in the government-controlled radio broadcasts. The prolonged strikes against the regime encouraged some migrants to return to the villages for extended stays in late autumn and early winter, often with the specific purpose of organizing demonstrations there. Of course, it was necessary to contend with village elites who were inclined to be pro-shah and very suspicious of the migrants, whom they accused of having no respect for authority and of having been corrupted by living in the cities. While a majority of villagers were unprepared to support the shah and his local partisans, neither were they ready to join the opposition movement; thus, in many instances activists were encouraged to depart from the villages, or even were forcibly expelled. The collapse of the government's power in December left rural elites without the means to enforce their political views and paved the way for unimpeded anti-government organizing in the villages. Visiting migrants now played a significant role in mobilizing general village support for the revolution during January and February 1979.

CONCLUSION: RURAL IRAN, CIRCA 1980

A primary reason why a minority of anti-shah activists were successful in mobilizing the support of a majority of villagers for the revolution was the absence of any deep feelings of allegiance to the shah and his government. For seventeen years, following the Land

Reform Law of January 1962, the bureaucracy's progressively expanding involvement in rural affairs had led to increasingly widespread disappointment in, and resentment of, Tehran. The net result
of this process was a willingness on the part of most villagers to accommodate the government, but a simultaneous inability to feel
any genuine loyalty toward it, or its symbol, the shah. Once it had
been demonstrated that the shah no longer controlled the government, then it was perceived as unnecessary to obey those who acted
in his name. Rather, the expedient course was to accommodate the
new personnel who seemed to wield the power of the government:
those acting in the name of Ayatollah Khomeini. Thus, by the time
the revolution succeeded on February 11, 1979, a majority of villagers had indicated their support for the new political order. However, the genuineness of that support was another matter altogether.

In the early part of 1979, the majority of villagers, who in the
past had seemed indifferent to politics, were rather ambivalent in
their views of the revolutionary government. On the one hand, there
were positive aspects: the new leader was a religious figure who had
a reputation for piety, honesty, and moral uprightness; furthermore,
he lived simply like a villager and talked constantly of the need to
help the poor and to revitalize agriculture. On the other hand, past
experience with the government had taught most villagers to be
wary of its promises and policies; the shah had spoken of the necessity of aiding villages for years, but only the rich had benefited. Villagers did believe Ayatollah Khomeini to be a more "sincere" man
than Mohammed Reza Pahlavi had been. However, the former's religious credentials were as much a matter of concern as they were of
approbation. For example, during the winter and spring of 1979, I frequently heard villagers pose, in reference to Khomeini, this rhetori-
cal question: "What does he know about politics?" Reinforcing this
concern was a general ignorance about the role of the clergy in
society. Typically, villager contacts with religious personnel were
limited to mendicant dervishes and itinerant mullahs who would
appear in the villages at harvest time to "share" the crop; while tol-
erated, they were held in very low esteem. In contrast the formal
clergy was an almost exclusively urban-based group; at most, only
10 percent of all villages were served by resident mullahs. Thus, as
late as February 1979, many villagers would confess to not really understanding the meaning of the term *ayatollah*, nor why there were
so many ayatollahs, or how they differed from mullahs. Given their
confusion, it perhaps was inevitable that many villagers would be
reserved in their attitude toward the new government, waiting for it
to demonstrate on behalf of whose interest it would act.

Not all villagers were prepared to await the formulation of policies by the new government; rather, they actively tried to influence it in order to secure their own interests. This was especially true of the village elite. Although as a group the elite had been champions of the shah almost to the moment he had left for exile on January 16, 1979, subsequently, they sought to ingratiate themselves with the supporters of Khomeini. While many of them found it difficult to participate in anti-shah demonstrations personally, they endorsed such activity by their sons; conveniently, sons of rich peasants emerged as conspicuous revolutionaries in numerous villages.[10] Thus, by the time the last royal government fell in February, most of the pre-revolutionary village elite had publicly displayed their support for the new order. Their efforts to retain their positions initially seemed successful: in villages where new revolutionary committees were set up to replace the village councils, a significant number of elected members were in fact from the families of rich peasants and their allies.

The principal organizers of the revolution in the villages had come from the non-elite groups, especially the middle peasants, and in larger villages the *khwushnishin* traders. Consequently, the activists were generally dissatisfied with the ability of the rich peasants to retain influence. By February, these activists had survived months of political demonstrations which had effectively transformed them into committed revolutionaries. Thus they interpreted revolution in the village to mean a fundamental change in the local political and economic status quo. However, in the immediate aftermath of the revolution, Tehran was admonishing caution, specifically appealing for respect for the sanctity of property. In the villages this was translated to mean no land expropriations, an action which rural revolutionaries believed essential in order to initiate the changes they desired.

One of the areas in which pre-revolutionary confrontations between pro-shah and anti-shah forces had been especially intense was Kurdistan. Inevitably, this became the first region where village activists, bitter about the lack of real change, attempted to implement the revolution locally. Generally, large landowners were more concentrated in Kurdistan than in other provinces. Significantly, a high proportion of these owners actually resided in the villages. As representatives of the shah's government, they continued to wield power in the villages as oppressively after land reform as they had before. Their hasty rapprochement with the new revolutionary government infuriated many village revolutionaries, who were determined that the large landowners should pay for their collaboration with the shah and their exploitation of the villagers. Consequently, as early as March, only one month after the success of the revolution, activists organized peasant and *khwushnishin* groups for the purpose of expropriating large landholdings. The landowners attempted to defend their properties by enlisting the aid of Tehran. The rural land struggle eventually became intertwined with the urban-based struggle for Kurdish provincial autonomy which the government has tried to suppress forcibly since August 1979.

Tehran's preoccupation with Kurdistan was one of many factors preventing the successful re-establishment of central governmental authority in rural areas during 1979 and 1980. As villagers gradually became aware of the government's essential weakness, they realized that it had limited power to enforce its decisions. Thus, a majority of villagers once again were willing to listen to the arguments of the activists and support them in challenging the prevailing status quo; i.e., to participate in popular land expropriations. Generally, expropriated land has been the property of absentee owners, especially the larger ones.[11] The villagers have sought to justify land expropriations on one or more of these grounds: (1) that the land had been acquired illegally; (2) that the owner had collaborated with the shah's secret police; (3) that the owner had fled the country; (4) that the land was not being cultivated; and (5) that the land had been originally confiscated from the peasants.

In the absence of significant data, it is not possible to estimate what percentage of all land has been expropriated since the revolution. Nor have any general patterns emerged with respect to the redistribution of such land. My own personal observations in Fars province indicate a variety of practices have been followed. In some villages, for example, the land initially was farmed collectively with the intent that profits be shared equally among all heads of households. In certain villages, all *khwushnishin*s were excluded from obtaining land, while in others they were among the eligible beneficiaries. In still other villages, only peasants whose holdings were below a specified minimum could acquire any of the expropriated land; in contrast, expropriated property was divided equally among all landowners in some villages.

The Iranian government has yet to adopt an official policy for dealing with the question of land expropriations. Generally, local bureaucrats have opposed seizures, but often have been powerless to prevent them. There have been some cases in which the government's revolutionary guards intervened to halt expropriation efforts; but in other instances security forces would not or could not interfere.[12] In villages where land has been expropriated, peasants are aware that the overall weakness of the central government assured their success. There is concern that the authorities eventually may order the restitution of all agricultural property; in the interim, peasants are collecting evidence about the "un-Islamic" character of expropriated owners as justification for their actions. There is also hope that the passage of time will make their *faits accomplis* more difficult to reverse.

The immediate cause of popular land expropriations, government weakness, and peasant fears of a possible return to the status quo ante if a powerful central authority is re-established emphasize one of the most important legacies of the land reform program: the deeply engrained suspicion of the government in the villages. The underlying cause for the expropriations, the rural poverty and underdevelopment, which also are legacies of land reform, tend to reinforce the mistrust because in the past government policies failed to alleviate barely tolerable socioeconomic conditions despite the persistent expounding of expectation-arousing rhetoric. Consequently, the revolutionary government of Iran confronts a formidable challenge with respect to agricultural development, which it has repeatedly professed to be one of its main priorities. That is, it must convince cynical villagers that it is sincerely interested in their welfare in order to secure their cooperation, which is essential for any successful rural development effort.

Notes

Abbreviations

IJMES: International Journal of Middle East Studies.
IS: Iranian Studies.
MEJ: Middle East Journal.
MERIP Reports: Middle East Research and Information Project Reports.
TE: Tahqiqat é Eqtesadi.

Introduction

1. The reference is to D. R. Denman, *The King's Vista: A Land Reform Which Has Changed the Face of Persia.* The propagandistic value of this book is attested by the fact that Iranian government officials gave gratis —and unsolicited—copies of it to persons doing scholarly and journalistic research on villages in the mid-1970's.
2. Ann K. S. Lambton, *The Persian Land Reform, 1962–1966.*

1. The Rural Setting

1. The statistics on land utilization are based upon Table A.1, "Estimated Land Use, 1971," in Oddvar Aresvik, *The Agricultural Development of Iran,* p. 247.
2. There has never been a separate census of the tribally organized nomadic population. One Iranian anthropologist who spent many years studying the customs and migration patterns of pastoralists calculated their numbers at around 2 million. See Nader Afshar-Naderi, *The Settlement of Nomads and Its Social and Economic Implications,* p. 10. In both the 1966 and 1976 censuses, the category "unsettled" presumedly includes the pastoral nomads.
3. See Iran, Plan Organization, *National Census of Population and Housing, November, 1966.*
4. Detailed results of the 1976 census had not been published as of autumn 1981 when this manuscript was completed; thus it was not possible to compare village statistics for the two periods.
5. Some districts of the Caspian provinces of Gilan and Mazandaran are exceptional in that villages consist of detached houses.

6. For a more detailed description of peasant homes and household furnishings, see Robert C. Alberts, "Social Structure and Cultural Change in an Iranian Village" (Ph.D. dissertation, University of Wisconsin at Madison, 1963), pp. 144–163.

7. Ann K. S. Lambton, *Landlord and Peasant in Persia*, p. 5.

8. George Cressey, "Qanats, Karez and Foggaras," *Geographical Review* 48 (1958): 28.

9. For more detail, see ibid., pp. 27–44, and Hans E. Wulff, *The Traditional Crafts of Persia*, pp. 251–254.

10. For more detail, see Lambton, *Landlord and Peasant*, pp. 356–368.

2. Agrarian Society, Circa 1960

1. For an excellent discussion of the differences between medieval European feudalism and later Iranian feudalism, see Ervand Abrahamian, "European Feudalism and Middle Eastern Despotisms," *Science and Society* 39 (Summer 1975): 129–156; for descriptive accounts of Iranian feudalism historically, see Lambton, *Landlord and Peasant*, and Farhad Nomani, "The Origin and Development of Feudalism in Iran: 300–1600 A.D." (Ph.D. dissertation, University of Illinois at Urbana-Champaign, 1972).

2. The impact of the international economy upon Iran from ca. 1850 to 1950 has been inadequately studied to date. A pioneering study which deals with the agricultural sector is Nikki Keddie, "Stratification, Social Control, and Capitalism in Iranian Villages: Before and after Land Reform," in *Rural Politics and Social Change in the Middle East*, ed. Richard Antoun and Iliya Harik, pp. 364–402.

3. For more insight into crop changes in nineteenth-century Iran, see Charles Issawi, ed., *The Economic History of Iran, 1800–1914*, especially Chapter 3, "Foreign Trade," pp. 70–151, and Chapter 5, "Agriculture," pp. 206–257.

4. Keddie, "Stratification, Social Control, and Capitalism in Iranian Villages," p. 368.

5. Ibid., pp. 366–367.

6. Keddie discusses the deterioration of standards in ibid., pp. 365–367.

7. Abolghassem Dehbod, "Land Ownership and Use Conditions in Iran," in *Central Treaty Organization, Symposium on Rural Development at Tehran, 25–30 September 1963*, p. 62.

8. There are no statistics or even authoritative estimates available on the number of large owners during the twentieth century. At most they numbered no more than two or three thousand, perhaps only several hundred.

9. For a general discussion of *khāliseh* villages, see Lambton, *Landlord and Peasant*, pp. 238–258.

10. See ibid., pp. 230–237.

11. For more detail, see Shahrough Akhavi, *Religion and Politics in Contemporary Iran*, pp. 56–59.

12. For more detail on *bigāri*, see Lambton, *Landlord and Peasant*, pp. 330–333.

13. Ibid., p. 263.

14. For a more detailed discussion of the nature of landlord-peasant relations, see Paul Vieille, "Un Groupement féodal en Iran," *Revue Française de Sociologie* 2 (1965): 175–190.

15. Javad Safi-nezhad, *Tālebābād: Nimunih-i Jām'i az Barrisi-i yek deh*, p. 115.

16. For examples, see F. A. C. Forbes-Leith, *Checkmate: Fighting Tradition in Central Persia*, pp. 71–72. The author was a retired British military officer hired by an Iranian landlord to supervise his extensive estates.

17. For an example, see Mostafa Azkia, *Monugrāfi-yi Hājjiābād*, p. 84.

18. For more detail concerning peasants' dues and services, see Lambton, *Landlord and Peasant*, pp. 338–341.

19. George J. Jennings, "A Development Project and Culture Change in an Iranian Village," *Proceedings of the Minnesota Academy of Science* 25–26 (1957–1958): 314–315.

20. These laws are treated in detail in Lambton, *Landlord and Peasant*, pp. 190–191.

21. Safi-nezhad, *Tālebābād*, p. 114.

22. Lambton, *Landlord and Peasant*, p. 386.

23. E. Sunderland, "Pastorialism, Nomadism, and the Social Anthropology of Iran," in *The Land of Iran*, ed. W. B. Fisher, vol. 1 of *The Cambridge History of Iran*, p. 629.

24. I am indebted to Hushang Keshavarz for this idea.

25. One authority estimated that there may have been as many as 2 million small landowners with holdings under 100 hectares (241 acres). See Khosrou Khosrovi, "La Stratification social rurale en Iran," *Etudes Rurales* 22–24 (1966): 245. This figure seems excessively high; a more realistic estimate is probably between 500,000 and 1 million small owners.

26. See ibid.

27. Benno Sternberg-Sarel, "Revolution blanche dans les compagnes iraniennes," in *Terre, paysans, et politique*, ed. H. Mendras and Y. Travernier, p. 471.

28. See further the discussion in Eric J. Hooglund, "The *Khwushnishin* Population of Iran," *IS* 6 (Autumn 1973): 229–231.

29. The few studies of pre–land reform villages contain meager information about these various individuals. Village shopkeepers have received more attention than the others; see, e.g., Alberts, "Social Structure and Culture Change," pp. 513–519.

30. For an example of the variety of goods found in a typical village shop around 1960–1962, see Safi-nezhad, *Tālebābād*, pp. 63–64.

31. Lambton, *Landlord and Peasant*, p. 380.

32. There was (and still is) a wide variety of weights and measures used in rural Iran. A great number have been collected and explained in terms of

the international metric system, the official standard of Iran. See Husayn Malek and Javad Safi-nezhad, *Vāhadhā-yi andāzeh giri dar rustāhā-yi Iran*. The *mann* which will be referred to frequently in this study will always be the *mann-i Tabrizi*, the most common of the several varying *mann*s. The *mann-i Tabrizi* consists of 40 *sir*s and is equivalent to 2.97 kilograms, or 6.5464 pounds; 100 *mann*s equals 1 *kharvār*.

33. Cf. Vieille, "Un Groupement féodal," p. 182.
34. William G. Miller, "Hosseinabad: A Persian Village," *MEJ* 18 (1964): 485.
35. A particularly notorious example is cited by William O. Douglas, *Strange Lands and Friendly Peoples*, pp. 47–48.
36. The *misqāl* is traditionally the smallest measurement of weight in Iran. There are 640 *misqāl*s in the *mann-i Tabrizi*. Each *misqāl* equals approximately .1635 ounces.
37. Cf. Miller, "Hosseinabad," p. 485.
38. The *gāvband*s as a separate group in Iranian rural society have not yet been the subject of detailed research. They are not found in all villages, or even all areas. They are particularly important in villages near Tehran and Kermanshah and in the provinces of Khuzistan and Sistan. Javad Safi-nezhad has dealt with *gāvband*s in *Buneh*, 2d ed., pp. 90–155.
39. The five factors were land, water, plough animals, seed, and labor. See further Lambton, *Landlord and Peasant*, pp. 306–329.
40. In some areas, notably Kermanshah, sharecropping agreements were not between landlord and peasant, but between landlord and *gāvband*. *Gāvband*s recruited peasants to do all the work associated with cultivation, giving them a share of the harvest retained by the *gāvband*s after division with the landlord.
41. The results of this survey are discussed in Research Group in Agricultural Economics, "A Review of the Statistics of the First Stage of Land Reform," *TE* 2 (March 1964): 144. It should be noted that this is a survey, not an actual census. The total of rural households was estimated from samples and thus differs from figures which will be cited in subsequent chapters.
42. Practice varied considerably from one village to the next. In some cases, the initial invitation from the landowner coupled with the successful completion of one season of work was considered sufficient for the peasant to have acquired *nasaq*.
43. Extensive scholarly work on *buneh*s during the past twenty years has been undertaken by Professor Javad Safi-nezhad of the University of Tehran; for more detail, see his book, *Buneh*, 2d ed. It should be noted that while *buneh* has become the standard term in Iran for scholarly purposes, its use by peasants is common only in the area from Qazvin southeastward to Garmsar; at least a dozen different words are employed in various parts of the country to refer to these teams. For some examples of equivalent terms, see ibid., "Moqadameh" (Introduction), p. ten.
44. For more details, see Safi-nezhad, *Buneh*, 2d ed., pp. 8–15.

45. Lambton, *Land Reform*, p. 7.
46. Personal communication from peasants.
47. *Sarbuneh* is the term for a *buneh* head in the Qazvin and Garmsar areas; *ābyār* or *oyār* is used in Varamin, and *sarsalar* in Khurasan. In parts of Kermanshahan, the term *gāvband* is synonymous with *sarbuneh*. Many other terms are encountered with less frequency than the above. My preference for *sarbuneh* follows general academic usage in Iran.
48. Cf. M. Mossane, "A Pilot Study and Evaluation in Qazvin Plain Villages," in *Seminar on Evaluation of Directed Social Change*, ed. Nader Afshar-Naderi, p. 115; and Khosrou Khosrovi, *Jām'ehshināsi-yi rustā'i-yi Iran*, p. 80.
49. Safi-nezhad, *Tālebābād*, p. 116.
50. Ibid., p. 117.
51. For a convenient list of the various tasks for which *sarbuneh*s were typically responsible, see Safi-nezhad, *Buneh*, 2d ed., pp. 46–47.
52. Cf. Azkia, *Hājjiābād*, p. 153.
53. Safi-nezhad, *Tālebābād*, p. 119; for a listing of the typical duties of assistants, see Safi-nezhad, *Buneh*, 2d ed., pp. 47–48. In April 1972, Safi-nezhad told me he discovered in certain villages men who were called assistants but had no supervisory functions. All *buneh*s exhibiting this characteristic were ones which had two or more members in addition to the *sarbuneh* and the men in charge of the oxen teams. Safi-nezhad believes that the practice was to assign surplus men the title of assistants so as not to confuse the members who were responsible for the oxen with those who were not. In terms of work, the assistants and peasants shared all other tasks equally in these special cases.
54. A peasant did not necessarily own the pair of oxen with which he worked. If he owned only one ox or none at all, it was necessary to rent from a *sarbuneh*, *gāvband*, or landlord. The importance of oxen ownership is discussed in Alberts, "Social Structure and Culture Change," pp. 273–275.
55. For an excellent discussion of the various ploughs used in Iran, see Wulff, *Traditional Crafts*, pp. 262–266.
56. Land which was not going to be irrigated was ploughed more quickly, since the soil was not tilled to any depth, but rather simply scratched. Normally, 4–6 hectares (about 10–15 acres) of *daymi* land could be ploughed in one day.
57. See Wulff, *Traditional Crafts*, pp. 266–268.
58. Safi-nezhad, *Tālebābād*, pp. 118–119.
59. For a more complete listing of the various jobs which were the peasants' responsibility, see Safi-nezhad, *Buneh*, 2d ed., pp. 48–49.
60. The division of the harvest based upon the five factors of production has been customary practice at least since Safavid times (1499–1722) and probably even earlier. See further, Muhammad 'Ali Ibadi, *Islāhat-i arzi dar Iran*, p. 15.
61. See further Lambton, *Landlord and Peasant*, pp. 306–329.

62. See further Safi-nezhad, *Buneh*, 2d ed., pp. 83–85.
63. Cf. Hushang Aliāsiān, *Moqadameh'i bar tahqiq-i ijtimā'i-yi rustāhā-yi Dasht-i Qazvin*, pp. 46–47.
64. Safi-nezhad, *Buneh*, 2d ed., p. 45.
65. See further Safi-nezhad, *Tālebābād*, pp. 204–209.
66. See further ibid., p. 116.
67. Significantly, *sarbuneh*s rarely were younger than thirty-five. For age statistics on *sarbuneh*s in the village of Kamalabad near Qazvin, see Aliāsiān, *Dasht-i Qazvin*, p. 43.
68. Other villagers considered as among the *rish sefid*s included *mubāshir*s, *kadkhudā*s, owners who resided in the villages, and prosperous *khwush-nishin* traders; see further Miller, "Hosseinabad," p. 489, and Benno Sternberg-Sarel, "Tradition et développement en Iran: Les Villages de la plaine de Ghazvin," *Etudes Rurales*, 22–24 (1966): 210 ff.
69. Aliāsiān calls these *buneh*s "family units of production" (see *Dasht-i Qazvin*, p. 44). This interpretation is inaccurate. Each member of a *buneh* is an adult peasant who must support his own nuclear family from the share of the harvest he receives; he is unable to contribute toward the maintenance of members of a wider extended family group, even though he may work with relatives in the *buneh*.
70. Figures for the percentages of *khwushnishin*s in the three groups have been estimated from official occupational statistics for the rural population during the 1960's. See Iran, Ministry of Labour and Social Affairs, *Barrisihā-yi masā'il-i niru-yi insāni*, vol. 3, pp. 2343–2438.
71. For an excellent discussion of the criteria peasants use in assigning status to villagers, see Alberts, "Social Structure and Culture Change," pp. 757–785.
72. The discussion of attitudes toward mullahs is based upon my field interview experiences in the 1970's. I believe it is reasonable to assume that these same attitudes prevailed twenty years earlier. Another writer did find somewhat similar attitudes during research in 1956–1958; see Alberts, "Social Structure and Culture Change," pp. 818–828.
73. See further Safi-nezhad, *Tālebābād*, p. 144.
74. Ibid., p. 155.
75. A detailed description of the various tools used in Iranian agriculture is in Wulff, *Traditional Crafts*, pp. 260–277.
76. Both blacksmiths and carpenters did accept special projects, such as shoeing horses and making furniture, for which they collected fees; the largest part of their work and income, however, was derived from servicing the *buneh*s.
77. Cf. Safi-nezhad, *Tālebābād*, pp. 144 and 155–156.
78. Apparently, it was standard in some villages for a carpenter's "salary" to be less than the blacksmith's; see Safi-nezhad, *Buneh*, 2d ed., p. 243.
79. In 1962 the average price of unground wheat was 6 *riāls* per kilogram. At an exchange rate of 75 *riāls* to $1.00, the equivalent monetary cost would be roughly $2.00 for a large pot or pair of shoes. In larger villages, barter transactions were relatively rare by 1962.

80. The information about barbers is based upon recollections of older peasants who were interviewed in the Varamin area during the spring of 1972.

81. Ibid.

82. Significantly, peasants said they would have no objection to giving their daughters in marriage to barbers, provided more suitable candidates were unavailable (ibid.).

83. Ibid.

84. For statistics, see Iran, Ministry of Labour and Social Affairs, *Niru-yi insāni*, vol. 3, pp. 2343–2438.

85. On the worsening economic situation of the peasantry throughout the nineteenth century, see further Lambton, *Landlord and Peasant*, pp. 143–145, and Nikki Keddie, *Historical Obstacles to Agrarian Change in Iran*, pp. 4–7.

86. In certain villages carpet and cloth weaving were important sources of income; see, e.g., Paul Ward English, *City and Village in Iran: Settlement and Economy in the Kirman Basin*, and Robert Dillon, "Carpet Capitalism and Craft Involution in Kerman, Iran" (Ph.D. dissertation, Columbia University, 1976).

87. Both peasants and agricultural workers stated that daily wage rates for reaping averaged between 6 and 8 *tumān*s throughout most of Western and Central Iran during the period 1961–1964.

88. The amounts of food allotted each reaper in the Tehran area are presented in Safi-nezhad, *Tālebābād*, pp. 125–126.

89. Ibid., pp. 124–125.

90. For an examination of the absence of widespread peasant rebellions in the twentieth century, see Farhad Kazemi and Ervand Abrahamian, "The Non-revolutionary Peasantry of Modern Iran," *IS* 11 (1978): 259–304.

91. Eric R. Wolf, *Peasant Wars of the Twentieth Century*, p. 291.

92. Ibid., p. 290.

93. A theory of rational decision-making by peasants is argued persuasively by Samuel Popkin, *The Rational Peasant*.

3. The Origins of Land Reform

1. See further Muhammad Taghi Bāhar, *Tārikh-i mokhtasar-i ahzab-i siyasi-yi Iran*, pp. 3–8.

2. For more detail about political groups and their activities during this period, see Ann K. S. Lambton, "Persian Political Societies, 1906–1911," in *St. Anthony's Papers No. 16*, ed. Albert Hourani, pp. 41–89.

3. For a brief history of the Jangali movement, see Ahmad Kasravi, *Tārikh-i hejdeh sāleh Azarbayjan*, 4th ed., vol. 2, pp. 812–828.

4. Kazemi and Abrahamian, "The Non-revolutionary Peasantry," p. 285.

5. Ibid., p. 286.

6. For details, see ibid., pp. 286–287, and Sepehr Zabih, *The Communist Movement in Iran*, pp. 19–45.

7. For more information about the relations between Reza Pahlavi and

Sayyid Ziā, see L. P. Elwell-Sutton, "Reza Shah the Great: Founder of the Pahlavi Dynasty," in *Iran under the Pahlavis*, ed. George Lenczowski, pp. 17–19.

8. Sayyid Ziā's interest in agriculture is discussed in Peter Avery, *Modern Iran*, pp. 235–237; see also Lambton, *Persian Land Reform*, p. 49.

9. For a study of Reza Shah's industrialization program, see Amin Banani, *The Modernization of Iran, 1921–1941*.

10. Ibid., pp. 122–124.

11. On the sale of state lands under Reza Shah, see Lambton, *Landlord and Peasant*, pp. 239–250, 253–255.

12. Ibid., pp. 256–257; Lambton, *Persian Land Reform*, pp. 49–50.

13. Ervand Abrahamian, "Communism and Communalism in Iran: The Tudeh and the *Firqah-i Dimukrat*," *IJMES* 1 (October 1970): 297–299; and Zabih, *Communist Movement*, pp. 64–70.

14. For an account of Arani's circle and the formation of the Tudeh written by one of the participants, see Bozorg Alavi, *Panjah-o-se nafar*.

15. Zabih, *Communist Movement*, pp. 81–82.

16. The best study of the Firqah-i Dimukrat-i Azarbayjan is Abrahamian, "Communism and Communalism," pp. 291–317.

17. For an account of the Azarbayjan insurrection, see Zabih, *Communist Movement*, pp. 98–122.

18. Cyrus Gharatchedaghi, *The Distribution of Land in Varamin*, pp. 37–38.

19. Abrahamian, "Communism and Communalism," pp. 306–310.

20. While living in Azarbayjan from 1966 to 1968, I encountered widespread favorable assessments among Azarbayjanis who could recall the Firqah-i Dimukrat period. Among the younger generation (ca. 18 to 25 in 1966–1968), there was an especially positive, even idealized, view of this time. Most Azarbayjanis, even those who expressed disapproval of the autonomous movement, resented bitterly the national holiday on December 12 to commemorate the "liberation" of Azarbayjan.

21. The Soviet Union and Great Britain jointly invaded Iran in August 1941 and occupied the country for the duration of World War II; they were later joined by the United States. The three wartime allies agreed to withdraw all their forces within six months of the cessation of all hostilities. The Soviet Union actually delayed its departure by two months, precipitating a minor international crisis. See further Richard W. Van Wagenen, *The Iranian Case, 1946*.

22. *Dāryā* (Tehran), 25 Dey 1329/January 15, 1951.

23. Ibid., 5 Bahman 1329/January 25, 1951.

24. The shah did not connect his decision to sell his properties to any influence except personal idealism. See Muhammad Reza Shah Pahlavi, *Mission for My Country*, pp. 201–203.

25. Nikki Keddie, "Stratification, Social Control, and Capitalism in Iranian Villages," p. 399, n. 9.

26. A brief treatment of landlord opposition to the shah's sale of royal estates is in Lambton, *Persian Land Reform*, pp. 53–55.

27. The best study of the National Front movement is Richard W. Cottam, *Nationalism in Iran.*
28. For an analysis of the Musaddiq government's policies, see Henry C. Atyeo, "Political Developments in Iran, 1951–1954," *Middle Eastern Affairs* 5 (1954): 249–259.
29. See further Lambton, *Persian Land Reform*, pp. 37–38.
30. Ibid., pp. 38–39.
31. Ibid., pp. 39–40.
32. For a contrasting view, see ibid., p. 40.
33. Cottam maintains that the National Front's agricultural program could have brought "fundamental" changes to the villages (see *Nationalism*, pp. 271–272); this optimism seems unjustified in view of the fact that there was no attempt to alter the tenure patterns.
34. Ibid., p. 283.
35. See further ibid., pp. 286–313.
36. The most comprehensive study of the shah's efforts to develop Iran on a capitalist model is Fred Halliday, *Iran: Dictatorship and Development.*
37. Cottam, *Nationalism*, p. 290.
38. Ibid., note 2.
39. The shah's relations with the military in the initial years after the 1953 coup have been inadequately studied. Most of the senior officers had risen through the ranks under Reza Shah and their loyalty had been to him; they tended to be contemptuous of the son's apparent lack of authoritativeness (in comparison to the father) in the 1941–1953 period. Many of the junior officers, in contrast, had been socialized in the post-1941 period and were influenced by the various reform ideas of the pre-coup years. Consequently, the military was divided into different factions, some of which had political ambitions. At least one major plot against the monarchy was foiled in 1958 (see ibid., pp. 314–315). The fact that a majority of the military stayed loyal during this coup attempt was an indication that the shah had succeeded in establishing the primacy of his own authority.
40. Lambton, *Persian Land Reform*, p. 56.
41. Ibid.
42. Ibid., p. 60.
43. See Cottam, *Nationalism*, p. 298.
44. Edward A. Bayne, *Persian Kingship in Transition*, p. 191.
45. I am grateful to William G. Miller, former political officer at the U.S. Embassy in Tehran, for this information. The history of U.S.-Iranian relations in the critical years 1960–1963 has not been investigated to date. For one brief overview, see Barry Rubin, *Paved with Good Intentions: The American Experience and Iran*, pp. 101–107.

4. The Land Reform Program

1. It has been fashionable for some authors to attribute its success to the fact that the law was issued as a decree while the parliament was dissolved (1961–1963), and thus the traditionally landlord-dominated *maj-*

lis was unable to obstruct the program. However, the presence or absence of the parliament would be irrelevant, since elections to it and its work while in session were controlled by the government, which in turn was controlled by the shah. Indeed, the parliament was dissolved because of the political turmoil related to charges of government election rigging in 1960 and 1961. For more on the former view, see Avery, *Modern Iran*, p. 499. For an interpretation similar to mine, see Hossein Mahdavy, "The Coming Crisis in Iran," *Foreign Affairs* 44 (October 1965): 137.

2. A thorough examination of Arsanjani's ideas and role has yet to be published. For two very favorable, but brief, discussions, see Lambton, *Persian Land Reform*, pp. 61–64, and Doreen Warriner, *Land Reform in Principle and Practice*, pp. 116–118. For a more balanced account, see Marvin Zonis, *The Political Elite of Iran*, pp. 53–60.

3. James Bill, Interview with Hassan-e Arsanjani, No. 2, August 19, 1966, p. 3. I am grateful to Professor Bill for providing me with a copy of his extensive notes of this interview.

4. Ibid., pp. 5–6.

5. Lambton, *Persian Land Reform*, pp. 57–58.

6. The following discussion of Arsanjani's goals is summarized from Hassan Arsanjani, "Mas'aleh islāhāt-i arzi dar Iran," *Majaleh-i masa'il-i Iran* 1 (Deh 1341/December 1962–January 1963): 97–104.

7. Lambton, *Persian Land Reform*, p. 64.

8. Research Group in Agricultural Economics, "An Analysis of the Law Governing the First Stage of Land Reform in Iran," *TE* 7 (Winter 1970): 71.

9. Lambton, *Persian Land Reform*, p. 64.

10. James Bill, personal communication, January 5, 1981.

11. Lambton, *Persian Land Reform*, p. 63.

12. Detailed analyses of the provisions of the law can be found in ibid., pp. 64–86; and Research Group in Agricultural Economics, "Analysis," pp. 49–74.

13. A discussion of procedures for determining compensation price and appeals is in Research Group in Agricultural Economics, "Analysis," pp. 62–63.

14. Based upon interviews with peasants in various regions between 1967 and 1972.

15. Interview, fall 1967.

16. For more details on cooperatives, see Ann K. S. Lambton, "Land Reform and Rural Cooperative Societies in Persia," *Royal Central Asian Journal* 56, Parts II & III (1969): 9–28.

17. Warriner, *Land Reform in Principle*, p. 119.

18. Ibid., p. 117.

19. Abbas Salour, "Land Reform Activities in Iran," in *Central Treaty Organization, Symposium on Rural Development at Tehran*, p. 56.

20. Ibid., pp. 52–53.

21. Lambton, *Persian Land Reform*, pp. 122–123.

22. K. S. McLachlan, "Land Reform in Iran," in *The Land of Iran*, ed. W. B. Fisher, p. 704.
23. Bill, Interview with Arsanjani, pp. 1–2.
24. Lambton, *Persian Land Reform*, p. 90.
25. The Land Reform Organization's report is summarized in ibid., pp. 90–91.
26. Warriner, *Land Reform in Principle*, p. 119.
27. A summary of the provisions of Arsanjani's Additional Articles is in Lambton, *Persian Land Reform*, pp. 104–107.
28. Zonis, *Political Elite*, pp. 58–60.
29. James A. Bill, *The Politics of Iran: Groups, Classes, and Modernization*, p. 142.
30. Cf. ibid., p. 144.
31. For an analysis of the White Revolution as a means of preserving the shah's system of rule, see ibid., pp. 139–156.
32. See Research Group in Agricultural Economics, "Analysis," pp. 54–55.
33. Lambton, *Persian Land Reform*, p. 101.
34. Interviews with former land reform officials, Tehran, summer 1970.
35. When the 1962 Land Reform Law was enacted, Arsanjani had anticipated the completion of land reform by September 1963. After his departure, the completion date was repeatedly advanced. Officially, the government had purchased and transferred to the peasants all affected villages by September 1971. However, I encountered villages which were still in the process of being settled under the provisions of the 1962 law as late as the summer of 1972.
36. Sāzamān-i islāhāt-i arzi, *Guzāresh az aval-i bahman, 1340 tā pāyān-i shahrivar 1342*, pp. 5–8.
37. Ibid.
38. Sāzamān-i islāhāt-i arzi, *Guzāresh-i sāl-i 1344*, passim.
39. *Keyhan International* (Tehran), February 3, 1973, p. 12.
40. Arsanjani was actually "promoted" to ambassador to Italy, a post he held for one year. He resigned from government service completely in 1964.
41. Keddie, "Stratification, Social Control, and Capitalism in Iranian Villages," p. 392.
42. Bill, *Politics of Iran*, p. 123.
43. The main provisions of the Additional Articles are discussed in detail in Lambton, *Persian Land Reform*, pp. 194–215.
44. Ibid., pp. 198–200.
45. Ibid., pp. 200–201.
46. Ibid., pp. 201–202.
47. Ibid., pp. 202–204.
48. Ibid., pp. 204–206.
49. Ibid., pp. 206–207.
50. Ibid., p. 207.
51. Ibid., p. 196.
52. *Keyhan International* (Tehran), February 3, 1973, p. 12.
53. Sāzamān-i islāhāt-i arzi, *Guzāresh-i sāl-i 1345*, pp. 3 ff.

54. In fairness, it should be stated that there was no legal prohibition against payment in kind provided both parties were in agreement.
55. Interviews, various villages of western Iran, 1967–1968.
56. Information based upon interviews with one of the owners and several of the peasants, summer 1972.
57. For an analysis of the shah's agricultural development policies from a Marxist perspective, see Halliday, *Iran*, pp. 103–137.
58. The interpretation in this paragraph is based upon interviews conducted with various officials in Tehran and Meshhed during 1971–1972.
59. Kenneth B. Platt, *Land Reform in Iran*, p. 41.
60. Ibid.
61. Bāqir Parahān, *Islāhāt-i arzi va natā'ij-i ān*, pp. 54–55. Much of the disputed land consisted of those areas formerly used communally for pasturing animals.
62. Ibid.
63. James A. Bill and Carl Leiden, *The Middle East: Politics and Power*, p. 144.
64. Interviews with land reform officials, Tehran, December 1971.
65. Sāzamān-i islāhāt-i arzi, *Guzāresh-i sāl-i 1351*, pp. 1–3.
66. Official explanations have been unconvincingly varied: 1.25 million was an inflated figure due to overzealous reporting; the 1.25 million figure was a printing error; the 738,119 figure was a printing error; between 1969 and 1971, 400,000 tenants migrated to the cities and abandoned their land and rights (interviews with various officials in Tehran, summer 1977).
67. Quote from *MEJ* 26 (Winter 1972): 42.

5. Land Tenure after Redistribution

1. Of course, there are regional variations upon this 7-hectare average. In the rainfall abundant areas along the Caspian Sea coast, for example, less than 5 hectares is considered sufficient for basic subsistence; at the other extreme, in parts of Baluchistan even 10 hectares may be inadequate.
2. See further, Shoko Okazaki, "Shirang-Sofla: The Economics of a Northeast Iranian Village," *Developing Economies* 7 (September 1969): 281.
3. In this chapter the term *absentee* is used in a general sense to refer to all owners who did not personally work their land but either rented it out to tenants or hired wage labor to cultivate it. Most of these owners were also "absentees" in a residential sense, although some of them lived in the villages where their properties were located.
4. Government activities in the villages will be analyzed in Chapter 7.
5. For a more detailed discussion of post–land reform ownership patterns and statistical tables, see Khosrovi, *Jām'ehshināsi-yi rustā'i-yi Iran*, pp. 169–174. It should be pointed out here that beginning in 1968 government statistics record agricultural holdings in hectares.
6. For more detail, see Chapter 2, note 25.

7. For some reasonably accurate statistics, see Aresvik, *Agricultural Development*, pp. 101–102.
8. For more detailed data, see table in Akhavi, *Religion and Politics*, p. 133.
9. See further Lambton, *Persian Land Reform*, pp. 234–235.
10. Some *vaqf* properties were distributed to peasants in cases where the administrators decided it would serve the purposes of the endowment if the properties were sold and the proceeds reinvested in more profitable undertakings.
11. Based upon interviews, summer 1972 and summer 1977.
12. With respect to the latter point, it can be mentioned that during the Pahlavi period the government's Endowments Organization had exercised effective control over *vaqf* properties, much to the resentment of the *shi'i* clergy. See further Akhavi, *Religion and Politics*, pp. 132–134.
13. The estimates and information in this and the following paragraphs are based upon personal observations during field work in 1971–1972, 1977, and 1978–1979.
14. Many large-scale private farms had over 1,000 hectares (2,471 acres); however, rarely was more than 500 hectares cultivated in irrigated field crops at any one time. This may explain why most official government statistics do not provide detail on size of holdings over 500 hectares.
15. An excellent study of large-scale landownership is Shoko Okazaki, *The Development of Large-Scale Farming in Iran: The Case of the Province of Gurgan*. See especially pp. 14–21 for a discussion of agricultural entrepreneurs.
16. For an evaluation of the general success of commercial farming, see Mostafa Azkia, "The Effect of Rural Development Programmes on the Iranian Peasantry between 1962 and 1978, with Special Reference to Farm Corporations" (Ph.D. dissertation, Aberdeen University, 1980), pp. 117–125.
17. For a case study of a postrevolutionary expropriation, see Mary Hooglund, "One Village in the Revolution," *MERIP Reports* 87 (May 1980): 10–12.
18. For examples of the revolutionary government's contradictory attitudes toward land expropriations, see "Documents," *MERIP Reports* 87 (May 1980): 12–14.
19. For more details on this law, see Azkia, "Rural Development Programmes," pp. 126–127.
20. For more detail on government expropriation of land in Khuzistan, see ibid., pp. 128–129.
21. For more detail about international corporate interests, see Helmut Richards, "Land Reform and Agribusiness in Iran," *MERIP Reports* 43 (December 1975): 12–18, and F. R. C. Bagley, "A Bright Future after Oil: Dams and Agro-industry in Khuzistan," *MEJ* 30 (Winter 1976): 33–34.
22. See further Azkia, "Rural Development Programmes," pp. 129–130.
23. See further John Freivalds, "Farm Corporations in Iran: An Alternative to Traditional Agriculture," *MEJ* 26 (Spring 1972): 190–191.

24. M. A. Katouzian, "Oil versus Agriculture: A Case of Dual Resource Depletion in Iran," *Journal of Peasant Studies* 5 (April 1978): 361.
25. Richards, "Agribusiness in Iran," p. 17.
26. Azkia, summarizing the results of a study by Fatemeh Etemad-Moghaddam, in "Rural Development Programmes," p. 131.
27. Ibid.
28. Richards, "Agribusiness in Iran," p. 18.
29. The goals of the law are summarized in Azkia, "Rural Development Programmes," p. 139.
30. Ibid., pp. 141–146.
31. Detailed statistical data for eighty-nine farm corporations is provided in ibid., Appendix I, Table 5.5, pp. 416 ff.
32. For a detailed evaluation of the performance of farm corporations, see ibid., pp. 213–272.
33. Sāzamān-i barnāmeh, *Barrisi-yi masā'il-i rustā'i-yi Iran*, p. 5.
34. Hushang Keshāvarz, J. Safi-nezhad, and V. Hājjabi, *Shirkat-i sahāmi-yi zirā'ati-yi Rezā Pahlavi (Qasr-i Shirin)*, pp. 30–33, 62–69.
35. Interviews with officials and rural sociologists in Iran, summer 1978.
36. The following information is based upon field research during 1971–1972.
37. Field research, summer 1977.
38. Sāzamān-i chirikhā-yi fadā'i-yi khalq, *Barrisi-yi sakht-i iqtisādi-yi rustāhā-yi Kirman*, pp. 85–88.
39. Based upon field research, 1971–1972, 1977.
40. I encountered several such examples in the summer of 1977; these cases seemed much more frequent in remoter villages than in ones near major highways and/or towns.
41. The following observations are based upon field research, 1971–1972, 1978–1979.
42. The practice of *salaf-khari* seems to have increased significantly since land reform; see Khosrou Khosrovi, "La Réforme agraire et l'apparition d'une nouvelle classe en Iran," *Etudes Rurales* 34 (1969): 123.
43. The role of rural cooperatives and government credit agencies is discussed in Chapter 6.
44. Institute for Social Studies and Research, *Barrisi-yi iqtisādi va ijtimā'i-yi rustāhā-yi Arāk*, p. 189; *Turbat-i Jām*, p. 138; *Birjand*, p. 144; *Quchān*, p. 141; and *Turbat-i Haydari*, p. 91.
45. For more detail on the fate of artisans since 1962, see E. Hooglund, "The *Khwushnishin* Population," pp. 234–236.
46. See further Bill, *Politics of Iran*, p. 146.

6. Rural Socioeconomic Changes

1. For more detailed information, see Eric J. Hooglund, "Rural Socioeconomic Organization in Transition: The Case of Iran's Bunehs," in *Modern Iran: The Dialectics of Continuity and Change*, ed. Michael Bonine and Nikki Keddie, pp. 191–207.
2. Safi-nezhad, *Buneh*, 2d ed., p. 178.

3. Ibid., pp. 179–180.
4. Ibid., pp. 180–187.
5. See especially Part Two of ibid., pp. 171–234.
6. For examples of conflicts over the sharing of *buneh* work, see Sternberg-Sarel, "Revolution blanche," p. 497.
7. For examples, see Aliāsiān, *Dasht-i Qazvin*, pp. 42–44.
8. Safi-nezhad, *Buneh*, 2d ed., pp. 188–189.
9. See further Mostafa Azkia, "Fardis," *Ulum-i Ijtimā'i* 1976: 180–188.
10. For more detailed information, see the following studies: Peter Dorner, ed., *Land Reform in Latin America: Issues and Cases*; H. Mendras and Y. Travernier, eds., *Terre, paysans, et politique*, and Sein Lin, ed., *Readings in Land Reform.*
11. This interpretation is based upon extensive interviews with senior officials during the winter of 1972 and the summer of 1977. There were a few, but notable, exceptions, such as Ismail Ajami, a rural sociologist, who served in the Ministry of Agriculture during 1977.
12. For statistics on rural cooperative societies, see the various year-end reports from 1964 through 1972: Iran, Ministry of Cooperatives and Rural Affairs, *Annual Report on Rural Cooperative Societies*. As with other government statistics, these should be considered guides rather than absolute facts.
13. Following paragraph based upon personal observations during field research, 1971–1972, 1978–1979.
14. A detailed study of the structure of rural cooperatives is Ahmad 'Arāghi, *Tashkil va idārah-yi shirkathā-yi t'āvuni.*
15. Following information based upon ibid., pp. 107–142.
16. In the early 1960's government control was much less effective, and consequently independent and voluntary activities were evident in some cooperatives. See further Lambton, *Persian Land Reform*, pp. 303–346 passim.
17. A detailed study of the paucity of activities in seventy-nine randomly selected cooperatives is Mostafa Azkia, ed., *Shirkathā-yi t'āvuni rustā'i dar shish mantiqeh.*
18. In the mid-1970's the cooperatives were marketing less than 1 percent of agricultural output; see Aresvik, *Agricultural Development*, p. 145.
19. Generally, the division of shares among members is as follows: 1–9 shares (9 percent); 11–30 shares (5 percent); 31–60 shares (30 percent); 61–100 shares (40 percent); and over 100 shares (16 percent). See Azkia, ed., *T'āvuni*, pp. 80–85.
20. The original name of this bank was the Agricultural Credit and Rural Development Bank. It was changed successively to the Agricultural Development Bank, the Agriculture Bank, and Agricultural Cooperative Bank. Hereafter, it simply will be referred to as the Agriculture Bank. It should not be confused with the Agricultural Development Bank established in 1969.
21. For details, see Azkia, ed., *T'āvuni*, pp. 190–208 passim.
22. For statistics on total cooperative loan disbursements, total number of

loan recipients, etc., for various years up through the Iranian year ending in March 1978, see Iran, Ministry of Cooperatives and Rural Affairs, *Annual Statistics*.

23. See Azkia, ed., *T'āvuni*, pp. 203 ff.
24. In certain areas this was interpreted to apply not just to cooperative debts, but also to those from any other government source; see Lambton, *Persian Land Reform*, p. 314.
25. Azkia, ed., *T'āvuni*, p. 203.
26. There are no comprehensive statistics on cooperative credit as a percentage of total peasant borrowing. For regional surveys, see Azkia, ed., *T'āvuni*, pp. 95–139; and Paul Vieille, "Les Paysans, la petite bourgeoisie, et l'état après la réforme agraire en Iran," *Annales* 27, No. 2 (1972): 349–372.
27. Based upon personal observations and interviews, 1971–1972, 1977.
28. See further International Labour Office, *Employment and Incomes Policies for Iran*, pp. 9–19.
29. For one good, but generally uncritical, study, see Aresvik, *Agricultural Development*. For a Marxist interpretation, see Halliday, *Iran*, pp. 103–137.
30. See statistical tables in Aresvik, *Agricultural Development*, pp. 169–170.
31. In the case of the Agricultural Development Bank, this minimum limit was actually 1 million *riāl*s; see further ibid., p. 172. In this period, 100,000 Iranian *riāl*s was equivalent to roughly $1,500.
32. The following is based upon personal observation during 1978 and Aresvik, *Agricultural Development*, pp. 143–148.
33. For purchases, 1958–1975, see ibid., Table 7.6, p. 144.
34. For statistics, see ibid., p. 144.
35. Ibid., p. 149.
36. A fascinating fictional account of village migrants in Tehran during the 1960's is Samad Behrangi, "24 Restless Hours," in *The Little Black Fish and Other Modern Persian Short Stories*, trans. Mary and Eric Hooglund.
37. A study of rural migrants in Tehran's slums is Farhad Kazemi, *Poverty and Revolution in Iran: The Migrant Poor, Urban Marginality and Politics*.
38. Halliday, *Iran*, p. 184.
39. These calculations are derived from Table 14 in ibid., p. 176.
40. Information in this paragraph is based upon interviews and personal observations during the summers of 1977 and 1978.
41. Halliday, *Iran*, pp. 184–185.
42. Ibid., p. 182.
43. See Iran Statistical Organization, *Preliminary Report of the 1976 Census*.
44. Between 1966 and 1976 the urban population increased from 9.8 million to 15.7 million. Assuming a natural growth rate of 3.1 percent per annum such growth would provide an increase of only 3 million persons.

The additional 2.9 million would be the increase due to migration from rural areas, primarily of villagers, but also including some of the nomads, listed euphemistically in census reports as the "unsettled population" and enumerated separately at 1.87 million in 1976.

45. Data on village migrants was obtained from sample surveys which I conducted in western Iran during the summer of 1977 and in Fars in south central Iran during the summer of 1978. For more detail, see E. Hooglund, "Rural Participation in the Revolution," *MERIP Reports* 87 (May 1980): 4.

46. Cities offered not simply better jobs, but a better quality of life in general. Educational, medical, and social services were available in urban areas, in contrast to their virtual absence in villages. Rural and urban disparities in consumption, incomes, and general economic growth also were marked. Indeed, by the mid-1970's, the average per capita consumption expenditure of urban families was four times that of rural households. See further Manoucher Parvin and Amir Zamani, "Political Economy of Growth and Destruction: A Statistical Interpretation of the Iranian Case," *IS* 12, Nos. 1–2 (Winter–Spring 1979): 46–49.

47. Ibid.

48. The total national production of the principal food grains of wheat and rice actually increased marginally during the 1970's. However, since the majority of commercial farmers invested in non-edible cash crops such as cotton, opium, and tobacco rather than less profitable grains, their output of wheat and rice was insufficient to offset the loss from subsistence farms. Consequently, the annual increase in the production of food grains was less than 2 percent per year. See further Katouzian, "Oil versus Agriculture," pp. 361–364.

49. I interviewed three of the participants in this conference during the summer of 1977. All information is based upon their recollections.

50. See further Robert Graham, *Iran: The Illusion of Power*, pp. 77–125.

7. Caesar's Will

1. Compare Miller, "Hosseinabad," p. 489.

2. For a more detailed discussion, see Grace Goodell, "The Elementary Structures of Political Life" (Ph.D. dissertation, Columbia University, 1977), pp. 113–124.

3. Cf. John Hanessian, Jr., "Yosouf-Abad, an Iranian Village," *American Universities Field Staff Reports Service*, Southwest Asia Series, No. 12 (1963): 17.

4. Villagers did not always passively accept the new political status quo, and certain peasants did try to challenge it, usually unsuccessfully. For an interesting case study of one such peasant activist, see Reinhold Löffler, "The Representative Mediator and the New Peasant," *American Anthropologist* 73 (October 1971): 1077–1091.

5. For the pre–land reform history of village councils, see Lambton, *Persian Land Reform*, pp. 37–43.

6. See further Research Group in Agricultural Economics, "Community Development and Land Reform," *TE* 4 (January 1967): 207–209.

7. As early as 1967, village councils had been found in 72 percent of a sample survey of sixty-eight villages in central Iran. See Institute for Social Studies and Research, *Arāk*, p. 68.

8. Research Group in Agricultural Economics, "Community Development," p. 209.

9. See, e.g., Miller, "Hosseinabad," pp. 489–490.

10. Sternberg-Sarel, "Revolution blanche," p. 500; idem, "Tradition et développement," p. 215.

11. Interviews, 1978–1979.

12. Sternberg-Sarel, "Revolution blanche," pp. 499–500.

13. *Kayhan International* (Tehran), February 3, 1973, p. 12.

14. Interviews, 1977 and 1978.

15. Interviews, summer 1972.

16. This interpretation and the following passage are based upon extensive personal observations in 1967–1968, 1970, 1971–1972, 1977, and 1978.

17. 'Azziz Rakhsh-Khurshid, *Nizari bih zindagi-yi ijtimā'i va iqtisādi-yi dihnishinhā-yi Dasht-i Mughān*, p. 88.

18. For assessments of the White Revolution, see Bill, *Politics of Iran*, pp. 133–156, and R. K. Ramazani, "Iran's 'White Revolution': A Study in Political Development," *IJMES* 5 (April 1974): 124–139.

19. For a concise summary of twelve points of the White Revolution, see "The Revolution of the Shah and the People," *Kayhan International* (Tehran), February 3, 1973, pp. 12–13.

20. For a favorable assessment of the Literacy Corps, see François Tripet, "Les Bouleversements de l'univers rural en Iran," *L'Afrique et l'Asie* 95–96 (1971): 27–40; for a more cautious view, see Sternberg-Sarel, "Revolution blanche," pp. 471, 500–594.

21. *Kayhan International* (Tehran), February 3, 1973, p. 12.

22. Ibid.

23. Institute for Social Studies and Research, *Turbat-i Jām*, p. 37.

24. William H. Bartsch, *Problems of Employment Creation in Iran*, p. 56.

25. Ibid., p. 55.

26. Ibid., p. 56.

27. This and following interpretations are based upon extensive personal observation.

28. Statistics from Graham, *Iran*, Appendix F, p. 262.

29. Government statistics claim 40 percent of adult (male) peasants attended Literacy Corps classes between 1963 and 1978. Adult male illiteracy may have been higher than 60 percent, since official statistics recorded only numbers enrolled in classes, not whether they actually learned to read and write. For statistics, see Iran, Ministry of Education, *Report for 1356*.

30. See further Halliday, *Iran*, p. 120.

31. Interview, 1972.

8. Villages and the Revolution

1. In all the years I have been carrying out research in Iranian villages, I never encountered any genuine enthusiasm for the shah or his government on the part of a majority of villagers. Curiously, however, journalists and certain other writers—none of whom had ever been in an Iranian village—contended that there was widespread rural support for the shah right up to the collapse of the monarchy in February 1979.

2. Unless otherwise noted, all the material for this chapter is based upon personal observations in Iran's villages during the revolution.

3. See further Barrington Moore, Jr., *Injustice: The Social Origins of Obedience and Revolt*, pp. 3–31.

4. An interesting analysis of the role of middle peasants in one village is Mary Hooglund, "Peasants and the Process of Revolution: An Iranian Case Study" (paper presented at the Annual Meeting of the Alternative Middle East Studies Seminar, Washington, D.C., November 8–9, 1980).

5. Ervand Abrahamian, "Structural Causes of the Iranian Revolution," *MERIP Reports* 87 (May 1980): 25.

6. Ibid.

7. For a brief but excellent analysis of the pre-revolutionary period, see ibid., pp. 21–26.

8. I undertook sample surveys in western Iran in 1977 and in Fars in 1978–1979. I used the resultant data to present some general observations in E. Hooglund, "Rural Participation in the Revolution."

9. For an examination of political attitudes before and during the revolution among Tehran's migrants, see Kazemi, *Poverty and Revolution*, pp. 68–96.

10. For one example, see M. Hooglund, "One Village in the Revolution," pp. 7–10.

11. For an example of land expropriations in one village, see ibid., pp. 10–12.

12. For details, see "Documents," *MERIP Reports* 87 (May 1980): 12–14; and Manijeh Dowlat, B. Hourcade, and Odile Puech, "Les Paysans et la Revolution Iranienne," *Peuples Méditerranéens* No. 10 (January–March 1980): 34–41.

Glossary

ābi   irrigated crop land.

ayatollah   honorific title given to *shi'i* theologians whose outstanding erudition in religious matters has been demonstrated through the publications of widely recognized commentaries upon such subjects as the Koran, the authenticated traditions of the Prophet Muhammad and the twelve *imāms*, and the accepted codices of *shi'i* canonical law. Ayatollahs are considered competent to interpret Islamic law for *shi'i* Muslims.

āyish   fallow crop land.

bāgh   an orchard, specifically one containing fruit and/or nut trees or a vineyard.

baksh   an administrative district of a county; each *baksh* is subdivided into *dehestān*s.

bazaar   covered market area of Iranian towns.

bāzāri   one who owns a shop in a bazaar.

bigāri   compulsory labor service which landlords demanded of peasants before land reform.

buneh   peasant work team responsible for cultivation of specified plots under the pre–land reform sharecropping system.

dāng   one of six parts into which village agricultural land is divided.

daymi   crop land which is dry-farmed.

dehestān   rural administrative district within a county.

dehyār   official in charge of supervising a group of villages within a *dehestān*.

gāv   general term for cattle, especially an ox.

gāvband   a cattle owner, especially one who owns the oxen used for ploughing.

hammāmi   bath house attendant.

juft   a team of oxen; also the amount of land which such a team can plough in one day.

kadkhudā   village headman.

khāliseh   state-owned land.

kharvār   a common unit of weight in rural Iran equivalent to 297 kilograms, or approximately 655 pounds.

khwushnishin   a landless villager.

majlis   a representative assembly, or parliament.

mann   unit of weight equivalent to 2.97 kilograms, or 6.55 pounds; 100 *mann* equal one *kharvār* (see above).

misqāl   the smallest unit of weight commonly used in Iran; each *misqāl* is equivalent to approximately 4.64 grams, or .16 ounces.

mubāshir   a landlord's agent, or bailiff.

mullah   popular term for a member of the clergy.

nasaq   a cultivation right under the pre–land reform sharecropping system.

qanāt   an artificial underground water channel which is a special feature of irrigated farming in Iran.

riāl   the unit of currency in Iran; during most of the 1960's and 1970's, approximately 75 *riāls* were equivalent to $1.00.

rish sefid   a village elder, especially one who has influence on account of his popularity and / or wealth.

salaf-khari   the practice of buying crops in advance of their actual harvest; dealing in futures.

sarbuneh   head of a *buneh* (see above).

sarparast   a government agent responsible for supervising the activities of rural cooperative societies.

sayfi   general term for all crops which are planted and harvested during the summer.

sepāhi   a soldier serving in one of the military units specially created for development work in rural areas; member of the Extension and Development, Health, or Literacy Corps.

shahrestān   county. Each of Iran's provinces is comprised of several counties, each centered upon a town of at least 5,000 population.

Shi'ā   the general designation for Muslim sects which believe that the religious and political leadership of the Islamic community passed upon the death of the Prophet Muhammad to his cousin and son-in-law 'Ali, in contrast to the Sunni sects which recognize the legitimacy of the caliphs. Approximately 90 percent of Iranians are adherents of the sect of Shi'ā, referred to as "12 Imāms"; that is, they believe that beginning with 'Ali, the first *imām*, leadership of the community passed by hereditary succession to eleven of his direct descendants.

shi'i   adjective pertaining to Shi'ā (see above).

Sunni   see Shi'ā (above).

Tudeh   literally, the masses; Iranian Marxist political party formed in 1941.

tumān   common designation for 10 *riāls* of currency. Thus, 1,000 *riāls* is referred to as 100 *tumāns*.

vaqf   land endowed for religious or charitable purposes.

zanjiri   the practice of making a group collectively responsible for the debts of its individual members.

Selected Bibliography

Persian Sources

Afshar-Naderi, Nader. *Monugrāfi-yi il-i Bahmeh'i* (Monograph of the Bahmeh'i tribe). Tehran: University of Tehran, 1347/1968–1969.

'Ajami, Ismā'il. "Khalqiyāt, mu'tiqidāt va ārazuhā-yi shoghli-yi rustāiyān" (Characteristics, beliefs and occupation aspirations of peasants). *'Ulum-i ijtimā'i* 1 (Bahman 1348/January–February 1970): 26–47.

———. *Shishdāngi: Pazhuhishi dar zaminah-yi jam'āhshināsi-yi rustā'i* (Six *dāng*s: An inquiry in the field of rural sociology). Shiraz: Pahlavi University, 1348/1969–1970.

'Ajami, Ismā'il, et al. *Asarāt-i iqtisādi va ijtimā'i-yi Sad-i Dāryush Kabir* (The economic and social effects of the Daryush Kabir Dam). 2 vols. Shiraz: Pahlavi University, 1354/1975–1976.

Alavi, Bozorg. *Panjah-o-se nafar* (Thirty-one persons). Tehran, 1944.

Āl-i Ahmad, Jalāl. *Tātnishinhā-yi baluk-i Zahrā* (The residents of the Zahra district). Tehran: Danish, 1340/1961–1962.

———. *Urazān* (The village of Urazan). Tehran: Dānish Co., 1333/1954–1955.

Aliāsiān, Hushang. *Moqadameh'i bar tahqiq-i ijtimā'i-yi rustāhā-yi Dasht-i Qazvin* (Introduction to the social study of the villages of Dasht-i Qazvin). Tehran: Qazvin Development Organization, 1348/1969–1970.

'Arabzadah, Muhsin. *Fihrist-i jam'at-idihāt-i Qazvin* (Population index of the Qazvin villages). Qazvin: Umrān Organization, 1347/1968–1969.

'Arāghi, Ahmad. *Tashkil va idārah-yi shirkathā-yi t'āvuni* (Organization and management of cooperative societies). Tehran, 1347/1968–1969.

Arsanjani, Hassan. "Mas'aleh islāhāt-i arzi dar Iran" (The land reform problem in Iran). *Majaleh-i masa'il-i Iran* 1 (Deh 1341/December 1962–January 1963): 97–104.

Azkia, Mostafa. "Fardis" (Fardis village). *Ulum-i Ijtimā'i* 1976: 180–188.

———. *Monugrāfi-yi Hājjiābād* (Monograph of Hajjiabad village). Tehran: Institute for Social Studies and Research, 1346/1967–1968.

———. *Shirkat-i Sahami-yi Zirā'i-i Dargazin* (The Dargazin Agricultural Corporation). Tehran: Institute for Social Studies and Research, 1350/1971–1972.

———, ed. *Shirkathā-yi t'āvuni rustā'i dar shish mantiqeh* (Rural cooperative societies in six regions). Tehran: Institute for Social Studies and Research, 1348/1969–1970.

Azkia, Mostafa, A. Nikkhulq, and K. Bābā'i. *Barrisi-yi natā'ij-i islāhāt-i arzi dar shish mantiqah-i Iran* (A study of the result of land reform in six regions of Iran). Tehran: Institute for Social Studies and Research, 1348/1969–1970.

Azkia, M., A. Nikkhulq, M. Muhājir-Yervāni, and M. 'Askari. *Khwushnishin-i Kurdistan* (The *khwushnishin*s of Kurdistan). Tehran: University of Tehran, 2535/1977.

Bāhar, Muhammad Taghi. *Tārikh-i mokhtasar-i ahzab-i siyasi-yi Iran* (A brief history of Iran's political parties). Tehran, 1321/1942–1943.

Bahrāmi, Taqi. *Farhang-i rustā'i* (Rural directory). Tehran, 1316–1317/1937–1939.

———. *Joghrāfi-yi keshāvarzi-yi Iran* (Agricultural geography of Iran). Tehran: University of Tehran, 1333/1954–1955.

Behrangi, Samad. *Qasehhā-yi Behrang* (Collected stories of Behrangi). Compiled by Hassan Kayvān. 3d ed. Tehran: Intashārāt-i Ruz Bahār, 2536/1977–1978.

Bihnām, Jamshid, and Shāhpur Rāsekh. *Muqadamah bar jam'ahshināsi-yi Iran* (Introduction to Iranian sociology). Tehran: Khwārazami, 1348/1969–1970.

Huran, Ahmad. *Iqtisādi-yi kishavārzi* (Agricultural economics). Vol. 1. Tehran, 1334/1955–1956.

Ibadi, Muhammad 'Ali. *Islāhāt-i arzi dar Iran* (Land reform in Iran). Tehran, 1340/1961–1962.

Institute for Social Studies and Research. *Barrisi-yi iqtisādi va ijtimā'i-yi rustāhā-yi Arāk* (A social and economic study of the villages of Arak). Tehran: University of Tehran, 1346/1967–1968.

———. *Barrisi-yi iqtisādi va ijtimā'i-yi rustāhā-yi Birjand* (A social and economic study of the villages of Birjand). Tehran: University of Tehran, 1348/1969–1970.

———. *Barrisi-yi iqtisādi va ijtimā'i-yi rustāhā-yi Bujnurd* (A social and economic study of the villages of Bujnurd). Tehran: University of Tehran, 1346/1967–1968.

———. *Barrisi-yi iqtisādi va ijtimā'i-yi rustāhā-yi Khalkhāl* (A social and economic study of the villages of Khalkhal). Tehran: University of Tehran, 1346/1967–1968.

———. *Barrisi-yi iqtisādi va ijtimā'i-yi rustāhā-yi Quchān* (A social and economic study of the villages of Quchan). Tehran: University of Tehran, 1348/1969–1970.

———. *Barrisi-yi iqtisādi va ijtimā'i-yi rustāhā-yi Sabzavār* (A social and economic study of the villages of Sabzavar). Tehran: University of Tehran, 1346/1967–1968.

———. *Barrisi-yi iqtisādi va ijtimā'i-yi rustāhā-yi Turbat-i Haydari* (A social and economic study of the villages of Turbat-i Haydari). Tehran: University of Tehran, 1349/1970–1971.

———. *Barrisi-yi iqtisādi va ijtimā'i-yi rustāhā-yi Turbat-i Jām* (A social and economic study of the villages of Turbat-i Jam). Tehran: University of Tehran, 1348/1969–1970.

Iran, Ministry of Labour and Social Affairs. *Barrisihā-yi masā'il-i niru-yi insāni* (Studies of manpower problems). Vol. 3. Tehran, 1344/1965–1966.

Jamalzadah, S. M. A. *Zamin, arbāb, dihqān* (Land, landlord, and peasant). Tehran: Pocket Books Co., 1340/1961–1962.

Kasravi, Ahmad. *Tārikh-i hejdeh sāleh Azarbayjan* (Eighteen-year history of Azarbayjan). 4th ed. 2 vols. Tehran: Amir Kabir, 1346/1967–1968.

Kayhān, M. "Arziābi-yi natā'ij-i 'islāhāt-i arzi az bāla'" (An assessment of the results of "land reform from above"). *Donyā* (Khurdād 1356/May–June 1977): 34–43.

————. "Jām'eh'i-yi rustā'i-yi Iran dar āstāneh-yi islāhāt-i arzi" (Iran's rural society on the eve of land reform). *Donyā* (Esfand 1355/February–March 1977): 42–51.

Keshāvarz, Hushang. *Masā'il va mushkilāt-i kudakān va javānān-i rustā'i-yi Iran* (The problems of rural children and youth in Iran). Tehran: Plan Organization, 1350/1971–1972.

Keshāvarz, Hushang, J. Safi-nezhad, and V. Hājjabi. *Shirkat-i sahāmi-yi zirā'ati-yi Rezā Pahlavi (Qasr-i Shirin)* (The Reza Shah Pahlavi Agricultural Corporation of Qasr-i Shirin). Tehran: University of Tehran, 1350/1971–1972.

Khosrovi, Khosrou. "Ābyāri va jām'eh-yi rustā'i dar Iran" (Irrigation and rural society in Iran). *Ulum-i ijtimā'i* 1 (February 1970): 48–56.

————. *Jām'ehshināsi-yi rustā'i-yi Iran* (Rural sociology of Iran). Tehran: University of Tehran, 1351/1972–1973.

————. *Jām'eh-yi dehghāni dar Iran* (Peasant society in Iran). Tehran: Peyam Publications, 1357/1978–1979.

Malek, Husayn, and Javad Safi-nezhad. *Vāhadhā-yi andāzeh giri dar rustāhā-yi Iran* (Units of measure in the villages of Iran). Tehran: University of Tehran, 1349/1970–1971.

Mirheydar, Hussein. *Az tuyul tā inqalāb-i arzi* (From land assignment to land revolution). Tehran: Amir Kabir, 2535/1976–1977.

Muhajirāni, Mostafa, ed. *Barrisi-yi iqtisādi va ijtimā'i-yi rustāhā-yi Darreh Gaz* (A social and economic study of the villages of Darreh Gaz). Tehran: Institute for Social Studies and Research, 1348/1969–1970.

Muhājirāni, Mostafa, and A. Nikkhulgh. *Baqirābād va islāhāt-i arzi* (Baqirabad and land reform). Tehran: University of Tehran, 1345/1966–1967.

Mu'meni, Hamid. *Darbāreh-yi mobārzāt-i Kurdistan* (About the struggle in Kurdistan). Tehran: Intashārāt-i Shabāhang, 1357/1978–1979.

Nikkulgh, 'Ali Akbar. *Hassanlingi, dihkadah az Bandar-i 'Abbās* (Hassanlingi, a village of Bandar-i 'Abbas). Tehran: Institute for Social Studies and Research, 1345/1966–1967.

Parahān, Bāqir. *Islāhāt-i arzi va natā'ij-i ān* (Land reform and its results). Tehran, 1349/1970–1971.

Purkarim, Hushang. *Fishinak* (The village of Fishinak). Tehran: Institute for Social Studies and Research, 1345/1966–1967.

Rakhsh-Khurshid, 'Azziz. *Nizari bih zindagi-yi ijtimā'i va iqtisādi-yi dih-nishinhā-yi Dasht-i Mughān* (A view of the social and economic life of the villagers of the Dasht-i Mughan). Tehran: University of Tehran, 1340–1341/1961–1963.

Sā'di, Gholāmhusayn. *Ahl-i havā* (People of the outdoors). Tehran: University of Tehran, 1345/1966–1967.

Sā'dlu, Hushang. *Masā'il-i keshāvarzi-yi Iran* (Iran's agricultural problems). 2d ed. Tehran: Intashārāt-i Ravāq, 1357/1978–1979.

Safi-nezhad, Javad. *Asnād-i bunehhā* (Buneh documents). 2 vols. Tehran: Institute for Social Studies and Research, 2536/1977–1978.

————. *Atlas-i ilāt-i Kuhgiluyeh* (Atlas of the tribes of the Kuhgiluyeh). 2d ed. Tehran: University of Tehran, 1347/1968–1969.

————. *Buneh* (A study of Bunehs). 1st ed., Tehran: University of Tehran, 1351/1972–1973. 2d ed., Tehran: Intashārāt-i Tus, 1353/1974–1975. 3d ed., Tehran: University of Tehran Press, 2535/1977.

————. *Sisakht-i Boir-i Ahmad* (The Boir Ahmad village of Sisakht). Tehran: Institute for Social Studies and Research, 1345/1966–1967.

————. *Tālebābād: Nimunih-i Jām'i az Barrisi-i yek deh* (Talebabad: A detailed example of the study of one village). Tehran: University of Tehran, 1345/1966–1967.

Safi-nezhad, Javad, V. Hajjabi, and Hushang Keshāvarz. *Shirkat-i sahāmi-yi zirā'ati-yi Nivān Nār (Golpaygān)* (The Nivan Nar Agricultural Corporation of Golpaygan). Tehran: Institute for Social Studies and Research, 1350/1971–1972.

Sāzamān-i barnāmeh. *Barrisi-yi masā'il-i rustā'i-yi Iran* (A study of the problems of rural Iran). Tehran, 1350/1971–1972.

Sāzamān-i chirikhā-yi fadā'i-yi khalq. *Barrisi-yi sakht-i iqtisādi-yi rustāhā-yi Fars* (A study of the economic structure of the villages of Fars). Rural Studies Series, No. 3. N.p., 1352/1973–1974.

————. *Barrisi-yi sakht-i iqtisādi-yi rustāhā-yi Kirman* (A study of the economic structure of the villages of Kerman). Rural Studies Series, No. 4. N.p., 1353/1974–1975.

————. *Barrisi-yi shirkathā-yi sahāmi-yi zirā'i* (A study of the agricultural corporations). Rural Studies Series, No. 2. N.p., 1352/1973–1974.

————. *Islāhāt-i arzi dar Iran va natā'ij-i mustaqim-i an* (Land reform in Iran and its direct results). Rural Studies Series, No. 1. N.p.: Intashārāt-i Tondar, 1357/1978–1979.

Sāzamān-i islāhāt-i arzi. *Guzāresh az aval-i bahman, 1340 tā pāyān-i shahrivar, 1342* (Report from the beginning of Bahman, 1340, to the end of Shahrivar, 1342). Tehran, 1342/1963–1964.

————. *Guzāresh-i sāl-i, 1340–1350* (Reports for the years 1961–1962 to 1971–1972). Tehran, annually, 1962–1972.

Tahabāz, Sirus. *Yush* (The village of Yush). Tehran: Institute for Social Studies and Research, 1346/1967–1968.

Tālib, Mehdi. *Dih-i naw Arāk* (The Arak village of Dih-i naw). Tehran: Institute for Social Studies and Research, 1346/1967–1968.

Tālib, Mehdi, and P. Mourinano. *Monugrāfi-yi dihkadah-yi Ibrahimābād*

(Monograph of Ibrahimabad village). Tehran: Institute for Social Studies and Research, 1347/1968–1969.

Tālibbeygi, Firuz. *Shirkat-i t'āvuni* (Cooperative societies). Tehran, 1339/1960–1961.

Taqipur, Husayn. *Monugrāfi-yi Qal'eh Barbar* (Monograph of Qal'eh Barbar). Tehran: Institute for Social Studies and Research, 1347/1968–1969.

Vadi'i, Kāzim. *Joghrāfi-yi iqtisādi-yi umumi* (General economic geography). Vol. 1, *Joghrāfi-yi keshāvarzi* (Agricultural geography). Tabriz: University of Tabriz, 1340/1961–1962.

European Language Sources

Books, Government Documents, Theses, and Dissertations

Afshar-Naderi, Nader. *The Settlement of Nomads and Its Social and Economic Implications.* Tehran: Institute for Social Studies and Research, 1971.

———, ed. *Seminar on Evaluation of Directed Social Change.* Tehran: Institute for Social Studies and Research and UNESCO, December 1966.

Akhavi, Shahrough. *Religion and Politics in Contemporary Iran.* Albany: State University of New York Press, 1980.

Alberts, Robert C. "Social Structure and Culture Change in an Iranian Village." Ph.D. dissertation, University of Wisconsin at Madison, 1963.

Allen, H. B. *Rural Reconstruction in Action.* Ithaca: Cornell University Press, 1953.

Amirsadeghi, Hossein, ed. *Twentieth Century Iran.* New York: Holmes and Meier, 1977.

Amuzegar, Jahangir. *Technical Assistance in Theory and Practice: The Case of Iran.* New York: Praeger, 1966.

Amuzegar, J., and A. Fekrat. *Iran: Economic Development under Dualistic Conditions.* Chicago: University of Chicago, 1971.

Antoun, Richard, and Iliya Harik, eds. *Rural Politics and Social Change in the Middle East.* Bloomington: Indiana University Press, 1972.

Aresvik, Oddvar. *The Agricultural Development of Iran.* New York: Praeger, 1976.

Avery, Peter. *Modern Iran.* New York: Praeger, 1965.

Azkia, Mostafa. "The Effect of Rural Development Programmes on the Iranian Peasantry between 1962 and 1978, with Special Reference to Farm Corporations." Ph.D. dissertation, Aberdeen University, 1980.

Badeau, John S., and Georgiana G. Stevens. *Bread from Stones: Fifty Years of Technical Assistance.* Englewood Cliffs: Prentice-Hall, 1966.

Banani, Amin. *The Modernization of Iran, 1921–1941.* Stanford: Stanford University Press, 1961; reprint ed., 1969.

Bartsch, William H. *Problems of Employment Creation in Iran.* Geneva: International Labour Office, 1970.

Bayne, Edward A. *Persian Kingship in Transition.* New York: American Universities Field Staff, 1968.

Behrangi, Samad. *The Little Black Fish and Other Modern Persian Short Stories.* Translated by Mary and Eric Hooglund. Washington, D.C.: Three Continents Press, 1976.

Bémont, Frédy. *L'Iran devant le progrès.* Paris: Presses Universitaires de France, 1964.

Bharier, Julian. *Economic Development in Iran, 1900–1970.* London: Oxford University Press, 1971.

Bill, James A. *The Politics of Iran: Groups, Classes, and Modernization.* Columbus: Charles Merrill, 1972.

Bill, James A., and Carl Leiden. *The Middle East: Politics and Power.* Boston: Allyn and Bacon, 1974.

Bonine, Michael, and Nikki Keddie, eds. *Modern Iran: The Dialectics of Continuity and Change.* Albany: State University of New York Press, 1981.

Brown, James R., and Sein Lin, eds. *Land Reform in Developing Countries.* Hartford: University of Hartford, 1968.

Central Treaty Organization. *Symposium on Rural Development at Tehran, 25–30 September 1963.* Ankara, n.d.

Chelkowski, Peter, ed. *Iran: Continuity and Variety.* New York: New York University Press, 1971.

Connell, John, ed. *Samnan, Persian City and Region.* London: University College, 1969.

Cook, M. A., ed. *Studies in the Economic History of the Middle East from the Rise of Islam to the Present Day.* London: Oxford University Press, 1970.

Costello, Vincent. *Kashan: A City and Region of Iran.* New York: R. R. Bowker, 1976.

Cottam, Richard W. *Nationalism in Iran.* Pittsburgh: University of Pittsburgh Press, 1964; reprint ed., 1979.

Critchfield, Richard. *The Golden Bowl Be Broken: Peasant Life in Four Cultures.* Bloomington: Indiana University Press, 1973.

Denman, D. R. *The King's Vista: A Land Reform Which Has Changed the Face of Persia.* Berkhamsted: Geographical Publications, 1973.

Dillon, Robert. "Carpet Capitalism and Craft Involution in Kerman, Iran." Ph.D. dissertation, Columbia University, 1976.

Dorner, Peter, ed. *Land Reform in Latin America: Issues and Cases.* Madison: University of Wisconsin Press, 1971.

Douglas, William O. *Strange Lands and Friendly Peoples.* New York: Harper Bros., 1951.

English, Paul Ward. *City and Village in Iran: Settlement and Economy in the Kirman Basin.* Madison: University of Wisconsin Press, 1966.

Feder, Ernest. *The Rape of the Peasantry: Latin America's Land Reform System.* Garden City: Doubleday and Co., 1971.

Fisher, W. B., ed. *The Land of Iran.* Vol. 1 of *The Cambridge History of Iran,* A. J. Arberry, gen. ed. Cambridge: Cambridge University Press, 1968.

Forbes-Leith, F. A. C. *Checkmate: Fighting Tradition in Central Persia.* London: McBride, 1927.

Gharatchehdaghi, Cyrus. *The Distribution of Land in Varamin.* Opladen: Laske, 1967.

Ghassemlou, Abdul Rahman. *Kurdistan and the Kurds.* Prague: Czechoslovak Academy of Science, 1965.

Gittinger, J. Price. *Planning for Agricultural Development: The Iranian Experience.* Center for Development Planning Series in Planning Experience, No. 2. Washington, D.C.: National Planning Association, 1965.

Goodell, Grace. "The Elementary Structure of Political Life." Ph.D. dissertation, Columbia University, 1977.

Graham, Robert. *Iran: The Illusion of Power.* New York: St. Martin's Press, 1979.

Guerrilla Organization of the People's Fedaee. *Land Reform and Its Direct Effects in Iran.* London: Iran Committee (British Section), 1976.

Gunderson, Kathryn Hubbs. "The Dynamics of Rural Relationships in Iran: Change and Modernization." M.A. thesis, University of Texas at Austin, 1968.

Halliday, Fred. *Iran: Dictatorship and Development.* Harmondsworth: Penguin Books, 1979.

Hirsch, Etienne. *Employment and Income Policies for Iran.* Geneva: International Labour Office, 1973.

Hooglund, Eric. "The Effects of the Land Reform Program on Rural Iran." Ph.D. Dissertation, Johns Hopkins University, 1975.

Hourani, Albert, ed. *St. Anthony's Papers No. 16.* London: Chatto and Windus, 1963.

Hunter, Guy. *Modernizing Peasant Societies: A Comparative Study in Asia and Africa.* London: Oxford University Press, 1969.

International Labour Office. *Employment and Incomes Policies for Iran.* Geneva, 1973.

Iran, Land Reform Organization. *Report on Land Reform Activities, 1965–1966.* Tehran, June 1966.

Iran, Ministry of Education. *Report for 1356.* Tehran: Iran Statistical Organization, 1978.

Iran, Ministry of Cooperatives and Rural Affairs. *Annual Report on Rural Cooperative Societies.* Tehran, 1964–1972 (annually).

——. *Annual Statistics.* 1964–1972.

Iran, Plan Organization. *Ghazvin Area Development Project, Reconnaissance Report.* 2 vols. Tel Aviv: Tahal Water Planning, August 1963.

——. *National Census of Population and Housing, November, 1966.* Tehran: Iranian Statistical Center, 1968.

Iran Almanac and Book of Facts. Tehran: Echo of Iran Press, 1970–1977 (annually).

Iran Statistical Organization. *Preliminary Report of the 1976 Census.* Tehran, 1978.

Irons, William G. "The Yomut Turkmen: A Study of Kinship in a Pastoral Society." Ph.D. dissertation, University of Michigan at Ann Arbor, 1969.

Issawi, Charles, ed. *The Economic History of Iran, 1800–1914*. Chicago: University of Chicago Press, 1971.

Jacobs, Norman. *The Sociology of Development: Iran as an Asian Case Study*. New York: Praeger, 1966.

Jacoby, Erich H. *Man and Land*. London: Andre Deutsch, 1971.

Jacqz, Jane, ed. *Iran: Past, Present, and Future*. New York: Aspen Institute, 1976.

Kazemi, Farhad. *Poverty and Revolution in Iran: The Migrant Poor, Urban Marginality and Politics*. New York: New York University Press, 1980.

Kazemian, Gholam H. *Impact of U.S. Technical Aid on the Rural Development of Iran*. Brooklyn: Theo. Gaus' Sons, 1968.

Keddie, Nikki. *Historical Obstacles to Agrarian Change in Iran*. Claremont, Calif.: Asian Studies, 1960.

Lambton, Ann K. S. *Landlord and Peasant in Persia*. London: Oxford University Press, 1953; reprint ed., 1969.

———. *The Persian Land Reform, 1962–1966*. Oxford: Clarendon Press, 1969.

Lappé, Frances Moore, and J. Collins. *Food First: Beyond the Myth of Scarcity*. New York: Ballantine, 1978.

Lenczowski, George, ed. *Iran under the Pahlavis*. Stanford: Hoover Institution Press, 1978.

Lin, Sein, ed. *Readings in Land Reform*. Hartford: University of Hartford Press, 1970.

Looney, Robert E. *The Economic Development of Iran, 1959–1981*. New York: Praeger, 1974.

McLachlan, K. S., and Brian Spooner. *A Preliminary Assessment of Potential Resources in Khurasan Province, Iran*. Rome: Italconsult, 1963.

Mansfield, Peter, ed. *The Middle East: A Political and Economic Survey*. 4th ed. London: Oxford University Press, 1973.

Mendras, H., and Y. Travernier, eds. *Terre, paysans, et politique*. 2 vols. Paris: SEDEIS, 1969.

Moore, Barrington, Jr. *Injustice: The Social Origins of Obedience and Revolt*. White Plains, N.Y.: M. E. Sharpe, 1978.

———. *Social Origins of Dictatorship and Democracy: Lord and Peasant in the Making of the Modern World*. Boston: Beacon Press, 1966.

Nirumand, Bahman. *Iran: The New Imperialism in Action*. Translated by Leonard Mins. New York: Monthly Review Press, 1969.

Nomani, Farhad. "The Origin and Development of Feudalism in Iran: 300–1600 A.D." Ph.D. dissertation, University of Illinois at Urbana-Champaign, 1972.

Okazaki, Shoko. *The Development of Large-Scale Farming in Iran: The Case of the Province of Gorgan*. Tokyo: Institute of Asian Economic Affairs, 1968.

Pahlavi, Muhammad Reza Shah. *Mission for My Country*. New York: McGraw Hill, 1961.

———. *The White Revolution*. Tehran: Imperial Library, 1967.

Parsons, K. H., R. J. Penn, and R. M. Raup, eds. *Land Tenure.* Madison: University of Wisconsin Press, 1956.

Paydarfar, Ali. *Social Change in a Southern Province of Iran.* Chapel Hill: North Carolina Institute for Research in Social Science, 1974.

Platt, Kenneth B. *Land Reform in Iran.* Washington, D.C.: Agency for International Development, June 1970.

Popkin, Samuel. *The Rational Peasant.* Berkeley: University of California Press, 1979.

Potter, J. M., N. N. Diaz, and G. M. Foster, eds. *Peasant Society: A Reader.* Boston: Little, Brown, 1967.

Price, O. T. W. *Towards a Comprehensive Iranian Agricultural Policy.* Tehran: International Bank for Reconstruction and Development, 1975.

Rubin, Barry. *Paved with Good Intentions: The American Experience and Iran.* New York: Oxford University Press, 1980.

Saikal, Amin. *The Rise and Fall of the Shah.* Princeton: Princeton University Press, 1980.

Sandjabi, Karim. *Essai sur l'économie rurale et le régime agraire de la Perse.* Paris: Domat-Montchristien, 1934.

Shanin, Teodor, ed. *Peasants and Peasant Societies.* Harmondsworth: Penguin Books, 1971.

Smith, Anthony. *Blind White Fish in Persia.* London: Unwin Books, 1966.

Smith, Harvey H., et al. *Area Handbook for Iran.* Washington, D.C.: Government Printing Office, 1971.

Stavenhagen, Rodolfo, ed. *Agrarian Problems and Peasant Movements in Latin America.* Garden City: Doubleday and Co., 1970.

———. *Les Classes sociales dans les sociétés agraires.* Paris: Edition Anthropos, 1969.

Sweet, Louise, ed. *Peoples and Cultures of the Middle East.* 2 vols. New York: Natural History Press, 1970.

Tai, Hung-chao. *Land Reform and Politics: A Comparative Analysis.* Berkeley: University of California Press, 1974.

Tapper, Richard. *Pasture and Politics: Economics, Conflict, and Ritual among Shahseven Nomads.* New York: Academic Press, 1979.

Tuma, Elias H. *Twenty-six Centuries of Agrarian Reform: A Comparative Analysis.* Berkeley: University of California Press, 1965.

United Nations, Department of Economic and Social Affairs. *Progress in Land Reform, 4th Report.* E/4020/Rev. 1, 1966.

Upton, Joseph M. *The History of Modern Iran: An Interpretation.* Harvard Middle Eastern Monographs. Cambridge: Harvard University Press, 1960.

Van Wagenen, Richard W. *The Iranian Case, 1946.* New York: Carnegie Endowment for International Peace, 1952.

Vieille, Paul. *La Féodalité et l'état en Iran.* Paris: Editions Anthropos, 1975.

Warne, William E. *Mission for Peace: Point Four in Iran.* New York: Bobbs-Merrill, 1956.

Warriner, Doreen. *Land and Poverty in the Middle East.* Middle East Economic and Social Studies of the Royal Institute of International Affairs. London: Oxford University Press, 1948.

———. *Land Reform and Development in the Middle East: A Study of Egypt, Syria, and Iraq.* 2d ed. London: Oxford University Press, 1962.

———. *Land Reform in Principle and Practice.* Oxford: Clarendon Press, 1969.

Weulersse, Jacques. *Paysans de Syrie et du Proche-Orient.* Paris: Gallimard, 1946.

Wolf, Eric R. *Peasants.* Englewood Cliffs: Prentice-Hall, 1966.

———. *Peasant Wars of the Twentieth Century.* New York: Harper and Row, 1969.

Wulff, Hans E. *The Traditional Crafts of Persia.* Cambridge: Massachusetts Institute of Technology, 1966.

Yar-Shater, Ehsan, ed. *Iran Faces the Seventies.* New York: Praeger, 1971.

Zabih, Sepehr. *The Communist Movement in Iran.* Berkeley: University of California Press, 1966.

Zonis, Marvin. *The Political Elite of Iran.* Princeton: Princeton University Press, 1971.

Periodical Literature and Unpublished Papers

Abbreviations

IJMES: International Journal of Middle East Studies.
IS: Iranian Studies.
MEJ: Middle East Journal.
MERIP Reports: Middle East Research and Information Project Reports.
TE: Tahqiqat é Eqtesadi.

Abrahamian, Ervand. "Communism and Communalism in Iran: The *Tudeh* and the *Firqah-i Dimukrat.*" *IJMES* 1 (October 1970): 291–316.

———. "European Feudalism and Middle Eastern Despotisms." *Science and Society* 39 (Summer 1975): 129–156.

———. "Structural Causes of the Iranian Revolution." *MERIP Reports* 87 (May 1980): 21–26.

"The Agrarian Reform Law in Iran." *International Labour Review* 86 (August 1962): 173–175.

Ajami, Ismail. "Social Class, Family Demographic Characteristics and Mobility in Three Iranian Villages: A Pilot Study." *Sociologia Ruralis* 9 (1969): 62–71.

Antoun, Richard. "The Gentry of a Traditional Peasant Community Undergoing Rapid Technological Change: An Iranian Case Study." *IS* 9 (Winter 1976): 2–21.

Askari, H., J. Cummings, and J. Toth. "Land Reform in the Middle East: A Note on Its Redistributive Effects." *IS* 19 (1977): 267–280.

Atai, Mansour. "Economic Report on Agriculture in the Isfahan and Yazd Areas." *TE* 3 (August 1965): 69–152.

———. "Economic Report on Cultivation in the Region of the Sixth Province (District 2)." *TE* 4 (January 1967): 71–137.

Atyeo, Henry C. "Political Developments in Iran, 1951–1954." *Middle Eastern Affairs* 5 (1954): 249–259.

Azadeh, B. "L'Iran aujourd'hui." *Temps Modernes* 27 (May 1971): 2031–2066.

Bagley, F. R. C. "A Bright Future after Oil: Dams and Agro-industry in Khuzistan." *MEJ* 30 (Winter 1976): 25–35.

Beckett, P. H. T., and E. D. Gordon. "Land Use and Settlement Round Kerman in Southern Iran." *Geographical Journal* 132 (1966): 476–490.

Bharier, J. "The Growth of Towns and Villages in Iran, 1900–1966." *Middle East Studies* 9 (1972): 51–62.

Black, Jacob. "Tyranny as a Strategy for Survival in an 'Egalitarian' Society: Luri Facts versus an Anthropological Mystique." *Man* 7 (December 1972): 614–634.

Black-Micaud, J. "An Ethnographic and Ecological Survey of Luristan, Western Persia: Modernization in a Nomadic Pastoral Society." *Middle Eastern Studies* 10 (May 1974): 210–228.

Brun, Thierry, and R. Dumont. "Iran: Imperial Pretensions and Agricultural Dependence." *MERIP Reports* 71 (October 1978): 15–20.

Carey, J., and A. Carey. "Iranian Agriculture and Its Development." *IJMES* 7 (July 1976): 359–382.

Connell, John. "Economic Change in an Iranian Village." *MEJ* 28 (Summer 1974): 309–314.

Cordonnier, Jean C. "Les Tendances nouvelles de l'agriculture irriguée dans l'oasis d'Ishahan (Iran)." *Revue Geographique de l'Est* 4 (1964): 387–392.

Craig, Daniel. "The Impact of Land Reform on an Iranian Village." *MEJ* 32 (1978): 141–154.

Cressey, George. "Qanats, Karez, and Foggaras." *Geographical Review* 48 (1958): 27–44.

Delavalle, J. P. "La réforme agraire en Iran." *Orient* 7 (1963): 37–54.

D'Encausse, Hélène Carrère. "L'Iran en quête d'un équilibre." *Revue Française de Science Politique* 17 (April 1967): 213–236.

DePlanhol, X. "Un Village de montagne de l'Azerbaidjan iranien, Lighwan (versant nord du sahend)." *Revue Geographie Lyon* (1960): 395–418.

"Documents." *MERIP Reports* 87 (May 1980): 12–14.

Dowlat, Manijeh, B. Hourcade, and Odile Puech. "Les Paysans et la Revolution Iranienne." *Peuples Méditerranéens* No. 10 (January–March 1980): 19–42.

Eghtedare, Ali Muhammad. "Management of Rural Community Development." *TE* 4 (August 1967): 52–70.

Fitzgerald, Frances. "Giving the Shah Everything He Wants." *Harpers*, November 1974, pp. 55–82.

Freivalds, John. "Farm Corporations in Iran: An Alternative to Traditional Agriculture." *MEJ* 26 (Spring 1972): 185–193.

Friedl, Erika. "Division of Labor in an Iranian Village." *MERIP Reports* 95 (March–April 1981): 12–18.

Ghadiri, B. "The Experience of Rural Cooperatives and Cooperative Unions in Iran." *TE* 10 (1973): 80–105.

Goblot, H. "Le Problème de l'eau en Iran." *Orient* 23 (1962): 43–50.

Goodell, Grace. "Agricultural Production in a Traditional Village of Northern Khuzestan." *Marburger Geographische Schriften* 64 (1975): 245–289.

Grapachet, S. "Populations rurales et développement en Iran." *Communates: Archives Internationales de Sociologie de la Cooperation et du Developpement* No. 26 (July–December 1969): 159–172.

Gruessing, K., and J.-H. Grevemeyer. "Peasant Society: Organization-krisewiderstand." *Mardom Nameh* 3 (1977): 86–111.

Hadary, Gideon. "The Agrarian Reform Problem in Iran." *MEJ* 5 (Spring 1951): 181–196.

Hanessian, John, Jr. "Yosouf-Abad, an Iranian Village." *American Universities Field Staff Reports Service*. Southwest Asia Series, No. 12 (1963).

Hayden, Lyle J. "Living Standards in Rural Iran." *MEJ* 3 (April 1949): 140–150.

Homayoun, Daryush. "Land Reform in Iran." *TE* 2 (1963): 18–31.

Hooglund, Eric J. "Iran's Agricultural Inheritance." *MERIP Reports* 99 (September 1981): 15–19.

———. "The *Khwushnishin* Population of Iran." *IS* 6 (Autumn 1973): 229–245.

———. "Rural Participation in the Revolution." *MERIP Reports* 87 (May 1980): 3–6.

Hooglund, Mary. "One Village in the Revolution." *MERIP Reports* 87 (May 1980): 7–12.

———. "Peasants and the Process of Revolution: An Iranian Case Study." Paper Presented at the Annual Meeting of the Alternative Middle East Studies Seminar. Washington, D.C., November 8–9, 1980.

Inlow, E. Burke. "Iran: The Politics of Reform." *Middle East Forum* 47 (1971): 103–114.

Issawi, Charles. "Iran's Economic Upsurge." *MEJ* 21 (1967): 447–462.

Jennings, George J. "A Development Project and Cultural Change in an Iranian Village." *Proceedings of the Minnesota Academy of Science* 25–26 (1957–1958): 309–325.

———. "Economy and Integration in a Changing Iranian Village." *Proceedings of the Minnesota Academy of Science* 27 (1960): 112–119.

Katouzian, M. A. "Land Reform in Iran: A Case Study in the Political Economy of Social Engineering." *Journal of Peasant Studies* 2 (January 1974): 220–239.

———. "Oil versus Agriculture: A Case of Dual Resource Depletion in Iran." *Journal of Peasant Studies* 5 (April 1978): 347–369.

Kazemi, Farhad, and Ervand Abrahamian. "The Non-revolutionary Peasantry of Modern Iran." *IS* 11 (1978): 259–304.

Keddie, Nikki R. "The Iranian Village before and after Land Reform." *Journal of Contemporary History* 3 (July 1968): 69–91.

———. "Oil, Economic Policy, and Social Conflict in Iran." *Race and Class* 21 (Summer 1979): 13–29.

Keddie, W. "Fish and Futility in Iranian Development." *Journal of Developing Areas* 6 (1971): 9–28.

Khamsi, F. "Land Reform in Iran." *Monthly Review* 21 (July 1969): 20–28.

Khosrovi, K. "La Réforme agraire et l'apparition d'une nouvelle classe en Iran." *Etudes Rurales* 34 (1969): 122–126.

———. "La Stratification social rurale en Iran." *Etudes Rurales* 22–24 (1966): 243–246.

Lambton, Ann K. S. "Land Reform and Rural Cooperative Societies in Persia." *Royal Central Asian Journal* 56, Parts II & III (1969): 1–28.

———. "Some Reflections on the Question of Rural Development and Land Reform in Iran." *TE* 3 (August 1965): 3–9.

Löffler, Reinhold. "The National Integration of Boir Ahmad." *IS* 6 (Spring–Summer 1973): 127–135.

———. "Recent Economic Changes in Boir Ahmad: Regional Growth without Development." *IS* 9 (Autumn 1976): 266–287.

———. "The Representative Mediator and the New Peasant." *American Anthropologist* 73 (October 1971): 1077–1091.

Mahdavy, Hossein. "The Coming Crisis in Iran." *Foreign Affairs* 44 (October 1965): 134–146.

Mahdavy, H., H. Saedloo, F. Nasseri, and J. Arjmand. "A Study of Rural Economic Problems of Gilan and Mazandaran." *TE* 4 (January 1967): 135–204.

Malek, H. "Essai d'estimation des dépenses ostentations d'un village du Khorassan (Iran)." *Economies et Sociétés* 2 (April 1968): 893–898.

Miller, William G. "Hosseinabad: A Persian Village." *MEJ* 18 (1964): 483–498.

Najafi, B. "Farm Corporations in Iran: A Case Study." *Zeitschrift für Ausländische Landwirtschaft* 17 (1978): 38–45.

Okazaki, Shoko. "Shirang-Sofla: The Economics of a Northeast Iranian Village." *Developing Economics* 7 (September 1969): 261–283.

Ōno, Morio. "On Socio-economic Structures of Iranian Villages." *Developing Economics* 5 (1967): 446–462.

Op't Land, C. A. "Land Reform in Iran." *Persica* 2 (1966): 80–122.

Parvin, Manoucher, and Amir Zamani. "Political Economy of Growth and Destruction: A Statistical Interpretation of the Iranian Case." *IS* 12, Nos. 1–2 (Winter–Spring 1979): 43–78.

Ramazani, R. K. "Iran's 'White Revolution': A Study in Political Development." *IJMES* 5 (April 1974): 124–139.

Research Group in Agricultural Economics. "An Analysis of the Law Governing the First Stage of Land Reform in Iran." *TE* 7 (Winter 1970): 49–74.

———. "Community Development and Land Reform." *TE* 4 (January 1967): 205–209.

————. "Reasons for the Decline in Iran's Agricultural Production in the Farming Year 1963–64." *TE* 4 (January 1967): 210–232.

————. "A Review of the Statistics of the First State of Land Reform." *TE* 2 (March 1964): 139–150.

————. "Rural Economic Problems of Khuzistan." *TE* 3 (August 1965): 153–233.

————. "A Study of the Rural Economic Problems of East and West Azarbayjan." *TE* 5 (January 1968): 149–238.

————. "A Study of the Rural Economic Problems of Sistan and Baluchestan." *TE* 7 (Summer–Autumn 1970): 140–211.

————. "A Survey of Rural Cooperatives up to Mehr 1342 (September 1963)." *TE* 2 (March 1964): 151–160.

————. "A Survey of the Rural Economic Problems of Kurdistan." *TE* 7 (Spring 1970): 92–136.

Richards, Helmut. "Land Reform and Agribusiness in Iran." *MERIP Reports* 43 (December 1975): 3–18.

Scarcia, G. "Governo, riforma agraria e opposizione in Persia." *Oriente Moderno* 42 (1962): 731–801.

Schewizer, G. "The Aras-Moghan Development Project in Northwest Iran and Problems of Nomad Settlement." *Applied Science and Development* 4 (1974): 134–148.

Springborg, Robert. "New Patterns of Agrarian Reform in the Middle East and North Africa." *MEJ* 31 (1977): 127–142.

Sternberg-Sarel, Benno. "Tradition et développement en Iran: Les Villages de la plaine de Ghazvin." *Etudes Rurales* 22–24 (1966): 206–218.

Stickley, S. T., and B. Najafi. "The Effectiveness of Farm Corporations in Iran." *TE* 8 (Winter 1971): 18–28.

Tripet, François. "Les Bouleversements de l'univers rural en Iran." *L'Afrique et l'Asie* Nos. 95–96 (1971): 27–40.

————. "Cinq ans de revolution blanche en Iran." *Etudes* (August–September 1969): 206–220.

Van Nieuwenhuijze, C. A. O. "Iranian Development in a Sociological Perspective." *Der Islam* 45 (June 1969): 64–80.

Vieille, Paul. "Un Groupement féodal en Iran." *Revue Française de Sociologie* 2 (1965): 175–190.

————. "Les Paysans, la petite bourgeoisie, et l'état après la réforme agraire en Iran." *Annales* 27, No. 2 (1972): 349–372.

Warriner, Doreen. "Employment and Income Aspects of Recent Agrarian Reforms in the Middle East." *International Labour Review* 101 (1970): 605–626.

Weinbaum, M. G. "Agricultural Policy and Development Politics in Iran." *MEJ* 31 (1977): 343–450.

Westwood, Andrew. "Reform Government in Iran." *Current History* 42 (1962): 227–232.

Index